SWEETER
than
Honey

SWEETER

than *Honey*

Daily Devotions *for* Disciples

❧ VOLUME TWO ❧

GREG HINNANT

CREATION
HOUSE

SWEETER THAN HONEY: DAILY DEVOTIONS FOR DISCIPLES, VOLUME 2
   by Greg Hinnant
Published by Creation House
A Charisma Media Company
600 Rinehart Road
Lake Mary, Florida 32746
www.charismamedia.com

Unless otherwise noted, all Scripture quotations are from *The New Scofield
Reference Bible*, King James Version (New York: Oxford University Press, 1967).
The New Scofield Reference Bible contains introductions, annotations, subject
chain references, and some word changes in the King James Version that will help
the reader.

Scripture quotations marked AMP are from the Amplified Bible. Old Testament
copyright © 1965, 1987 by the Zondervan Corporation. The Amplified New
Testament copyright © 1954, 1958, 1987 by the Lockman Foundation. Used by
permission.

Scripture quotations marked ESV are from the English Standard Version of the
Bible, copyright © 2001, Crossway Bibles, a division of Good News Publishers.
Used by permission.

Scripture quotations marked GNT are from the Good News Translation of the
Bible, copyright © 1992 by American Bible Society. Used by permission.

Scripture quotations marked GW are from God's Word Translation, copyright
© 1995 by God's Word to the Nations. Used by permission of Baker Publishing
Group.

Scripture quotations marked KJV are from the King James Version of the Bible.

Scripture quotations marked NAS are from the New American Standard Bible–
Updated Edition, Copyright © 1960, 1962, 1963, 1968, 1971, 1972, 1973, 1975, 1977,
1995 by The Lockman Foundation. Used by permission. (www.Lockman.org)

Scripture quotations marked NCV are from The Holy Bible, New Century Version.
Copyright © 1987, 1988, 1991 by Word Publishing, Dallas, Texas 75039. Used by
permission.

Scripture quotations marked NIV are from the Holy Bible, New International
Version. Copyright © 1973, 1978, 1984, International Bible Society. Used by
permission.

Scripture quotations marked NKJV are from the New King James Version of the
Bible. Copyright © 1979, 1980, 1982 by Thomas Nelson, Inc., publishers. Used by
permission.

Design Director: Bill Johnson
Cover design by Terry Clifton

AUTHOR'S NOTE: Some Scripture quotations have specific words and/or phrases that I am emphasizing. I have added italics to these verses to show that emphasis. Also, in some of the Scripture quotations, with the exception of the Amplified Bible, I have inserted in brackets explanatory text to help with the understanding of certain words and phrases.

Visit the author's website: www.greghinnantministries.org.

Library of Congress Control Number: 2013930879
International Standard Book Number: 978-1-62136-356-9
E-book International Standard Book Number: 978-1-62136-357-6

First edition

13 14 15 16 17 — 987654321
Printed in Canada

DEDICATION

To my coworkers and friends at Greg Hinnant
Ministries. Your wonderfully faithful prayers, support,
and assistance have made this book possible.

CONTENTS

Preface xi
1 The Union 1
2 In One Miraculous Moment! 3
3 Christian Abandonment 6
4 Spiritual Resilience 9
5 Show Mary's Devotion 12
6 Lovers of Truth 15
7 Rest in His Recognition 18
8 Let's Go! 20
9 Reach Out to "Samaritans" 23
10 Don't Judge the Wrong Person 26
11 The First Duty of the Faithful 29
12 Sing While You Suffer 31
13 Seeking Spiritual Unity 33
14 Are You on Fire? 36
15 Like a Rushing Mighty Wind! 38
16 A Prodigious Parade of Prodigals 40
17 The Prime Principle of Preachers 42
18 Will You Be Taken? 45
19 A Fresh Revelation of Jesus Is Near! 48
20 How Far Will You Go? 50
21 Occupying in the Valley of Delay 53
22 The Benefits of Cross Bearing 55
23 All Nations Are Before Him 57
24 Obsessed! 59
25 Courageous Faith! 62
26 Unmoved by Satan's Subtlety 64
27 God's Flood Management Plan 67
28 When Prophets Come… 69
29 Reset This Vision Before You 72
30 Strengthen Your Hull 74
31 Secret Believers 77
32 The Probing, Prompting Questions of God 79
33 Springs, Builders, Repairers, Restorers 82
34 Looking for a Way Out? 85
35 They Watched Him—and Watch Us 87
36 Abandoned, Yet Stronger! 90
37 Caring for Christ's Body 92
38 Heaven's Humble Messengers 94
39 He Meets Us as We Go 97
40 Walking Alone to Assos 100
41 The Wayless Wilderness 102

42 Don't Keep Jesus in a Tomb!............................ 104
43 Prepare to Be Taken Up 107
44 Revival, the Simple Way 110
45 Receiving Christ's Consolations.........................113
46 Complete Your Spiritual Résumé........................116
47 Ready to Rise?..119
48 Stand Up, Speak Up! 122
49 Perfecting the Prayer of Faith......................... 124
50 Transformative Teaching.............................. 127
51 Calling Christian Armor-Bearers!...................... 130
52 Christ Our Security 133
53 Holding Jesus—Tightly!............................... 136
54 Ready for Launch? 138
55 Offering Prayer With Worship......................... 140
56 Triumphant Twosomes!................................143
57 Do You See Your Opportunity?........................ 146
58 The Rich Rewards of Repentance 149
59 Content in His Courts................................152
60 Pentecostal Peril 155
61 A Few Thoughts on Self-Pity 158
62 Shadowed by the Savior...............................161
63 Determined Disciples of Jesus 163
64 Has Your City Fallen? 166
65 Thus Far, No Farther!.................................169
66 Follow the Wisest Wisdom.............................172
67 Hands Up!...175
68 Are You Nesting in God? 178
69 The Divine Drawing.................................. 180
70 The Burning Book 183
71 Learn From a Lame Man 186
72 Child Sacrifice, Our Way............................. 188
73 Hope for Cripples—and Carriers! 191
74 From Walking to Worrying to Worshipping.............. 194
75 His Work Will Go On... 196
76 Firm Up Your Foundation 198
77 Blessed at Jesus' Feet 200
78 Philip Went Down—Will You?......................... 203
79 The New Wine Is Better 206
80 Inverted Christians.................................. 209
81 Must We Tithe?......................................212
82 About Overcoming Christians and Churches.............215
83 He Knows Where to Find You.........................218
84 Refocusing on the Family of God 221
85 Amazing Grace Incarnate............................ 224

86 Our Original Denominations 227
87 Just a Mustard Seed 230
88 Ananias' Extraordinary Character 233
89 Go With a Straight Course! 235
90 Key Time 238
91 The Walls Will Come Down! 241
92 Memorial Day Is Coming! 244
93 Reestablishing the Head 247
94 All That Call on Thy Name 250
95 Will You See Judge Jesus? 252
96 Calling Consummate Congregants 255
97 Ecclesiastical Excellence 258
98 Re-Crown Him Lord of All 261
99 Reminded by the Spirit 263
100 Need a Friend? 266
101 Praying Until… 268
102 Be Christian or Die! 271
103 He Gives Light in Prisons 274
104 Obey Your Angel! 277
105 Sleeping the Sleep of Folly? 280
106 On the Sidelines? 283
107 Seek Confirmation 286
108 Rapid Righteous Reversals 289
109 Lord, Open My Eyes! 292
110 Whose Heart Are You After? 295
111 Philadelphia Christians in a Laodicean Era 297
112 Bless Him by Night 300
113 Shake Off That Dust! 303
114 Mistaken, Mesmerizing, Maddening Materialism 306
115 Marvelous Municipal Miracles Manifesting 309
116 Are You Awake to God's Plan? 312
117 He Hasn't Given Up on Us 315
118 Lord, Fully Enlighten Me! 318
119 Only Fifty Miles to Derbe! 321
120 Are You Rooted? 324
121 If God Converted Paul… 327
122 If John Were Here… 330
   Notes 333
   Contact the Author 341
   Other Books by This Author 343

PREFACE

*T*HE MOST ANCIENT natural sweetener, honey isn't just sweet. It's very useful.

It's a food, spread, and sauce (honey mustard). It's a key ingredient in drinks, bread, and other foods. It's used to make honey wine. It's even a remedy for coughs, burns, and sores. Scripture affirms honey's usefulness.

Jacob sent a gift of "a little honey" to Egypt's royal grain master, who was Joseph (Gen. 43:11)! Thus honey is a royal gift, or gift fit for a royal. When weary, Jonathan tasted some honey, and "his eyes brightened" (1 Sam. 14:27, NIV). Thus it gives energy—and joy, smiles, and sharper vision. Honey was a staple of John the Baptist's diet (Matt. 3:4). So it's the food of prophets and reformers. David's friends brought honey to sustain him during Absalom's rebellion (2 Sam. 17:27–29). So honey sweetens bitter times. God promised to satisfy His people with honey if they'd obey (Ps. 81:16). So it satisfies or contents obedient ones. The Promised Land was filled with "milk and honey" (Exod. 3:8). So honey should be plentiful among God's people. Solomon urged, "Eat thou honey, because it is good [beneficial]; and...sweet" (Prov. 24:13). So God wants us to enjoy, not neglect, the honey He provides—whether from our beehives or Bibles.

The latter contains spiritual honey. Manna, a symbol of God's Word, tasted like "wafers made with honey" (Exod. 16:31, NIV). Ezekiel said God's Word tasted like honey (Ezek. 3:3). Thus God's Word is our soul-honey.

The scriptures above imply the honey of God's Word is His royal gift to us, proof we're in His royal family. It brightens our inner eyes with spiritual energy, joy, and clearer discernment. A steady diet of it makes prophets and reformers. If we'll obey it, it will content us in "whatsoever state" we're in (Phil. 4:11) and sweeten our bitterest times. It should be found abundantly among us, in our minds, conversations, and churches. God wants us enjoying, not neglecting, our soul-honey daily. Why?

It's so uniquely sweet! While bees' honey is sweet, biblical honey is even sweeter:

> How sweet are Your words to my taste! Yes, sweeter than honey
> to my mouth!
> —PSALM 119:103, NAS

Truly the timely comfort, wisdom, correction, and guidance the Spirit gives through God's Word are more gratifying than any human joy or pleasure. The Book of Psalms is the Bible's central honeycomb, devotional writings yielding sweet, useful soul-honey in every verse. They've sustained countless souls and continue doing so. May God make these biblical devotionals, however imperfect, psalmic—gratifyingly sweet, useful, and sustaining.

Sweeter Than Honey is the second book in my devotional trilogy that, together with its companion works, *Not by Bread Alone* and *Water From the Rock*, provides a full year of daily readings. Now, please, have some honey.

—GREG HINNANT

Chapter 1

THE UNION

THE MOST PRECIOUS thing in Jesus' earthly life was His union with His heavenly Father: "I and my Father are *one* [one in essence or nature; also at one, or unified]" (John 10:30). It was everything to Him.

That sacred bond preceded all His other relationships, sustained His rich spiritual life, and empowered His diverse and dynamic teaching, preaching, mentoring, healing, and charity ministries. Every decision Jesus made, every action He undertook, every word He spoke, every new course He chose or declined was motivated by His determination to preserve His union with His Father. Whatever His Father willed, Jesus agreed with it so He would always be at one with Him: "I do always those things that please him" (John 8:29). He maintained that oneness, that mystical connection, that marvelous intertwining of His and His Father's Spirits, minds, and actions at all costs. The public could criticize or praise Him, His disciples could come or go, but Jesus always nurtured and protected the union—His unique closeness, fellowship, harmony, and alliance with heaven—every day in every situation. It began in Nazareth.

Though Jesus preached no sermons and worked no miracles for thirty years, He nevertheless served, faithfully nourishing, growing, and guarding the union by consistently obeying His Father. After Jesus' stunning debut before the nation's religious leaders at age twelve, rather than start His ministry He opted to return to Nazareth to continue submissively serving Joseph and Mary. Why? It was His Father's will. Years later He did the opposite, refusing to leave His growing ministry to return with His mother and family to Nazareth (Mark 3:21, 31–35). Why? It was His Father's will. Seeing Jesus' focus, Satan aimed to break it.

In the temptation he attempted to separate Father and Son by persuading Jesus to change His focus. He offered Him several alluring alternatives—pleasing Himself physically, empowering Himself politically, or promoting Himself religiously—but they all contradicted His Father's will. He sent Jesus not to serve the flesh but the Spirit, not to rule but to be rejected, not to be crowned but to be crucified to redeem the world. When Jesus said no, the union prevailed and the tempter failed. But only "for a season" (Luke 4:13).

1

Persistent, Satan kept trying to disrupt the union and abort God's plan during Jesus' ministry. He moved Jewish nationalists, after seeing Jesus' miracles, to suggest He establish His kingdom immediately by force of arms (John 6:15), but Jesus again said no. When Jesus announced He was going to the cross, His closest disciple strongly objected. Finally, when Jesus was on the cross, the religious leaders taunted Him to come down to save Himself. But again He refused. Why? The union.

Jesus prayed our union with Him would be like His and His Father's: "Father...that they may be one, even as we are one" (John 17:21–22). He taught our alliance would be like a vine's bond with its branches—a constant vital dependency yielding life, fruit, and honor for the vinedresser (John 15:1–8). He said loving, trusting obedience keeps our connection strong and growing: "If ye keep my commandments, ye shall abide in my love [union], even as I have kept my Father's commandments, and abide in his love" (v. 10). If wise, we'll cherish our alliance as He did His.

We'll nourish our union daily with private prayer, Bible reading, and worship. We'll maintain it by constantly following His Spirit's guidance. We'll grow it by living faithfully for Jesus in our home, church, neighborhood, and workplace. We'll protect it by training ourselves to think scripturally, not secularly; humbly, not haughtily; kindly, not callously; generously, not selfishly. We'll preserve it by forgiving offenders and reconciling with those we offend. We'll keep it unencumbered by quickly confessing sins to Christ and laying aside burdens of anxiety. We'll strengthen it by loving those Jesus loves most—Christians—by fellowship, patience, and assistance. We'll keep it "first" (Matt. 6:33) by favoring it over any relationship that could hinder or ruin it. When the tempter presses, we'll follow Jesus' example: refusing allurements, though they strongly stir our desires; rejecting distractions, lest they waste our time, energy, or resources; enduring crosses, accepting these negative situations as positive opportunities to obey God and prove our loyalty to Him. Why? The union.

In these last days God is raising up a new body of believers like Jesus—a taught, tested, transformed, purified bride church (Eph. 5:25–27). Every choice they make, every word they speak, every action they take or decline, will be decided by one question: Will it help or hinder the union? Be among them.

Today, commit yourself unswervingly to the union.

Chapter 2

IN ONE MIRACULOUS MOMENT!

*B*EFORE MEETING PETER and John at the Beautiful Gate of the Jewish temple, the beggar "lame from his birth" had never walked (Acts 3:2). Not one day. Not one minute. Not one step! But in one miraculous moment this changed.

When Peter gripped the cripple's hand and in Jesus' name challenged him to "rise up and walk," suddenly he leaped up and walked with them into the temple courts (Acts 3:1–11). There he "held [fast] Peter and John" (v. 11). There is rich symbolism here.

The temple courts, where the Jews worshipped, symbolize the church, where Christians worship: "Ye [the church] are the temple of God" (1 Cor. 3:16). The man "lame from his birth" symbolizes sinners and immature Christians. Though different in many respects, sinners and immature Christians share this trait: both are spiritually lame, having never walked in the Spirit since their physical or spiritual birth.

Specifically they've never:

1. Walked with God closely and consistently

2. Walked with believers in loving fellowship

3. Walked with spiritual leaders (Peter and John), holding fast their mature teaching, counsel, and fellowship

The sudden raising of this lame man to walk with God, His people, and their leaders sends an encouraging message: As He did with this cripple, the all-powerful Holy Spirit can raise the spiritually lame—sinners, immature Christians, backsliders, dead churches, and entire generations of lukewarm, worldly Christians—to walk closely with God, one another, and their spiritual leaders. And quickly!

He's done it periodically in church history. When His people were very low and needy, Christ poured out His Spirit afresh, and suddenly, in one miraculous moment:

- Spiritually crippled medieval Christians rose to begin walking with God, and embracing Luther and other Reformation leaders

- Sinners and backslidden Christians rose to walk with God during the Great Awakening, holding fast Whitefield's evangelism and Edwards' instruction

- Spiritually lame Englishmen rose to walk with God during the Wesleyan revival, clinging to the Wesley brothers' sermons and songs

All these walked through the Beautiful Gate of divine visitation to worship in the joyful courts of revived churches. God did the same in Israel.

In Elijah's day, after God's supernatural fire fell on Mount Carmel, His Spirit convicted the lukewarm Israelites, consumed their bonds of iniquity, and moved them to unanimously acclaim, "The LORD, he is God!" (1 Kings 18:39). Thus an entire nation turned from idols to God in a moment. He's done this for the possessed.

When Jesus met a man hopelessly bound by many demons, He spoke one word—"Go!"—and instantly a demoniac became a disciple (Matt. 8:32). God can even do this with our worst enemies.

Raging as he hastened to persecute more Christians in Damascus, Saul of Tarsus ran head-on into Jesus—and fell headlong! The next moment he rose to walk with the Lord, people, and leaders he had persecuted (Acts 9:1–9, 19, 27–28).

Isaiah foresaw his nation's astonishingly sudden rebirth: "Shall the earth be made to bring forth in one day? Or shall a nation be born at once?" (Isa. 66:8). After the Rapture Jesus will appear to, convert, and send 144,000 Jews to evangelize "all Israel" (Rom. 11:26). Thus the nation of Israel, restored naturally in 1948, will be reborn spiritually in one miraculous moment!

The parable of the ten virgins foresees Christians being spiritually asleep in these last days due to disappointment over His delayed coming (Matt. 25:1–13). But a "midnight cry" suddenly awakens us and sparks a powerful "lamp-trimming" revival. After it runs its course, the Bridegroom appears and takes away His revived, refined, and "ready" bride church, "in a moment, in the twinkling of an eye" (1 Cor. 15:52).

Though diverse in time, location, and subjects, these miraculous moments share this: they required faith! Peter prayed confidently. The lame man "gave heed…expecting to receive something" (Acts 3:5). Luther,

Whitefield, Edwards, the Wesleys, Elijah, even the demoniac "expected to receive something." In these last days the bride church will eagerly expect Jesus' appearing. So faith is the Beautiful Gate through which we receive miraculous moments. Are you willing and ready to open it?

Who is the spiritual cripple, "lame from birth," for whom you pray daily? Your spouse? Child? Parent? Neighbor? Friend? Coworker? Fellow student? Are you discouraged because they've never walked with God? Not one day. Not one minute. Not one step! No sinner, backslider, or struggling Christian is beyond the Spirit's supernatural, creative, restorative power. As shown above, He can raise spiritually lame individuals, churches, nations, and generations to walk closely with God, other believers, and mature spiritual leaders. So don't doubt.

Pray expectantly and persistently for your one miraculous moment!

Chapter 3

CHRISTIAN ABANDONMENT

*A*FTER THE NATION's highest court for the second time forbade the apostles, with threats, to preach Jesus, they gathered for prayer. They asked for boldness to continue their witness—and got it (Acts 4:23–33)! But they forgot to request escape.

Their omission is revealing. These original Christians—Christ's loyalists—were so given to God, so trusting in Him, they desired only to move forward with Christ's work (Great Commission) regardless of the difficulties. Like the three Hebrews, who were so content with Jesus in Nebuchadnezzar's furnace they had to be called out (Dan. 3:25–26), the apostles seemed oblivious to their very dangerous predicament. But they weren't oblivious.

They were abandoned. Entirely yielded to God's will, they were aware of, yet unmoved by, the possible adverse consequences of their obedience. Radically dedicated, they embodied Christian abandonment. They surrendered themselves entirely and without condition to obey God and gave themselves over completely to His all-powerful control and faithful, loving care. With their brave decision to continue preaching Jesus they overleaped the deadly bog of lukewarm Christianity with its entangling quagmire of timid, self-centered, self-protecting reasoning. Now fully proven "disciples indeed" (John 8:31), they walked steadily forward in bold, Christ-centered, kingdom-serving living, focused only on finishing the will of Him who sent them. This Christian abandonment is the very core, the throbbing heart, of New Testament discipleship. But though radical, they weren't fanatical.

They didn't practice reckless brinksmanship, desire martyrdom, resent authorities, crave sensationalism, or seek conflicts. Yet when conflicts came in the line of duty, they consistently and courageously pleased God. Knowing the Sanhedrin had recently executed Jesus, they still chose to defy its command rather than fail His commission, even if it meant:

- NATIONAL REJECTION, for defying Israel's highest council (Matt. 10:22)
- LOSS OF LIBERTY, by incarceration (Acts 5:18)

- BEATINGS, a common punishment in first-century synagogues (2 Cor. 11:24)
- LOSS OF PROPERTY, as many Christians later experienced (Heb. 10:34)
- LOSS OF LIFE, as Jesus warned (Matt. 10:21)

True leaders, the apostles led not only in word but also in deed. Subsequently brave thousands followed their lead, accepting and enduring these very sufferings from the Jews (AD 30–70) and the Romans (64–313). But few follow them today.

Seeking advantages, acquisitions, aggrandizement, or appeasement holds far too many of us back from abandonment. Crippled by our culture's comfortable conventions, we have a big "if" emblazoned on our Christian breastplates. We'll faithfully follow Jesus and do His will *if* He: gives us career or professional advantages; increases our money, goods, or property; enhances and defends our reputation; or helps us appease our critics and opponents. As long as Jesus grants these favors, we'll play the Christian. If not, the game is up, and we'll take our religious toys and go back, pouting and murmuring, to our old life. These conventional motivations are the opposite of the spirit of Christian abandonment. And Christ's apostles.

They abandoned their old lives to apprehend new lives in Christ. Peter said, "We have left [abandoned] all, and followed thee" (Luke 18:28). Paul did the same. When Christ called, he willingly set aside his heart's desire, a promising career as a Pharisee, to please Jesus' heart (Phil. 3:4–10). Conversely the rich young ruler, when Jesus called him, refused to abandon his worldly wealth to apprehend the riches of Christ. Or follow God's example.

The Father gave this world the ultimate example of abandonment. "God so loved the world, that he gave [surrendered, yielded, abandoned] his only begotten Son, that whosoever believeth in him should not perish, but have everlasting life" (John 3:16). Oswald Chambers said this verse reveals "God gave Himself absolutely," adding, "In our abandonment, we give ourselves over to God just as God gave Himself for us, without any calculation."[1] Why is this important?

Without Christian abandonment, God's work won't advance. If the apostles had appeased the Sanhedrin, Christ's gospel would have ceased and His church withered. But their abandonment kept them alive, the gospel growing, and the church steadily apprehending God's purpose.

Will we abandon and apprehend? Paul did: "What things were gain to me, those I counted loss...that I may apprehend that for which also I am apprehended of Christ" (Phil. 3:7, 12). Or will we settle into our lukewarm, comfortable cultural conventions and remain spiritually unfulfilled? Will we be radical yet not fanatical? Will we lead by our talk and our walk? Ultimately every Christian will adamantly insist on his own way or abandon to Christ.

Will you walk in adamant self-will or Christian abandonment?

Chapter 4

SPIRITUAL RESILIENCE

*A*FTER DENYING CHRIST three times, Peter, wounded in spirit, wandered off and "wept bitterly" (Matt. 26:75). After vowing to stand, he had fallen! Yet though he fell, he didn't fail. Why?

Spiritually resilient, Peter refused to stay down! Over the next forty-eight hours he rose, repented, confessed his sin to God, and rejoined the apostles in the Upper Room. Aware of Peter's response, Jesus responded just as quickly, initiating a series of vital encouragements.

After His resurrection He sent an angel to give Peter an uplifting message through Mary Magdalene: "Tell his disciples, and Peter, that he goeth before you into Galilee; there shall ye see him" (Mark 16:7). When Peter heard the words "and Peter," his heart leaped with joyful relief. All wasn't lost; the Lord hadn't rejected him, and he would yet be a "fisher of men!" Then Jesus appeared and talked with Peter privately, before visiting the other apostles: "He was seen of Cephas [first], then of the twelve" (1 Cor. 15:5). This hinted Peter hadn't been demoted but would resume his place as the leader of Jesus' specially commissioned messengers. Finally, some days later Jesus appeared to the apostles one morning and emphatically and publicly recommissioned Peter before his peers: "Feed my sheep" (John 21:17). Restored and reinstalled by grace, Peter went on to finish the race set before him and receive a full reward. Thanks to resilience!

Without spiritual resilience—the determination to bounce back after spiritual defeats—Peter would have gone on to failure, not fulfillment; aimlessness, not leadership; loss of rewards, not a rewarding life and ministry. Knowing spiritual resilience makes the difference between victorious and vanquished Christians, God, through His Word, repeatedly challenges us to possess and practice it:

A just man falleth seven times, and riseth up again.

—PROVERBS 24:16

The steps of a good man are ordered by the LORD...though he fall, he shall not be utterly cast down.

—PSALM 37:23–24

9

> Rejoice not against me, O mine enemy: when I fall, I shall arise.
>
> —MICAH 7:8

Numerous biblical overcomers illustrate this determination to rise again after every setback.

Moses stumbled by not circumcising his second son in Midian but recovered himself on the way to Egypt (Exod. 4:24–27). The Israelites' progress ceased when they complained in the wilderness, yet after chastening and confession they "set forward" again (Num. 21:10). David fell headlong into sin with Bathsheba but rose again immediately after Nathan's correction (2 Sam. 12:13–25). Paul sank briefly into despair in Asia Minor yet revived to resume his indomitable confidence and labors (2 Cor. 1:8). Mark's faithfulness failed on his first mission, yet he later became one of Paul's most reliable helpers (2 Tim. 4:11). Jonah's ministry lapsed when he rebelled, yet after discipline he rose and completed his mission (Jonah 3). John stumbled by callously invoking judgment on the Samaritans, yet he recovered to become the tender-hearted apostle who showed and taught us to "love one another" (1 John 4:7). All these overcomers exemplify spiritual resilience— and Peter's recovery.

If despite the bitterest failure Peter recovered, so may we. No Christian who falls need fail. Like Peter, we may rise to finish running the race set before us. But we must do our part.

In every spiritual restoration there are human and divine responsibilities. As Peter did, we must start this earthly-heavenly cooperation by confessing our sins or failures and turning from them...if necessary, seven times a day (Matt. 18:21–22)! Seeing our move, Jesus will move to meet us with vital encouragements: uplifting messages, signs of favor, visitations of His presence in prayer or worship, new insights in Bible study, and assistance as we resume our duties. In these and other ways He'll meet us, strengthening, helping, and upholding us with His powerful hand: "Though he fall, he shall not be utterly cast down; for the LORD upholdeth him with his hand" (Ps. 37:24). Thus, by our action and God's reaction, our repentance and His response, we bounce back to our normal faith and faithfulness. Have you fallen?

Failed to courageously confess or obey Jesus? Rejected His counsel? Despised His chastening? Indulged wrong attitudes? Spoken foolishly? Acted unkindly? Been unfaithful, lazy, carnal? Don't condemn yourself as worthless, for "indeed, we all make many mistakes" (James 3:2, NLT). The key is how you respond to your spiritual defeats. Falling is not failure; refusing to rise again is failure. Falling is your prompt to practice spiritual resilience—and go on to fulfillment, not failure; leadership, not aimlessness; a rewarding life, not loss of rewards. Listen!

Peter's Lord is calling you to overcome: "Rise, let us be going" (Matt. 26:46). Be going, and growing, in spiritual resilience.

Chapter 5

SHOW MARY'S DEVOTION

*I*F LOVE FOR Christ may be measured by acts of devotion to Him, extraordinary acts of devotion reveal extraordinary love. Mary of Bethany showed us this.

While Jesus reclined at table in the home of Simon the leper, Mary broke a very expensive alabaster vase of perfumed oil and poured it on Jesus' head and feet (Matt. 26:6–13). Overflowing with gratitude for Jesus' recent raising of her brother, Lazarus, she couldn't contain her love for Jesus. She had to express it—in a large, not a limited, way. Let's study her exceptional act of devotion.

It was an act of extravagant worship. Her gift was lavish, not economical. She gave with abandon what others wouldn't think of giving.

It was an act of exceptional faith. Stating her anointing was "for my burial" (v. 12), Jesus pointed to her full-orbed faith. She believed not only His pleasant promises and prophecies but also His unpleasant warning that He must soon die and rise again (Matt. 16:21).

It was a breaking. By breaking her treasured vase to bless Jesus, she taught us *we must break to bless*, and she proved she would give up any blessing to bless Jesus.

It was an outpouring. As Jesus came to earth "not to be ministered unto, but to minister and to give" (Matt. 20:28), so Mary came to supper not to receive but to release a rich ministry upon Jesus.

It was a giving of her best. She could have offered Him a less valuable possession, yet she chose to give her best, her "very precious [expensive] ointment" (Matt. 26:7), worth a typical yearly wage. Thus she declared her Prince, not her property, was her best possession.

It was not for a cause but for Christ. She could have set her devotion on popular social, religious, or nationalistic causes. Many sacrificed much for the Pharisees, Sadducees, Herodians, or Zealots. But, not misdirected, Mary's zeal was focused on always pleasing Jesus; His will was her cause.

It was a delight to Jesus, beautiful and sweet smelling. He said, "She has done a beautiful thing to me" (v. 10, NIV), and John added, "The house was filled with the fragrance of the perfume" (John 12:3, NIV).

12

It highly honored Jesus. According to existing customs, her anointing of Jesus' head and feet distinguished Him as Simon's honored guest and, more subtly, their nation's most honorable guest—their anointed One or Messiah. Therefore He highly honored her, ordering that believers retell the story of her devotion worldwide "for a memorial of her" (Matt. 26:13).

It paralleled Jesus' sacrifice for us. He "was rich, yet for your sakes he became poor, that ye through his poverty might be rich" (2 Cor. 8:9). By giving her riches, Mary became poor, yet she enriched us with an inspiring example of consummate love for Jesus.

It was misjudged and misrepresented—by believers! Moved by Judas' greedy murmurings, the Twelve mistook Mary's faith for folly. Instead of admiration they "had indignation"; instead of calling her act wonderful, they called it wasteful: "To what purpose is this waste?" (Matt. 26:8). Thus the brethren reproached a sister they should have respected. But Christ didn't.

Indignant, He immediately rebuked them and raved about Mary's sacrifice (vv. 10–13). His glowing praise and emphatic command that we honor her worldwide—something He did for no one else!—should make us pause. And think. And question, "Why this great honor?" Until the light dawns: He wants *us* to have and show Mary's extravagant love for Him! We have it, by grace, through the Cross.

But we rarely show it. Here's how to reenact her ancient devotion in this postmodern world:

- Worship Jesus lavishly, giving Him the very best of your time, strength, praise, and resources
- Believe everything His Word says, promises and warnings
- Realize you must break to bless, and break your hindering sins and self-interest so your life and labor will bless Jesus
- Pour yourself out "wholly" (1 Tim. 4:15) to seek Him, study His Word, and serve His people
- Focus your zeal not on good causes but God causes—Christ's revealed will for your life, nothing less, nothing other
- Honor Jesus highly by obeying His Word, correction, and guidance consistently

Then your life, like Mary's, will be a "beautiful thing" to Jesus, and "a sweet smell, a [living] sacrifice acceptable, well-pleasing to God" (Phil. 4:18). Lukewarm and hypocritical Christians may misjudge and misrepresent you, as Judas did, but in His time and way Jesus will silence them and honor you, as He did Mary of Bethany.

Mary has shown us extraordinary devotion, Jesus has given it, and we've studied it. So let's go show Mary's devotion.

Chapter 6

LOVERS OF TRUTH

*A*s PILATE ANXIOUSLY probed Him for the truth, Jesus said, "For this cause came I into the world, that I should bear witness unto the truth" (John 18:37). What did He mean?

One reason Jesus visited this world was to "bear witness," or testify, to the truth—to reveal, explain, clarify, and confirm eternal truth in all its forms to the darkened, searching hearts of sinful men. Why? So, as we believe, truth could be planted in our hearts and increasingly demonstrated in our lives as it was in His.

Continuing, Jesus said, "Every man who loves truth recognises my voice" (v. 37, PHILLIPS), or, "All who love the truth recognize that what I say is true" (NLT). Here Jesus further declares that true Christians are lovers and followers of truth. Pilate famously asked, "What is truth?" (v. 38). Truth consists of:

- FACTS, not uncertain, unverifiable, or refuted information
- ACCURACY, not mistakes, additions, or omissions
- REALITY, not imaginations, myths, or wishful thinking
- HONESTY, not partial information, distortions, or falsehoods
- FAITHFULNESS, not infidelity, fraud, or betrayal of trust

To love truth in all its forms is to reject all manifestations of falsehood—nonfactual information, inaccuracy, unreality, dishonesty, or infidelity. To perfectly love truth is to love the whole truth: the person, principles, precepts, patterns, and phases of truth.

The person of truth is Jesus. He is truth personified and incarnated: "I am...the truth" (John 14:6). With these words Jesus fully identified Himself with truth. He and truth are forever one, united, inseparable. Every form of truth, spiritual or natural, philosophical or practical, is but one aspect or facet of Christ. In Him eternal truth is openly displayed in time. As the Son of God Jesus shows us the truth about God: "He that hath seen me hath seen the Father" (v. 9). As the Son of man Jesus reveals the truth about redeemed mankind, what we shall be when redemption has run its course in our souls, churches, and social order.

The principles, precepts, and patterns of truth are found in the Bible. Jesus affirmed, "Thy word is truth" (John 17:17). Not just Jesus' sayings but also all biblical writings—its spiritual principles, practical proverbs, moral precepts, mystical parables, historical patterns, and prophecies—reveal the truth about everything they address. The psalmist affirmed, "The word of the LORD is right" (Ps. 33:4), and, "I esteem all thy precepts concerning all things to be right" (Ps. 119:128). As we study and obey biblical truth, God will give us more love for and insight into it.

The numerous phases of truth surround us. Religious truth identifies the only true God, Savior, and religion, not false deities, deliverers, and dogmas. Theological truth presents correct biblical creeds, doctrines, and expositions, not twisted interpretations and heretical teachings. Scientific truth presents proven facts, laws, and data, not dubious theories posing as indisputable explanations. Political truth discloses the real positions, policies, and beliefs of candidates, not partisan spin or slander. Conversational truth consists of pertinent, edifying, or worthwhile discussions, not malicious rumors, idle gossip, or trivia. Historical truth describes people, events, and patterns objectively, without the distortions of pride or prejudice. Relational truth consists of seeing others as they are, not as we wish they were, and acknowledging our real attitudes toward them. Societal truth speaks honestly of our culture's virtues and vices without ignoring unpleasant facts or trends. National truth faces our nation's brighter and darker sides, its righteous triumphs and tragic blunders, without the blinders of national pride. Racial truth celebrates the dignity of every race and equal opportunity and justice for all, not racial superiority and suppression. Financial truth seeks accurate, not falsified, data; a real, not an altered, accounting. Forensic truth focuses on physical evidence, not hunches, hearsay, or clairvoyance. Judicial truth rests on indisputable facts, impartial testimony, and rigorous cross-examination, not courtroom diversions, showmanship, or sensationalism. In public controversies truth is determined by the law, not by special interest propaganda, public protests, or celebrities' opinions. Prophetic truth is the Bible's revelations about the last things, not the visions of secular pundits, atheistic prognosticators, or entranced psychics. Do we love and look for truth in these areas?

We should. Why? Like Jesus, we're here to "bear witness" to truth: "You will be my [truth's] witnesses" (Acts 1:8, NLT). So let's bear a full witness to truth by loving it in all its forms: its person, principles, precepts, patterns, and phases. Wherever it is, whatever it concerns, whoever speaks it, if it's *truth*, let's love, live, profess, support, share, and cling to it—until the Lord of truth appears to catch away the lovers of truth.

Chapter 7

REST IN HIS RECOGNITION

C REATED WITH A need for recognition, we live our entire lives desiring to be appreciated, loved, or respected for who we are or what we do. This need for notice begins in our families.

From infancy to adolescence to maturity, we yearn for our parents' approval, time, and touch, and we fret or fear for want of it. To a lesser degree we seek and savor the interest and appreciation of our siblings.

Subsequently we crave credit in our school years. We hope to master our subjects and receive grades, and later degrees, that bring respect from teachers and peers. Or we hope our athletic, musical, artistic, leadership, or personality gifts will win us esteem.

When employed, we again pursue recognition. Will our labors, talents, and loyalty be noticed or ignored by our employers, managers, and coworkers?

If we marry, our hearts throb for the affectionate attention and admiration of our spouses—till death or divorce do us part.

Once saved, our quest for appreciation resurfaces in our church. We want our new brothers and sisters to respect and respond to us. And we hope our spiritual leaders—pastors, elders, teachers—will notice our faithfulness and give us personal care and counsel.

Even after entering ministry, we desire recognition. Openly or inwardly we want our work to be endorsed, our gifts esteemed, our calling confirmed, and our ministry recommended by fellow believers and ministers.

That's a long litany of longing. Sometimes these hungers are gratified, but not always. Most of us live with one or more of these yearnings deep in our souls. Though different, they're alike in this: we're seeking human recognition. Ponder this parable.

If we approached a powerful, famous, or wise person surrounded by a large, admiring crowd, how would the "great one" recognize us?

He (or she) may look our way, smiling and watching as we approached through the crowd. He may speak, calling our name and waving. He may approach us to give instruction, guidance, or encouragement. He may answer our questions relayed by mutual friends we sent ahead. He may give us gifts, as mementos or tokens of friendship. He may thank us for supporting his work or cause. He may summon us to join his team of coworkers. Or, if he specially favors us, he may invite us to spend time with him, giving us lengthy private audiences freely and frequently. These things would confirm the great man was personally aware and appreciative of who we are and what we do. Here's good news for committed Christians!

The greatest Man—Jesus, the Son of man—has noticed you among the masses milling around Him: "Ye have not chosen me, but I have chosen you" (John 15:16). And He's sending you signs of His recognition daily.

He's looking at you, watching you pray and work: "I saw thee under the fig tree" (John 1:50). He's smiling by giving you favor and success as you pursue His plans. He's speaking to you by His "still, small voice" as you pray, worship, study, or reflect. He approaches you often through pastors and counselors to instruct, guide, or encourage you. When mutual "friends" (angels) bring Him your secret requests and questions, He answers openly—granting your desires or purifying them; changing your adversaries or your attitudes; and creating escapes or giving more grace. He's given you precious gifts—His nature, Spirit, and spiritual gifts—as signs of your immense value to Him. To say thanks to you for supporting His cause and works, He "giveth [you] richly all things to enjoy" (1 Tim. 6:17). He calls you to join His co-laborers in churches and ministries carrying on His kingdom-building work. Best of all, He's invited you into His presence: "Come unto me, all ye that labor and are heavy laden, and I will give you rest" (Matt. 11:28). He wants you to be with Him daily, enjoying the powerful, re-creative, permeating peace of His sensed presence—for the rest of your life! Thus the greatest Man has recognized you with His affectionate attention and approval in this crowded world ceaselessly craving human recognition. Are you recognizing His recognition?

You can. Just tell Him every time you detect His notice. How? By thanksgiving, praise, worship, and obedience. Tell Him His recognition is better than any other. Why? He wants your recognition: "Lovest thou me?" (John 21:15).

Don't have someone's approval? Fret no more. You have the highest recognition possible: Christ's! Declare your quest for recognition finished and your soul satisfied: "In thy presence is fullness of joy" (Ps. 16:11). Remember, rejoice, and rest in His recognition.

Chapter 8

LET'S GO!

*J*ESUS' GREAT COMMISSION ordered all believers to go and evangelize, teach, baptize, and bear witness of Him in the Spirit's power worldwide. But how? We "go" by prayer, person, print, programs, or proxy.

Prayer precedes and prospers all Spirit-led works. Without persistent prayer God doesn't birth, bless, or establish kingdom works. Therefore we go to the "uttermost" (Acts 1:8) first by intercessory prayer. When Jesus commissioned the seventy, He ordered, "Pray ye," before charging them, "Go your ways" (Luke 10:1–3). Thus their praying preceded their preaching and prospered it. If they wouldn't pray, they wouldn't go with heaven's blessing. And if we won't pray, we won't go further—in knowing the Commissioner or fulfilling His commission.

Moravian missions significantly impacted eighteenth-century Christianity. They sent missionaries to many lands, from the West Indies to India. Their exemplary efforts prompted William Carey's call for Protestant missions. And Moravian immigrant-missionaries helped convert John Wesley, arguably the greatest Christian leader of the era. Their influential "going" began with a colossal intercessory prayer effort, a nonstop prayer vigil that lasted over a hundred years.[1] Thus the Moravians' persistent prayers preceded and prospered their missionaries' going and made their intercessors partners with their missionaries.

Ours will do the same if we set our hearts to live and pray faithfully. As our petitions ascend, angels will descend, God's Spirit will move, and His servants will work in every issue and nation for which we pray. And we'll go and work with them...by prayer.

Or we may go in person. The Commissioner may call us to launch out as His ambassadors to other cities, provinces, continents, or nations—or our own. After faithfully praying and serving in Antioch, Paul received this summons: "Separate me Barnabas and Saul for the work unto which I have called them" (Acts 13:2).

If Christ calls us to lengthy mission works or short-term trips, we too will go and share His light-giving Word with this sin-darkened world...in person.

Or we may go by print. Paul fulfilled Christ's commission not only by prayer and in person but also in print. His instructive, corrective, exhortative, and revelatory letters visited first-century churches more often than he did, as was the case with other apostles' and teachers' inspired writings. Since Paul's time countless Christian writers—church fathers, theologians, polemicists, reformers, revivalists, pastors, teachers, poets, and hymnists— have been going to the body of Christ worldwide by the handwritten or printed page.

If so called, our words will quietly talk where our feet can't walk. In books, magazines, tracts, or letters, we will go and feed and inspire hungry nations…by print.

Or we may go by programs. Today technology enables us to go to the "uttermost" by various kinds of media programming: radio, television, or Internet broadcasts; e-mail computer software programs; Web videos, podcasts, and MP3s; CDs, DVDs, and cassette tapes; or whatever electronic wonder appears next.

So without leaving our "Jerusalem," Christ's disciples may today fill the world with our words…by programs.

If not in person, print, or by programs, we may still go by proxy, or substitute. Our missionary stand-ins are any evangelists, churches, ministries, teachers, missionaries, or websites we support or assist. By giving our monies, counsel, manual assistance, or other aid to these who go, we go with them. Why?

They can't go without our help. So wherever they go, we go with them, evangelizing, teaching, training, healing, giving…by proxy.

However we go, we must go in God's ways. We must go fully dependent on God by prayer, asking His initiatives, guidance, protection, provision, and favor for every work and worker. We must go patiently, waiting for God to give "doors of utterance" so we may preach, teach, or witness in season. We must go courageously, not only to familiar territory but also to new cities, nations, cultures, and continents. We must go focused, with our hearts set on Christ's commission—pursuing no other causes, goals, or distractions. We must go persistently, around or through hinderers and hindrances, persecutors and persecutions, traitors and tribulations. We must go humbly, whether few or many respond, or we receive prosperity or bare provision. We must go faithfully, always moving forward, when fellow missioners lose faith and turn back. And we must go sacrificially, when, to make disciples, we must pass through valleys of sorrow with painful thorns and heavy crosses. Ready for your mission, God's way?

The Commissioner has called, the hour is late, and His return near. So don't moan that you lack education, credentials, connections, cash, or the charisma of Carey or Wesley. Ask Christ how He wants you to fulfill His Great Commission—by prayer, person, print, programs, or proxy. And let's go!

Chapter 9

REACH OUT TO "SAMARITANS"

*J*ESUS' GREAT COMMISSION charged His disciples
nesses "in Samaria" (Acts 1:8). These orders must '
very Jewish followers. Witness in Jerusalem, Ju
Fine, no problem. But Samaria?

Despised by the Jews, the Samaritans were a mixe
Gentile heritage. They practiced a false religion, taker
Judaism, that stubbornly rivaled and resisted the true Jev
4:19–22). Zeal for truth may have justified the disciples' former a
everything Samaritan, but now things would be different. Their Mast
ordered them to minister to Samaria! Leading by example, Jesus had mu.
istered two days to Samaritans in Sychar—while Jewish crowds anxiously
awaited Him in Galilee (vv. 3–4, 39–43). He further told an unflattering
story about a Samaritan layman whose mercy far exceeded that of the Jewish
clerics! And He counseled His apostles against anti-Samaritanism: when two
of them prayed fire would consume some inhospitable Samaritans, Jesus declared He had come to save, not scorch, Samaritans (Luke 9:51–56)!

So Christ's commission put His semi-holy followers to a holy test.
Would they lay down their former prejudice and minister to spiritually
hungry Samaritans as freely as they would Jews? He's putting us to the same
examination.

Since they were unlike Jews religiously, racially, and culturally,
"Samaritans" symbolize anyone who is different from us. The differences we
disdainfully discern may be one of many: racial, religious, political, ethnic,
national, vocational, educational, economic, social, denominational, or any
other excuse for unjustified rejection.

No minor issue, eradicating our prejudices is high on God's agenda. In
Scripture He declares His aversion for all forms of prejudice—a by-product
of pride—not once but seven times! Truly, "God is no respecter of persons"
(Acts 10:34). But, like Jesus' original followers, we're loaded with a wide
range of un-Christlike, unfair, pre-judgments. We may not consciously
consider ourselves superior, yet we indulge subtle notions that others, even
Christians are, for faults real or supposed, inferior.

I heard recently of a dear Baptist minister who, when asked what he would call himself if not Baptist, replied, "Ashamed." And he wasn't joking. He sincerely sees other Christian groups as "Samaritan"—different, deceived, devalued, and dismissed. (All Baptists are *not* like him; and his Pharisaic equal may be found in every denomination, non-denomination, and local church.) Let's neither crucify nor stone him just yet but instead call down a little holy fire—"hot coals" of God's conviction—on his sectarianism. And ours! This proud preacher was insolent or ignorant enough to belittle others aloud. With equal hubris but less honesty we do it in our minds. And this makes us, well, un-Christlike.

Outgoing, Christ's love reaches out to penitent sinners and sincere believers whatever their worldly or religious "camp." Jesus went "outside the camp" (Heb. 13:13) of Israel's prejudices to help needy Samaritans, Hellenists, Phoenicians, Syrians, and Romans—and suffered for it. The small-minded, small-hearted Pharisees denounced His large-heartedness as moral compromise, dubbing Him "a friend of publicans and sinners" (Matt. 11:19, KJV). When He didn't change, they called Him a Samaritan. When that didn't move Him, they called Him demonic. Jesus wasn't alone in suffering to purge prejudice.

When at God's direct order Peter preached Christ to Gentiles at Cornelius' house, some Jewish Christians, still bound by their prejudice, demanded an explanation! If as God leads we reach out to spiritually open people from different groups, we too will be criticized. But be hopeful. Very fruitful ministry awaits the unprejudiced!

When Philip reached out to the city of Samaria, God blessed his efforts greatly. Simon Magus' occult control was shut down and the entire population rejoiced at Jesus' saving, healing, and delivering power (Acts 8:5–13). Purged of prejudice, the Spirit-filled apostles recognized God and rushed to help the Samaritans receive the Spirit (vv. 14–17, 25).

Here's another thought. Whoever we are, wherever we're from, whatever our status, someone somewhere sometime will consider us "Samaritan"—different racially, culturally, nationally, vocationally, educationally, socially, denominationally, etc.—and treat us as we've treated others. "Be not deceived...whatever a man soweth, that shall he also reap" (Gal. 6:7). Pause and ponder this until your proud preconceptions wither and die. Some prejudices die hard, others easily.

So strong was Jonah's antipathy toward the bully-nation Assyria that he flatly refused God's commission to preach there—until God "persuaded" him. Do we need "persuasion"?

Or will we humbly obey Christ's commission? Reach out to and kindly receive "Samaritans"? Accept the criticism of our religious "camp"? Yet continue ministering until our unbiased Lord blesses our efforts as He did Philip's? Don't disappoint Him.

Freely receive and reach out to "Samaritans!"

Chapter 10

DON'T JUDGE THE WRONG PERSON

O NE OF THE most divisive sins among Christians is wrongful judging—inaccurate, unkind, and unconstructive criticism, whether verbal or mental. Jesus foresaw and spoke to this.

"Judge not, that ye be not judged" (Matt. 7:1). Jesus warned us to break our deeply rooted habit of ceaseless, senseless fault-finding—or He'll find fault with us! The context shows He's really saying we must not *misjudge* (vv. 2–5), or make unfair or unmerciful decisions about others' actions or characters, especially Christians, whom we should love passionately: "A new commandment I give…love one another; as I have loved you" (John 13:34). Let's consider ten ways we may "judge not."

First, we mustn't judge matters prematurely or based solely on rumors, gossip, or unconfirmed reports. Fair judgments rest on facts, not fiction. All the facts! So however rabidly, or rapidly, others rush to judgment, withhold your decision until you've heard the whole story.

Second, we mustn't judge people by first appearances. You've heard, "First appearances are usually right." But Jesus said, "Judge not according to the appearance" (John 7:24). Why? Under stress we all may speak or act uncharacteristically, doing what we normally don't do or failing to do what we normally do.

Third, we mustn't condemn others for the same faults and failures we've committed. It's unmerciful, even arrogant, to dismiss them as hopelessly useless and unworthy for falling today into the very pits we stumbled into yesterday. Yet we do just this.

Fourth, we mustn't criticize people for failing where we're still failing! If we haven't conquered a fault or sin, we've no right to correct others for it. Jesus called this blatant hypocrisy: "Thou hypocrite" (Matt. 7:5). Until we conquer, we shouldn't critique, for "with what measure ye measure, it shall be measured to you again" (v. 2); or volunteer counsel, "How wilt thou say to thy brother, Let me pull the mote out of thine eye" (v. 4).

Fifth, we mustn't criticize people because their besetting sins or faults differ from ours. "Condemning sins we've no mind to, while excusing those we're inclined to" is blind pride manifesting. All sins offend God, and the sins others practice are no more offensive than those we prefer.

Sixth, we mustn't judge sinners for not acting like saints. God doesn't expect the once-born to live like the twice-born. Biblical standards are for believers, not unbelievers. We should intercede for, not despise, the latter.

Seventh, we mustn't judge hearts, motives, or destinies (our imaginations aren't God's inspirations!) but should evaluate only factual issues, actions, and statements. Only the Lord "looketh on the heart" (1 Sam. 16:7); we can't read that secret book. But, like Him, we can know people by their consistent acts, words, and omissions (1 Sam. 2:3).

Eighth, we mustn't reject people merely for breaking our rules. Only God's Scriptures, not our private scruples, are binding.

Ninth, we should only judge matters within our jurisdiction, or sphere of personal responsibility. If it's not our duty to evaluate people or settle issues, let's leave them to their authorities and God.

Tenth, we should forget judging others so we can focus on judging ourselves—a colossal job! And diligently! We must forget others' "motes" (minor faults) and steadily remove the "beams" (large faults, sins) in our "eye" (soul and viewpoint) by responding to the Holy Spirit's conviction and correction daily. Until this humble habit is deeply rooted, we have neither the right nor moral authority to correct anyone. Sadly, few practice these correctives.

So our misjudging grows. And grows. And grows. Soon it becomes a monstrous, insatiable lust! We obsessively judge everyone everywhere every day about everything—but never ourselves! As Jesus warned, unpleasant consequences will follow.

Our excessive judging causes others to judge us excessively, because "with what judgment ye judge, ye shall be judged" (Matt. 7:2). For persistently and pitilessly critiquing others, we must reap the same, even from gracious folks who are normally kind and uncritical. And because we're consistently disobeying Jesus' teaching, we come under His judgment, or disapproval. Consequently our conscience is burdened with inescapable, justifiable guilt when it should be at peace. Furthermore, we harm the unity of the body of Christ. Jesus prayed we would be "one...perfect in one" (John 17:21, 23). This can't happen while we prefer walking in misjudgment to walking in mercy. Finally, instead of flourishing, our Christian friendships will fail. We can't enjoy conversations when one or both of us are putting the other through a mental CAT scan!

Therefore Jesus authorized us to judge only one person: ourselves! "Cast the beam out of thine own eye" (Matt. 7:5). Anyone else is the wrong person. Don't judge the wrong person.

Chapter 11

THE FIRST DUTY OF THE FAITHFUL

HE EVENTS SURROUNDING Jesus' resurrection weren't just surprising. They were shocking! (See Matthew 28:1–10.)

When two brightly shining angels appeared by Jesus' tomb, rolled away its door, shook the earth, and began speaking to Mary Magdalene, the Roman guards went into shock: "The keepers did shake, and became as dead men" (v. 4). They "trembled violently" (WEY) and collapsed, speechless, motionless, and still staring! Equally stunned, Mary and her companions were temporarily immobilized.

One angel's first words to these faithful females were, "Fear not" (v. 5). After this he ordered, "Go quickly, and tell…he is risen" (v. 7). As they went, Jesus met them. His first words? "Be not afraid" (v. 10).

This was vintage Jesus. In fearful circumstances His first words to His disciples were always some variation of "fear not." When He suddenly appeared one night as they battled a powerful storm on the lake of Galilee, His initial statement was, "It is I; be not afraid" (John 6:20). When Jairus heard the somber news, "Thy daughter is dead," Jesus immediately added, "Be not afraid" (Mark 5:35–36). When Peter was stunned by a boat-sinking haul of fish, Jesus quickly said, "Fear not" (Luke 5:10). After Jesus' ascension this pattern continued. When persecution was brewing in Corinth, Jesus spoke to Paul in a vision. His first words? "Be not afraid" (Acts 18:9).

Why did Jesus initially counsel His distressed followers to not yield to fear? It's the first duty of the faithful in fearful circumstances. Until we discharge it, we can't pursue other duties well: telling others Jesus has risen, or walking on life's stormy waters, or continuing to "only believe" when it seems too late, or catching not fish but men for Christ. Why does God allow fearful situations and seasons?

As we trust and obey, fearful situations and seasons develop full-orbed faith in us, confidence that God truly controls "all things," pleasant and unpleasant, for our "good" (Rom. 8:28). Subsequently we trust Him equally in prosperity and adversity. Jesus had this faith. His eternal soul-mate, the bride church, will have it too. Why does God forbid us, once frightened, to stay afraid?

Fear is an insulting "no confidence" vote in His rule. It implies He doesn't know what's happening or care; can't help us or won't; doesn't have the wisdom we need or won't share it. All forms of "the spirit of fear" (2 Tim. 1:7), from anxiety to full-blown panic, slur God's character—and the Word, which repeatedly declares He's all-powerful, ever-present, loving, faithful, and just. Fear also blocks God's help, because Jesus taught we must believe to receive: "According to your faith, be it unto you" (Matt. 9:29). If we trust God, He always helps in His time and way; if doubtful, we hinder the help we need and He wants to give. Jesus desired to heal His fellow Nazarenes, but couldn't "because of their unbelief" (Mark 6:1–6). Great leaders recognize this first duty of the faithful.

When Pharaoh's charioteers closed in, Moses ordered the terrified Hebrews, "Fear not, stand still" (Exod. 14:13). When Sennacherib's armies surrounded Jerusalem, Hezekiah told the trembling Judeans, "Be not afraid nor dismayed" (2 Chron. 32:7). Churchill exhorted the discouraged British, "Never give in, never, never, never." Roosevelt charged depression-weary Americans, "The only thing we have to fear is fear itself—nameless, unreasoning, unjustified terror that paralyzes needed efforts to convert retreat into advance."[1] Let's follow them.

When suddenly perplexed, frightened, or shocked, let's remember Christ's first words and our first duty! Then we won't be pushed in all the wrong directions—confusion, anxiety, foolish knee-jerk reactions, despair, depression—by that bully demon, fear. Rather, we'll reject fear—"perfect love expels all fear" (1 John 4:18, NLT), and stand firm, think clearly, pray confidently, speak graciously, act wisely, and overcome. And help others do so. (See Acts 27:20–21, 25.) This word is timely.

It's getting scary out there. Hard times have gripped America and the world. Economic instability is everywhere. Jobs are scarce. Disasters are increasing. Government is failing. Society's moral foundations—marriage, family, decency, responsibility—are broken. Terrorism continues. Weapons of mass destruction proliferate. And this is just the prelude to the final "distress of nations, with perplexity" (Luke 21:25). Things will get worse. Like Jesus' Roman guards, many unbelievers are in shock. Many Christians, like Mary, are also afraid. But we needn't be. The Good Shepherd has risen. In these faithless times He's as faithful as ever: "In the days of famine they shall be satisfied" (Ps. 37:19). In faith, let's rise and walk with Him, confident, joyful, fruitful, shining in this darkness!

But first, "Fear not!" That's the first duty of the faithful.

Chapter 12

SING WHILE YOU SUFFER

$\mathcal{D}$URING THE LAST Supper Jesus told His disciples that one of them would betray Him that very night. After dining, they "went out into the Mount of Olives," where He began suffering (Matt. 26:30). But not before they had "sung an hymn" (KJV).

So Matthew reveals as Jesus left the upper room to face His sufferings—betrayal, abandonment, injustice, public ridicule, physical abuse, scourging, and the indignity of crucifixion—He sang praises to His Father. Many scholars believe the "hymn" He sang was taken from the Jewish "Hallel,"[1] the part of the Psalter traditionally sung during Passover (Psalms 113–118).[2] Jesus' worship in song under such dire circumstances was a powerful demonstration of God's grace at work in a soul. But it wasn't unique.

The Bible showcases others who sang as they suffered. When Jehoshaphat's armies "began to sing and to praise" the Lord, the Lord began to confuse their enemies and turn one against another (2 Chron. 20:20–22). As David sank in the "deep mire" and "deep waters" of his long wilderness afflictions, he praised and pleased God "with a song" and "with thanksgiving" (Ps. 69:1–2, 30). Paul and Silas worshipped Christ with joyful, heavenly songs while wounded and bound in Philippi's depressing, hellish inner prison (Acts 16:22–25). Church history continues this amazing testimony of singing sufferers.

After being publicly declared a heretic, defrocked, mocked, bound in chains, surrounded by wood, and his pyre set aflame, the fifteenth-century Czech reformer, John Hus, sang to his Savior as he suffered martyrdom at the Council of Constance (1415). Before expiring, he sang three times, "Jesus, son of the living God, have mercy on me."[3] A group of Moravians bound for America calmly sang psalms in German during an Atlantic storm so fierce it broke their ship's mast—while a young ordained but unconverted John Wesley stood by, stunned by the storm but even more by their worship! Many African American slaves sang soul-lifting praises to God—"spirituals," we call them—while enduring backbreaking labor and heartbreaking abuse all their lives. Said one, "We would pick cotton and sing, pick and sing all day."[4] While The Salvation Army bands played, their workers sang praises to the Savior in the streets of nineteenth-century England and America, while many faced verbal and physical abuse from angry mobs.

These remarkable sacrifices of praise reaped remarkable benefits. Jehoshaphat's enemies fell at his feet, never again to rise against him. While David's circumstances sank, his spirit rose and soared until he recovered all he had lost. God miraculously loosed Paul and Silas from their bonds and jail and left a permanent faith impression on the prisoners, the jailer, and his family. Though I can't prove it, I'm sure Hus never felt the intense heat that engulfed and incinerated his mortal body. The Moravians came through their dark storm shining, and Wesley saw their Light and came to Him. The Salvation Army's brave evangelists stood in God's armor, shattered spiritual strongholds, and freed thousands to walk with the Savior. Why were these so blessed? They sang while they suffered!

Are you suffering misunderstanding, rejection, slander, harassment, injustice, or worse, for Christ's sake? For studying, obeying, sharing, or ministering His Word? Have you received the fullness of the Holy Spirit, who alone gives us the power to suffer and sing as Jesus did? (See Acts 1:8.) If so, follow Jesus' example. Rise and, with your crosses and thorns before you, sing praises to Him. He's waiting to receive you on your Mount of Olives: "Enter into his gates with thanksgiving, and…his courts with praise" (Ps. 100:4). Your special songs will release special benefits for you and others.

They'll greatly honor and please God, and He'll confuse your enemies and lift your spirit. They'll reveal Jesus' grace and glory in you, and others will see and receive the Light of your life. They'll shatter your shackles of doubt and prisons of fear, and you'll walk and work freely with God. They'll see you through the hottest fiery trials, and you won't feel any heat. They'll bring you through the stormiest tribulation in peace, while others panic. They'll make angels sing along and demons be silent, and keep you linked to God and the river of His sustaining wisdom, strength, and peace—all while your sufferings continue.

Suffering for Jesus? Remember this: if you mumble and grumble, you'll stumble; but if you stand and sing, you'll soar. And bless God. And be blessed. And bless others. Ready to worshipfully sing your "Hallel" to Jesus as He sang His to His Father? Select your "hymn" and sing while you suffer.

Chapter 13

SEEKING SPIRITUAL UNITY

*O*F CHRIST'S FOLLOWERS gathered in the Upper Room, Luke notes, "These all continued with *one accord* in prayer and supplication" (Acts 1:14). It's a significant statement.

Various qualifying factors were present among the 120 who sought the Holy Spirit—faith, obedience, waiting, prayer, persistence. All present believed Jesus, obediently waited for Him to send power from on high, and prayed persistently for it. But while these requirements were important, one was more important: spiritual unity. Therefore, when describing the great day the Spirit fell on them, Luke again notes their oneness and the absence of discord: "When the day of Pentecost was fully come, they were all with one accord in one place" (Acts 2:1). Let's ponder their "one accord."

It wasn't like any other kind of human union. Their unity wasn't merely religious, all being of the same religion; or denominational, all of a single sect; or institutional, all of one organization; or racial, all of one race; or ethnic, all of one tribe or culture; or national, all of a single nation; or political, all of one political party; or social, all of one socioeconomic class; or physical, all present in one place. Their unity was more. It was a remarkably rare oneness of spirit and soul.

This spiritual unity occurs today whenever and wherever believers have the same:

- BELIEFS: core views, of God, Christ, salvation, the world, and the Bible

- HEART: core spirit and sentiments, a regenerated spirit and transformed emotional drivers (loves, desires, motives)

- MIND: core psychology, a biblical way of thinking with renewed, humble, spiritual attitudes

- PURPOSES: core goals, ends that are neither worldly (selfish, materialistic, political, humanistic) nor temporal, but are focused on Jesus' appearing and God's eternal kingdom

- FELLOWSHIP: core interests, friendly association and conversation centered around the things of Jesus

Further emphasizing this, Acts refers to the young church's spiritual unity seven times in describing its first fifteen years. (See Acts 1:14; 2:1; 2:44–46; 4:24; 4:32; 5:12; 15:25.) This repetition is shouting to us, "Spiritual unity is central to the church's success!" It shows early Christians not only achieved but also protected and nurtured their oneness, and it hints this enabled God to continue working through them powerfully despite the various internal problems and external persecutions they faced. Why was unity a chief concern?

It's the main request in Jesus' high priestly prayer: "That they all may be one…perfect in one" (John 17:21, 23). Since the Holy Spirit has come to execute this, Christ's last will and testament, He is duty-bound to create and fully develop spiritual unity among believers worldwide. And to bless it!

Psalm 133 reveals God reserves His best blessings—the refreshing "dew of [Mount] Hermon" and the overflowing "precious ointment" of believer-priests, both symbols of the Spirit's fullness—for those who "dwell together in unity." How do we dwell together in unity?

Spiritual unity is built and preserved by love, humility, and unselfishness. Wherever these are, unity is; wherever they abound, it thrives; wherever they diminish, it dies. Conversely, the forces that destroy spiritual unity are pride, malice, and selfishness. Wherever they appear, divisions follow; wherever they disappear, churches reunite; wherever they grow, churches fail. And the Spirit and Son grieve: "Jesus wept" (John 11:35).

To avoid this, the apostles called us to spiritual unity. Paul revealed the nature of God's love in us and urged us to live in it (1 Cor. 13:4–8). He ordered us to "walk in love" as God's dear and endearing children (Eph. 4:30–5:2). He reminded us to consider ourselves "all one in Christ" (Gal. 3:28). He insisted we meekly maintain the "bond of perfectness" (Col. 3:12–14). And Peter called us all, leaders and the led, to humility (1 Pet. 5:5). Will we respond?

Even when congregations won't comply, leaders must walk in spiritual unity—so God's Spirit can "run down" on their congregations to unify them! (Ps. 133:2).[1] This explains why Paul maintained unity with Apollos though the Corinthians were divided (1 Cor. 3:1–4, 6–8) and why he urged two female leaders in Philippi to have the "same mind" (Phil. 4:1–2). It explains why God corrected Miriam and Aaron "suddenly" for misjudging Moses (Num. 12:1–16)—the three were Israel's leadership!

Listen, leaders! As a house divided cannot stand, so one united cannot fall. Nor can it fail to be filled with the Spirit—and mightily used to honor God, build His kingdom, and bless His people!

Listen, His people! Division disappoints Jesus, but spiritual unity delights Him! When the first Christians "continued with one accord," He rejoiced. In these last days let's delight Him again by seeking spiritual unity.

Chapter 14

ARE YOU ON FIRE?

HE TIME WAS right, the believers were ready, so the Baptizer acted. "Suddenly…from heaven," He filled His followers with the Holy Spirit, who appeared as flames of fire resting on each one. Why fire?

God, the "consuming fire," was igniting the church with spiritual fire. John the Baptist said fire would accompany the baptism with the Spirit. Jesus said He came to kindle "fire on the earth" (Luke 12:49). Recognizing this, Peter concluded the miracle of Pentecost was Jesus' personal work: "He hath shed forth this, which ye now see and hear" (Acts 2:33). What did His fire do?

Matthew Henry wrote, "The Spirit, like fire, melts the heart, burns up the dross, and kindles pious and devout affections in the soul."[1] Once received, the Spirit lights three core fires in us:

1. He melts our stubborn wills, so we'll consistently do God's will, first and willingly.

2. He consumes our sinful attitudes, actions, and reactions, so we'll walk in Christ's righteousness daily.

3. He kindles ardent love for Jesus, so we're neither "cold" nor "lukewarm" but "hot," fervently focused on Jesus till He comes (Rev. 3:15–16).

Are these fires glowing in us as they did in the early Christians?

As fire requires fuel, oxygen, and sparks, spiritual fire requires God's Word, Spirit, and faith. When present, they ignite three burnings in us.

Our wills flame up—and, as our stubbornness melts, we begin yielding quickly and joyfully to God's will: "I delight to do thy will, O my God" (Ps. 40:8). Our consciences ignite—and, as the Spirit and Word convict us, we begin quickly and truthfully confessing our sins and receiving correction. Then our hearts blaze with love for Jesus—and, as this passion grows, we start devoting ourselves to Him fully, eager now to spend time with Him in His Word, prayer, and worship. These three fires of will, conscience, and heart are closely linked.

The third grows only as we allow the first two. As our wills and consciences glow with the Spirit's fervor, our hearts burn brightly; or, as our refinement increases, our devotion grows. But if our wills remain stubborn and our consciences unresponsive, we'll never know the joy of a heart burning with love for Jesus. So Satan ceaselessly tries to douse these inner fires—and the Spirit works tirelessly to make them hotter, or re-kindle them when low (Matt. 25:7). Why? He wants these internal fires to spread. Wherever they burn steadily, four external fires eventually break out.

First, they spark revival fires, or instances of New Testament Christianity revisiting churches, cities, and nations. Pentecost's fire spread rapidly. Initially it engulfed Jerusalem, Judah, Samaria, Syria, Greece, and Asia Minor. Then Paul and Peter stoked fires already lit in Rome. Tradition says Andrew carried Christ's "torch" to Russia, Thomas to India, Bartholomew to Armenia, Jude to Persia, Matthew to Ethiopia, and James the Younger to Egypt.[2] Soon love for Jesus and His Word burned in every part of the Roman Empire.

Second, they kindle fires of judgment. Wherever revival fires go, they not only ignite souls but also burn Satan's works in and among them. John affirms Jesus came to "destroy the works of the devil" (1 John 3:8). In Jerusalem gospel fires burned up the highly respected facade of Christ-rejecting, Pharisaic Judaism, exposing it as a false religion. They consumed sorcery in Samaria, magic arts in Ephesus, and idolatry throughout Asia Minor.

Third, they light fiery controversies. When the Redeemer revives a land, its citizens hotly debate His revival. Of Jesus' glowing movement in Israel many said, "He hath a demon, and is mad," while others responded, "These are not the words of him that hath a demon" (John 10:20–21). Sometimes the disbelieving citizenry openly denounces God's visitation. In Ephesus the idol-makers' guild, enraged over their losses, ignited a three-hour citywide riot filled with burning condemnations and confusion! (Acts 19:28–34).

Fourth, they start fiery persecutions. Enraged by the gospel's exclusive claims and absolute truths, truth-rejecting religious and nonreligious groups often unite to incinerate the faith—or the faithful! Ironically Rome's worst fire (AD 64) began the church's worst fiery trial, the 250-year Roman persecution. Falsely blamed for the inferno, Christians were subsequently burned as human torches in Nero's garden and Coliseum. We're more likely to be burned in effigy or reputation. All these flames spread from Pentecost's original fire.

Jesus is ready to give us Upper Room fire, as He did two disciples near Emmaus: "Did not our heart burn within us?" (Luke 24:32). It's time we receive His fire, stoke it, and spread it, however fiery the consequences. Today, are you on fire?

Chapter 15

LIKE A RUSHING MIGHTY WIND!

S UDDENLY THERE CAME a sound from heaven like a rushing mighty wind" (Acts 2:2). "Rushing mighty wind" describes the Holy Spirit's work perfectly. He rushes, He's mighty, He's like wind.

Sometimes He "rushes" in His work, moving with great speed and suddenness, as at Pentecost: "Suddenly, there came..." Or He rushes in compassion, quickly aiding the weak, fallen, helpless, or oppressed. When waiting for God, it's comforting to remember that, when His time arrives and terms are met, His Spirit rushes in compassionate haste to help us.

His work is always "mighty," or irresistibly powerful in souls, bodies, and nature. Persuasive, He changes our minds, goals, and life paths. Reinvigorating, He restores our bodily strength and health. Supernatural, He intervenes with an awesome energy we can't fully comprehend or describe.

And He works "like...wind." Jesus affirmed this: "The wind bloweth where it willeth, and thou hearest the sound of it, but canst not tell from where it cometh, and where it goeth; so is every one that is born of the Spirit" (John 3:8). Let's examine this symbol further. How are the works of the Spirit like the ways of the wind?

Like wind, the Holy Spirit is invisible. No man has seen the wind, only its influence on clouds, water, or physical objects. Similarly, we see the Spirit's effects but not His essence, His influence on souls and bodies, but never His form. He's appeared like doves and flames, yet He's neither. Only the inner eyes of our understanding detect Him. So we know Him by faith, not sight; intuitively, not visually.

Like wind, He's irresistible. His work is often opposed but never controlled, limited, or stopped by human means or power, any more than a hurricane, typhoon, or tornado can be. "If it [this work] be of God [the Holy Spirit], ye cannot overthrow it," said wise rabbi Gamaliel (Acts 5:39). Evil spirits, Jewish priests, and Roman emperors tried but failed to stop the mighty wind from the Upper Room.

Like wind, He's mysterious. No finite creature fully understands the Spirit's infinite thoughts, ways, or power. His reason far outstrips ours: "As the heavens are higher than the earth, so are my ways higher than your ways, and my thoughts than your thoughts" (Isa. 55:9). However intelligent or inspired, we understand divine wisdom only "in part" (1 Cor. 13:9). So we're awed when He makes fishermen apostles, makes atheists believers, works creative miracles, revives dead churches, converts sinful nations, gives biblical insight, and speaks to us personally through public sermons. Indefinable yet undeniable, He's a mystery.

Like wind, He's unpredictable. Jesus affirmed, "Thou canst not tell…whither it [wind] goeth" (John 3:8). We can't tell when, where, or how the Spirit's next "new thing" will break out (Isa. 43:19). Who would have predicted a Messiah from the unspiritual region of Galilee? The conversion of Saul, the church's worst persecutor? The lethal judgment of Ananias and Sapphira in church? Brave Luther overturning a thousand years of church corruption and errors? Wesley, an unsuccessful Anglican missionary, successfully reviving England? Seymour, a poorly educated African American, leading a Pentecostal movement that, from unconventional beginnings, today encompasses the globe? Humble house church leaders guiding Chinese Christians through decades of Communist oppression and persecution to a promised land of explosive growth? Nobody foresaw these Spirit-winds!

Like wind, He's active. Never totally stagnant, wind is ever moving—in swift, high altitude "rivers" of air, like our jet stream; in updrafts or thermals of rising warm air, on which eagles rise and glide; in trade winds that cool tropical islands and power sailing vessels across the seas. The Spirit is equally active. He's always blowing truths through our lives and churches, stirring the sleepy to vigilance, lifting the weary with inspirational messages, cooling the angry with warnings, and powering our ministries and missions with hope.

Like wind, He's omnipresent. Whether in whispers or roarings, wind is constantly blowing all over the world. Likewise the Spirit's work can't be limited to one place. His saving gospel blows over all peoples, nations, and continents daily.

Like wind, He blesses and destroys. Gentle breezes delight us regularly, enriching our lives. But tornados, sand storms, and flash-freezing Antarctic blasts devastate us and our property. The Spirit also blesses and destroys. His kind winds of grace bring rapturous joy to penitent ones, while His sudden judgments blow away impenitent sinners and their oppressive injustices.

The dead world and sleeping church rarely recognize these Spirit-winds. But they're as real and ready as ever. I hear a new "sound." It's coming "from heaven." It's—He's—ready to revisit us, again, "like a rushing mighty wind"!

Chapter 16

A PRODIGIOUS PARADE OF PRODIGALS

*I*N LUKE 15:11–32 Jesus described two sons. The "elder" lived close to his father and served faithfully in his "field." But the "younger," or less mature, ignored his father's will and elected to live far from him.

The younger's notorious journey to nowhere began when he shifted his focus from his father to selfishness—"give me...[what] falleth to me"—and materialism: "give me...the goods" (v. 12). In a hurry for wealth, he asked his father to divide his estate early, and he obliged. Then the younger departed for a "far country" (v. 13) where he lived contentedly as long as he could please, serve, and indulge himself. True to his nickname, this prodigal "wasted his substance" (v. 13), until he "spent all" (v. 14). Then the times changed.

Not a mini but a "mighty famine" visited the land (v. 14), forcing everyone to seek help. Still unwise, the prodigal sought earthly, not heavenly, help, partnering with "a citizen of that country" (v. 15) instead of turning to his father's God. But man's help proved unhelpful, leading only to more humiliation, hunger, and hardship. Weary, desolate, and desperate, he repented: "He came to himself [his right thinking]" (v. 17).

Humbled and restored to reality, he now saw the folly of his unfaithfulness and the wisdom of those who faithfully served his father: "My father's hired servants have bread enough and to spare" (v. 17). He refocused again, not on "goods" but on his good father! "I will...go to my father" (v. 18). He thought the thoughts of the penitent: "I...am no more worthy" (v. 19). He spoke their rhetoric: "I have sinned" (v. 18). He evinced their surrender, abandoning all claims to his estate and humbly accepting the lower status of a hired servant: "Make me as one of thy hired servants" (v. 19). And he demonstrated their actions: "He arose, and came to his father" (v. 20). His penitent parade home from the "far country" was underway.

Soon he rediscovered what he had long forgotten—how uniquely loving and gracious his father was! Not apathetic, his father was attentive, watching persistently for his son's return: "A great way off, his father saw him" (v. 20). Not disdainful, he "had compassion" on him (v. 20). Not delaying to respond, he "ran" to meet him (v. 20). Not denying affection, he hugged and "kissed" him freely (v. 20). Not withholding blessings, he gave his restored son the best provisions, since he now loved his father more than his "goods" (v. 22). Not ashamed, he gave him a signet ring, symbolizing his restored family trust, authority, and privileges (v. 22). Not morose, he was merry: "Let us eat, and be merry... [with] music and dancing" (vv. 23–25). What a dad—and new beginning!

This remarkable restoration began when a "mighty famine" visited the "far country."

For decades too many American Christians have lived like this younger son. Some have indulged in "riotous living," but most have simply focused on materialism or selfish goals. Some have wasted money, but most have wasted precious spiritual riches—Christ in them, the Spirit's guidance, the Word, ministry gifts, callings, and intimacy with our heavenly Father. Millions attend church yet prefer not to live near Father or serve His kingdom interests "first" (Matt. 6:33). Our "far country" is this world. Its prince, people, and temporal values—lusts of the flesh and eyes and the pride of life—are far from God, as are Christians who live for what this world offers. But the times are changing.

A "mighty famine" has come. Prolonged wars, potential wars, massive national debt, legislative gridlock, high unemployment, bankruptcies and foreclosures, unstable fuel costs, teetering European economies, and other factors have weakened our long-bullish economy. Today few prodigal Christians can indulge their material lusts. Most have spent all their cash—and credit—and are in want. Weary, they're desperately seeking help. Some still look to men: economists, psychologists, pundits, politicians, presidents! But this too will pass. Soon millions will come to themselves and, whether our economy stabilizes or sinks, return to live close to the Father, humbly serve Him, and prepare for Christ's appearing. I hear a parade.

The prodigal's parade home was a small, unnoticed, one-man trek. Our parade of prodigals will be neither small nor overlooked but prodigious—a huge throng of carnal, backslidden Christians returning to their heavenly Father, changing churches and nations as they come.

Pray for this, interceding for every prodigal you know. Prepare for it, purging the prodigal in you—selfishness, materialism, or spiritual wastefulness. Watch for it, till you see a prodigious parade of prodigals.

Chapter 17

THE PRIME PRINCIPLE OF PREACHERS

O THE PROUD Pharisees Jesus said: "Whosoever shall exalt himself shall be abased; and he that shall humble himself shall be exalted" (Matt. 23:12). This was no passing thought.

Rather, this proverb was one of the primary themes Jesus taught while traversing Israel for three-plus years. The Gospels record Him speaking it on three separate occasions. As cited above, He included it in His final lecture to the preachers of His day, the scribes and Pharisees. He also wove it into two other sobering talks He gave them.

Once after watching a group of Pharisees select the most prominent seating for themselves at a dinner, Jesus advised they start choosing not the highest but the lowest places, and added: "For whosoever exalteth himself shall be abased; and he that humbleth himself shall be exalted" (Luke 14:11). To other Pharisees who imagined their righteousness was superior and despised others, He told a parable intended to deflate their overinflated self-esteem, ending it, again, with His prime principle: "For everyone that exalteth himself shall be abased; and he that humbleth himself shall be exalted" (Luke 18:14). Jesus' repetition of this theme, and the audience to whom He spoke, tells us that: (1) it's important, and (2) it applies first to preachers.

What does His proverb mean to us today?

It decrees whoever tries to climb higher will be put lower, but whoever peacefully accepts life's low places will be lifted higher. Everyone who tries to look big will ultimately appear small, while those who don't puff their image will have it enhanced. Those who try to build impressive reputations will eventually have them torn down, while those who focus on building good character will ultimately gain a good reputation. People who try to become influential will become insignificant, while those who accept their insignificance will grow to be influential. All who seek recognition will be overlooked, while those who accept being overlooked will be recognized. Thus Jesus vows every proud heart will be humiliated and every humble heart honored—and His Father, and ours, is behind this inevitable process.

We preachers should meditate on this principle until it grips us and transforms us from self-serving, honor-seeking, religious office holders to meek, Christ-honoring, people-serving caregivers of Jesus' life, truth, and compassion. One of Jesus' original student-followers and preachers, Peter, got the message. He urged all undershepherds, "Humble yourselves…under the mighty hand of God" (1 Pet. 5:6), or, "Humble yourselves [demote, lower yourselves in your own estimation]" (AMP). Why should this call to humility be directed first to preachers?

God's people follow, and to some degree imitate, their preachers. If Christ's ministers walk in pride, so will His people. But if they think, speak, and live humbly, the people will follow suit. While we may feel a little bored with this subject, it's no small issue to God. Why?

First, He hates pride more than any other sin since it reminds Him of His proud adversary, Lucifer:

> These six things doth the LORD hate; yea, seven are an abomination unto him. A proud look…
>
> —PROVERBS 6:16–17

Second, He doesn't want His people—His precious eternal inheritance—spoiled by pride. If we follow proud preachers, we'll become like them, and Christ will loathe us. To prevent that, Christ purposely humbles every preacher He calls. And the higher He plans to take them, the meeker they must be.

We see this clearly in the training of God's most prominent servants, such as Moses: "Now the man Moses was very meek, above all the men who were upon the face of the earth" (Num. 12:3). "As a man," Jesus also, "humbled himself and became obedient unto death, even the [lowly] death of the cross" (Phil. 2:8). Conversely, the prouder ministers are, the surer they fall.

Note how Jesus dealt with the incorrigibly vain Pharisees. Everything they did was intended to lift themselves up: "All their works they do to be seen of men" (Matt. 23:5). And why? "That they may have glory [recognition, praise] from men" (Matt. 6:2). Therefore God sent His Son to deliberately put them down by publicly exposing their erroneous traditions and denouncing their hypocrisy. Thus He abased these small-hearted, self-serving office holders.

To avoid their humiliation and receive Christ's approval, listen: People of God, are you seeking personal integrity or a public image? Is your preacher haughty or humble, self-promoting or Christ-exalting? And preachers of God, where are you leading God's people? Into humility, spiritual growth, divine approval, and promotion? Or into excessive self-esteem, spiritual stagnation, divine disapproval, and eventual humiliation? Don't relive the Pharisees' failure.

Ponder and practice the prime principle of preachers.

Chapter 18

WILL YOU BE TAKEN?

To GET OUR full attention, Jesus spoke of His appearing—our joyous great escape, the Rapture—with a sense of urgency. He warned solemnly, "One shall be taken, and the other left [behind]" (Matt. 24:40, 41). Immediately we dread being left behind and yearn to be sure we'll be "taken."

To be confident of translation, we must possess the biblical qualifications for this, the church's great exodus. According to the Word, we may be sure we'll be taken if:

1. WE DON'T NEGLECT OUR SALVATION. "How shall we escape, if we neglect so great salvation?" (Heb. 2:3). After conversion we begin developing, or "working out," our grace-given salvation. Daily we seek to know more of our Savior's Word, will, ways, and presence. We may neglect worldly interests but never our personal relationship with Him.

2. WE'RE WATCHING. Jesus repeatedly urged not unbelievers but *believers* to "watch" for His return—believing in it, looking for its "signs of the times," and cultivating a growing sense of expectation: "Watch...watch...watch" (Mark 13:32–37). So rather than "sleep" in doubt or disbelief, we "watch."

3. WE'RE READY. Since it may be mere prophetic curiosity, watching for Jesus' appearing isn't enough. We must also actively prepare for it: "Watch...[and] be ye also ready" (Matt. 24:42, 44). Being "also ready" involves steady obedience, diligently practicing the spiritual disciplines—walking in love, faith, honesty, humility, patience, exhortation, charity—that bring us to God's standard of readiness. Why? Christ's bride must be ready not only to leave here but also to live and rule with Him in perfect union forever.

4. WE PURIFY OURSELVES. "Every man that hath this hope [the Rapture] in him purifieth himself, even as he is pure"

(1 John 3:3). Determined to not let sin rest in us and rule us, we maintain self-examination, regularly facing our true thoughts, emotions, words, and acts; quickly confessing any sins; and humbly conforming to God's Word and will.

5. WE'RE WORTHY. Besides watching, we give ourselves continually to prayer: "Watch ye…and pray always, that ye may be accounted worthy to escape all these things" (Luke 21:36). This "praying always," thanking our heavenly Father, talking with Him, and interceding in the Spirit for others creates a worthy spiritual life in His sight.

6. WE'RE FAITHFUL. "Who, then, is a faithful and wise servant…whom his lord, when he cometh, shall find so doing [his duty faithfully]" (Matt. 24:45–46). While we watch, we pursue faithfulness, discharging our duties in our homes, jobs, and churches in a regular, responsible, and trustworthy manner. Our faithful Savior will take His faithful servants.

7. WE'RE FOCUSED ON ETERNITY. Spiritually focused, we seek Christ, our King, and His kingdom values and work "first" (Matt. 6:33). We "attend upon the Lord without distraction" (1 Cor. 7:35). Daily we reset our hearts on things above, not on things on the earth (Col. 3:1–2) and refuse to be distracted by seeking power, wealth, or fame in this world. When the focus of our life appears, then we focused ones shall "also appear with him in glory" (v. 4).

8. WE'RE TESTED. "Because thou hast kept the word of my patience [my order to endure, patiently awaiting my help], I also will keep thee from the hour of temptation, which shall come upon all the earth" (Rev. 3:10). We've experienced many tests of faith and patience, and at least one long test of endurance, without rebelling. Since we've passed our tests, we're exempt from the world's final test. Just before the Tribulation Jesus will take us, keeping us from it.

9. WE'RE OVERCOMERS. In Revelation Jesus repeatedly urged us to become full-fledged overcomers: "To him that overcometh [subdues] will I…" (Rev. 2:7, 11, 17, 26; 3:5, 12, 21). Responding, we refuse to accept any defeat or failure as final,

rising again by renewed trust and obedience to subdue every adversity and adversary Satan throws at us.

10. WE WALK WITH GOD. While some Christians walk away or afar from our Father, we draw near to learn His ways of living. Accepting a separated, Christ-centered lifestyle, we conform to Christ's goals, standards, correction, and guidance, not popular trends. Like Enoch, we "walk with God" in a godless society (Gen. 5:22, 24). So one day God will take us, as He did Enoch—leaving those who walk away or afar to endure the worldwide judgment.

No idle speculations, these are fixed biblical requirements. Everyone possessing them may be sure—rock-solid confident—they'll be taken whenever Jesus appears. He forewarned us these things to get our attention. Does He have it?

Pursue these prerequisites now, and you'll never waver when asked, "Will you be taken?"

Chapter 19

A FRESH REVELATION OF JESUS IS NEAR!

A CALL FOR RESTORATION and revival, Psalm 85 sheds the light of hope on these dark times. The unnamed psalmist was urgent in prayer.

First, he pleaded, "Restore us, O God" (v. 4). Then, he begged, "Wilt thou not revive us again?" (v. 6). Finally, and wisely, he waited for God's answer: "I will hear what God, the LORD, will speak" (v. 8). He didn't have to wait long.

So quick and strong was the Spirit's response that it filled him with confidence that a fresh visitation of God was at hand: "Surely his salvation is near those who fear him, that glory may dwell in our land" (v. 9). The psalmist saw this as God's promise to save Judah from sin and punishment and reestablish His glorious presence, worship, and blessing in the land. But let's interpret God's response as it speaks to us today.

To contemporary Christians, "His salvation" speaks of God saving us from our besetting sins and all the needless adversities, oppressions, and spiritual dryness they bring. This uplifting release comes when "glory...dwell[s] in our land" (v. 9).

Glory dwelling in our land means nothing less than our stale churches and sinful nations receiving a stunningly fresh revelation of God's greatness—the *magnificent fullness of Jesus*, His wondrously beautiful character, truths, grace, and works. Of Jesus' character John wrote, "We beheld his glory, the glory...of the Father, full of grace and truth" (John 1:14). Of His ministry Matthew wrote, "Jesus went about all Galilee, teaching in their synagogues, and preaching the gospel of the kingdom, and healing all manner of sickness" (Matt. 4:23). When glory visits our land, the same Jesus is marveled at living and ministering among us in our ordinary, unspiritual "Galilee" regions. How? By the power of His Spirit working through the revived members of His body.

This rare public exhibition of God's awesomeness is a visitation, a divinely appointed season in which God reveals His ever present but usually veiled presence, power, and passion to save. These "times of refreshing...from the presence of the Lord" (Acts 3:19) are marked by fresh outpourings of the Spirit that reenergize us and guide the Lord's "visit." During visitations, unusual becomes usual and extraordinary ordinary.

Ministers speak, but not of themselves. Christ's very voice speaks through their talks and writings. The Spirit's gifts reappear and flow. The Good Shepherd uses them to comfort and guide His sheep through perilous valleys of testing. The Spirit reemphasizes holiness. Penitent Christians are purified and impenitent ones exposed. This unmatched spectacle of Jesus among us attracts powerfully: "I, if I be lifted up from the earth, will draw all men unto me" (John 12:32). Sinners receive the Light and prodigals return to the Father. No other worldly, religious, or entertaining attractions are needed—no impressive institutions, high ritual, or enchanting music; no excellent programs, amazing technology, or promises of prosperity; no renowned ministers, popular politicians, or famous entertainers. Seeing Jesus is the only draw and knowing Jesus the only end. Such visitations endure.

With wise, courageous leadership, they "go on unto perfection [maturity]" (Heb. 6:1). The fear of God falls, creating respect for God's authority and resolve to avoid His discipline: "Let them not turn again to folly [sin] ... those who fear him" (Ps. 85:8–9). Bible instruction is enthusiastically received, and changed lives and Christlike characters spring up: "Truth [God's Word] shall spring out of the earth [our human "dust"]" (v. 11). More "rains" of the Spirit come: "The LORD shall give that which is [his] good ["treasure," spiritual rain[1]]" (v. 12). Churches in many nations yield God rich harvests of overcoming disciples: "Our land shall yield her [kingdom] increase," and God will "set us in the way of his steps [paths]" (vv. 12–13) or establish us in His spiritual ways of living and ministering. This is the visitation's goal: a revived body of Christians firmly established in a steady, close walk with God, whether prosperous or persecuted—His Word demonstrated in us, His Spirit guiding us, and the glorious light of Jesus shining through us illuminating nations with the knowledge of the only true Savior and salvation. That's visitation victory!

Since God revives His people cyclically, why bother praying? The church's last days have arrived. Before Jesus comes for us, He'll come to us and revive us. This is necessary to fulfill Christ's high priestly prayer and the prophetic portraits of the mature church;[2] also, to give this world one merciful, bright, final witness of Jesus before the triumphant church departs—and the Tribulation arrives.

So pray, and believe Psalm 85: a fresh revelation of Jesus is near!

Chapter 20

HOW FAR WILL YOU GO?

*H*OW FAR WILL you go to be a blessing? The Italian Christians went out of their way to bless the apostle Paul.

Upon Paul's arrival, the Christians of Puteoli begged him, Luke, and Aristarchus, and perhaps Paul's Roman guards also, to lodge and worship with them for a week (Acts 28:13–14). Hospitably they further notified the Roman Christians Paul was coming, so they too would prepare to receive him.

The Romans' response was threefold. Some stayed in Rome, presumably to greet the weary apostle after he settled into his new quarters and rested. Others went to meet Paul on the Appian Way. Some walked thirty-three miles to the Three Taverns area (Acts v. 15) in a loving gesture, expending considerable effort. Others went further, trekking forty-three miles to the Forum of Appius (v. 15) to warmly greet and minister to the man who had blessed so many worldwide and had recently blessed them with his Epistle to the Romans. This blessed Paul greatly: "When Paul saw them, he thanked God and was greatly encouraged" (v. 15, GNT). All these believers acted commendably, yet some showed more willingness to bless others. Like them, many Christians have gone far to be a blessing.

Philip left his thriving work in Samaria and ventured into a lonely, windswept desert to bless one Ethiopian official. Hudson Taylor sailed halfway around the world to convert the isolated, spiritually unenlightened, nineteen-century Chinese. Paul crossed the Aegean Sea to bless the praying Jewish women of Philippi. Patrick willingly returned to Ireland—where he had been enslaved six years—to evangelize the pagan, Druid-led Irish. The first Moravian missionaries crossed the stormy Atlantic and labored humbly to evangelize the oppressed slaves of the West Indies. George Mueller prayed constantly for the funds that supported many orphans, missionaries, and schools. Methodist circuit riders forsook their comforts to carry God's Word to the settlers of the American West through hostile weather, terrain, and natives. Billy Graham left his growing family for long periods of time to evangelize the nations. How far will you go to bless others? Or to bless Jesus, who is delighted whenever we do His will?

How far will you go in:

- HOSPITALITY? Will you receive and host fellow Christians, whether traveling or ministering, for extended visits?

- GIVING? Will you give tithes and offerings to spread God's Word and care for the poor, widows, orphans, and refugees?

- INTERCESSION? Will you fast and pray frequently so others may be converted, healed, or matured?

- BIBLE STUDY? Will you abandon trivial pursuits to dig deep into God's sayings for weeks? Months? Years?

- LOVE? Will you forgive offenses, show mercy, and consider others before yourself, whether among family and friends? Strangers? Enemies?

- FAITH? Will you believe and await God's promises despite contradictions and delays lasting months? Years? Decades?

- HUMILITY? Will you remain close to God and meekly non-resistant when for a season He permits you to be misunderstood? Criticized? Rejected?

- SUFFERING? Will you continue "overcoming evil with good" when your evildoer and evil day seem endless?

- COMFORTING SUFFERERS? Will you continue assisting the sick, weak, or elderly when their condition seems hopeless?

- MINISTRY? Will you continue faithfully teaching or counseling God's people though their response is lukewarm?

- WORK? Will you continue laboring long hours under difficult conditions for deficient pay, because you feel you're where God put you?

How many "miles" of sacrificial effort will you walk to bless souls or your Savior in these or other graces and duties? Jesus taught that if compelled to carry burdens one mile, we should go two. Though not compelled, the Roman Christians far exceeded that—and blessed not only Paul but also Jesus. Will you?

Will you delight Him who said, "It is more blessed to give than to receive" and who came "not to be ministered unto, but to minister, and to give" (Acts 20:35; Matt. 20:28). How many "miles" will you voluntarily walk in diligence, faithfulness, and perseverance to bless Him, a weary "Paul," a "little one," or the lowest sinner needing your help? Thirty-three miles? Forty-three? You can stay comfortably in "Rome" if you wish and let others carry the burden. Or at any point on your "Appian Way" you can turn back, justly concluding, "I've gone far enough with this demanding test, Lord. I'm not bearing this unfairness, indignity, or labor any further." Or you can see how far you've come and conclude, "I've gone too far to turn back now," and finish your course. The Roman Christians went all the way.

How far will you go?

Chapter 21

OCCUPYING IN THE VALLEY OF DELAY

*A*FTER JESUS PROMISED to appear as a thief in the night to take His people away, He spoke a parable teaching us how to be ready when He comes (Matt. 24:44–51).

His story reveals just how dangerous the disappointment of delay is. By describing two servants' reactions to their master's delayed return, it showcases our two reactions to deferred divine promises: foolish faithlessness and wise faithfulness.

The "evil" servant's sad slide into infamy began with one unexamined thought: "My lord delayeth his coming" (v. 48). His reaction was ruinous. Rather than reject this lying imagination that implied his master's indifference or unfaithfulness, he received it. Then, like leaven, his doubt grew: "He's delayed his coming" soon expanded into "He's canceled his return." Offended at his master's apparent breach of promise, this servant started losing ground. He began being callous and careless, mistreating his fellow servants, whom he formerly loved, and partying with foolish drunkards, whose company he had previously avoided (v. 49). When his master returned, this faithless servant was punished and denied advancement (vv. 50–51). But some servants reacted differently.

One "wise and faithful servant" who supervised the estate's food services (v. 45) chose to continue believing his master. While acknowledging his master's delay, he still believed he would keep his promise and watched faithfully for his arrival. Sustained by this hope, he kept loving his fellow servants, avoiding the foolish and their ways, and staying busy with his appointed tasks. When his master returned, he found him "so doing" and promptly promoted him to steward of the entire estate (vv. 45–46).

Like these two servants' reactions to delay, ours are crucial. When our hopes are deferred, we either use or abuse the time between their delay and their arrival.

If wise, we'll remain faithful, staying close to Jesus and pursuing the work He's given us. Christ will respond by empowering us from above. When the apostles asked Jesus when His kingdom—and their heart's desire—would come, He put them off: "It is not for you to know…" (Acts 1:7).

Then He gave them a concession. If they would faithfully occupy, He would faithfully empower them: "But ye shall receive power, after the Holy Spirit is come upon you; and...be witnesses" (v. 8). Like theirs, our delays are opportunities to receive more spiritual power and strength of character to witness and work more effectively—unless we too turn to folly.

Specifically, the folly of unfaithfulness seen in the "evil" servant. This begins when we get offended (angry) over Jesus delaying His promises, plans, or purposes and stop trusting in His faithfulness. Jesus promised special blessings to those who refuse to lose confidence in Him whatever their difficulties: "Blessed is he, whosoever shall not be offended in me" (Luke 7:23).

Once offended, we begin sliding into unbelief. We grow lukewarm (Rev. 3:16), or spiritually or morally indifferent, and, no longer sure biblical truth is absolute, we stop calling things clearly right or wrong. We turn from patience and kindness to impatience and intolerance, turning on others, including Christians, devouring them with selfish strife, criticism, slander, or betrayal. Paul warned of this spiritual cannibalism: "If ye bite and devour one another, take heed that ye be not consumed" (Gal. 5:15). We turn from diligence to indulgence, giving ourselves to excessive leisure, overeating, oversleeping, sexual lusts, alcohol, or drugs.

Failing to examine ourselves, we fall into spiritual sleep. This leaves us unaware of our true spiritual condition, sin's damaging effects on us, imminent dangers, and the nearness of Jesus' appearing. While asleep, our devotion, holiness, and zeal grow weak and ministry labors ineffective: "While the bridegroom tarried, they all slumbered and slept" (Matt. 25:5). When pressure floods in, we panic, losing our nerves, succumbing to persecutors' threats, and reversing our righteous confessions or stands. We abandon our divinely appointed places of service to pursue other things as, when discouraged, David fled to Philistia and Peter returned to fishing. Or we rebel, openly defecting from our Christian faith and profession and returning to our former worldly values and vices. However we react, valleys of delays will come.

They must. Our wise, loving heavenly Father sends these low seasons to temper our high times—mountaintop spiritual experiences and sweet worldly successes—and keep us balanced and sober-minded. Will our valleys of delays break or make us? Stunt or grow us? Will we be offended or occupy? Denied or granted promotion to higher service?

Here's some good advice. Better yet, here's some God advice. "Occupy till I come" (Luke 19:13). May the Lord, whenever He appears, find you occupying in the valley of delay.

Chapter 22

THE BENEFITS OF CROSS BEARING

*W*HILE SALVATION IS by grace through faith alone, Jesus declared true discipleship requires cross bearing: "Who soever doth not bear his cross…cannot be my disciple" (Luke 14:27). Christianity's original and greatest authority, His claim is too clear to deny, dispute, or ignore.

Indeed, unless we willingly accept and patiently carry our crosses, as He did His, though saved, we cannot be Jesus' disciples. Three questions naturally arise.

First, who are Jesus' "disciples"? A first-century disciple[1] was a very serious student of a Greek philosopher or Jewish rabbi. These young men gave themselves in submissive trust to live near and closely follow their teacher, dedicating their lives and disciplining their life habits to learn, live, and teach their master's beliefs. Ideally this devotion enabled them to become like their master and spread his fame through their words and ways. Will we be Jesus' disciples—deeply serious, irrevocably committed, self-disciplined student followers?

Second, what are our crosses? The Roman cross, reserved for the execution of Rome's lowest criminals, symbolized utter *rejection* by Roman society. In Jesus' case, crucifixion was also unjustified; He did nothing deserving of it. Of Persian origin, crucifixion was designed to prolong and thus maximize pain prior to death. Often victims agonized for days before expiring. Lethal, crosses were obviously the opposite of one's will—specifically one's desire to live. When faced with His cross, Jesus openly declared it was not His will: "Let this cup pass from me" (Matt. 26:39). However, He waived His will in favor of His Father's. Thus we conclude our crosses are unjust rejections that, because they're the opposite of what we want, cause us prolonged pain. Are we willing to bear our crosses?

Third, why do crosses come? The prince of darkness, Satan, prompts our crosses because we're developing into Christ's true disciples, obedient servants, and effective Word-light bearers in this sin-darkened world. He hopes to stop this development by offending us. Our Father, however, permits Satan to "cross" us to test our faith, patience, and loyalty. And there's more.

Our crosses benefit us richly. First, they authenticate us as Jesus' disciples. Many Christians say but don't pay, professing loyalty to the Master but evading or abandoning their crosses—forgetting that without them they cannot be His disciples. Second, accepted crosses conform our characters to Jesus' image (Rom. 8:29). By breaking our stubborn self-will, they prepare us to serve God's will without resistance, as Jesus did. As we endure rejections for not sin's or stupidity's but Christ's sake, they melt and remold us like Him who was "despised and rejected of men, a man of sorrows, and acquainted with grief" (Isa. 53:3). Third, they complete our calling. Everyone called to believe is also called to suffer: "Unto you it is given in the behalf of Christ, not only to believe on him but also to suffer for his sake" (Phil. 1:29). Fourth, they qualify us to rule with Christ in His kingdom: "If we suffer, we shall also reign with him" (2 Tim. 2:12). Fifth, they qualify us to receive a greater inheritance in Christ. We are "joint heirs with Christ—if...we suffer with him" (Rom. 8:17). So the more we suffer, the more we inherit. Sixth, they render us worthy of Christ's kingdom. Paul taught crosses come "that ye may be counted worthy of the kingdom of God, for which ye also suffer" (2 Thess. 1:5). Seventh, they create ministerial capacity in our souls, inner wells of knowledge, compassion, and power from which we draw effective help for other sufferers. The timely biblical passages and principles with which God comforts us become the ministry resources we use to "comfort them who are in any trouble" (2 Cor. 1:4). Thus our crosses benefit not only us but also others.

So when unjust rejections cause long-lasting pain in situations that are the opposite of your will, don't reject them. Fully embrace and patiently endure your crosses. The alternatives are unacceptable: No crosses, no true discipleship. No crosses, no Christlikeness. No crosses, no completed calling. No crosses, no ruling with Christ. No crosses, no full inheritance from Him. No crosses, no worthiness for His kingdom. No crosses, no capacity to minister to others effectively. But Christ will never overrule your free will.

The choice remains yours. You may carry or cast off your crosses, accept or abandon them, qualify or disqualify yourself for their wonderful benefits. Make the wise choice. To be an authentic disciple of Jesus Christ, check Satan's plan to stop your spiritual development, avoid the unpleasant alternatives to cross bearing, and bring rich blessings on yourself and others, ponder the benefits of cross bearing.

Chapter 23

ALL NATIONS ARE BEFORE HIM

*A*FTER RETURNING AND establishing His throne in Jerusalem, King Jesus will gather the Tribulation survivors from every nation: "Before him shall be gathered all the nations [Gentiles]" (Matt. 25:32). He will then judge them.

With perfect fairness Jesus will evaluate each surviving Gentile and assign him (or her) just what he's due. He'll invite some to enter and enjoy His millennial kingdom, because they've believed the gospel professed by His suffering brothers, the persecuted remnant of Jewish believers, and helped them endure the Great Tribulation: "Come, ye blessed of my Father, inherit the kingdom prepared for you from the foundation of the world" (v. 34). Others, however, He'll rebuke and expel from His glorious realm, because they've disbelieved the Jews' Messianic message, denied them aid, and worshipped the Antichrist: "Depart from me, ye cursed, into everlasting fire prepared for the devil and his angels" (v. 41). Jesus alone—who suffered and died to save all nations—has the right to judge the nations in that day.

And this day! Not just every generation but every day Jesus is actively judging nations, rendering decisions that give them the just consequences of their consistent national decisions and actions. He's constantly rewarding what He loves—righteousness, justice, and charity; and punishing what He loathes—immorality, injustice, and arrogance. During His first advent He announced His authority to judge all human beings, societies, and issues: "The Father...hath committed all judgment unto the Son...and hath given him authority to execute judgment" (John 5:22, 27). He carefully described this authority as not just a future but also a present reality: "The Father hath committed...hath given." At His ascension He reasserted His current authority over nations: "All authority is [now] given unto me in heaven and in earth" (Matt. 28:18). But what law serves as the basis for Judge Jesus' judgments?

Surprisingly, the code by which He reckons with nations is succinctly stated in one of Solomon's ancient wisdom sayings:

Righteousness exalteth a nation, but sin is a reproach to any people.

—PROVERBS 14:34

57

The words "any people" reveal this divine statute applies to all nations equally, without partiality—even Israel! When Solomon led Israel in righteousness during the initial years of his reign, God exalted, or raised and increased, Israel's spiritual life, economy, military strength, borders, and prestige. But when Solomon and his people turned to idolatry, exalting sin, God brought them low.

We often fail to recognize Jesus' hand when He blesses or punishes nations because He usually works through providential, not miraculous, means. We mistake His hand for natural occurrences or mere human causes and effects. National pride also makes us slow to admit He chastens our nation—and quick to claim He judges others! Consequently our faith in the omnipotence of His rulership is not strong enough. We're not sure Jesus is controlling all things that touch all nations at all times. But He is, every day. The Most High will never control the course of the nations any more than He does right now. Daniel repeatedly assured King Nebuchadnezzar: "The Most High ruleth [presently] in the kingdom of men...the heavens do [now] rule" (Dan. 4:17, 25, 26, 32). In the Millennium Jesus will rule manifestly, but now He rules providentially. And wherever He rules, He judges.

But always in love. Yes, even His punishments ultimately benefit us. They confirm His warnings and magnify His Word, dispel presumption and restore the fear of God, induce the repentance that fuels reforms and revivals, decrease sin and increase righteousness, destroy Satan's works so God's grow and prosper, end confusion and reestablish God's order, and enable God to restore His blessings. Consequently the times following His rod are always better than those preceding it—for God and us. Truly God causes all things, including His judgments, to work together for our good (Rom. 8:28). What things?

Triumphs or tragedies, bumper crops or crop failure, economic growth or recession, international favor or disfavor, domestic unity or division, social peace or strife, good or poor leadership, functional or dysfunctional government, outstanding or outrageous high courts, these are more than natural trends, conditions, or occurrences. They're veiled divine judgments—King Jesus' personal decisions to bless or chasten nations now in this time. If they aren't, He's not the Most High, nor presently ruling in the kingdoms of men. But the Bible has it right.

All authority and judgment belong to Jesus! Now! Are you watching for His decisions in your nation? Will you pray for its repentance and His mercy: "O Lord...in [executing] wrath remember [to show] mercy" (Hab. 3:2).

In the Millennium, and this moment, all nations are before Him.

Chapter 24

OBSESSED!

OBSESSIVE-COMPULSIVE DISORDER (OCD) is a mental illness in which a person obsessed by unreasonable anxious thoughts relentlessly repeats certain actions (e.g., hand-washing; rechecking things) in a vain attempt to relieve their anxiety. Few American Christians have full-blown OCD, yet many suffer obsessions.

For instance, many of us are obsessed with making money—always more! We must have income to pay bills and buy necessities, but should we spend every waking moment devising ways to get more money? Shopping obsesses others. We must purchase new consumer goods regularly, but should we run up massive credit card debts buying items we don't need and may never even use or sell? Sports dominate many. Enjoying athletic contests occasionally is good, clean entertainment and may help us learn key principles for overcoming life's challenges, but should we feed on sporting events as if they were vitally or permanently important? Electronics entrance others. Cell phones, computers, television, and the Internet are great work aids or life enhancements, but must we always be distracted by beeping gadgets and flashing images and never quiet and reflective? While most of these obsessions are relatively harmless, others are more overtly base and destructive.

Internet-driven extramarital sex of every kind has become America's most rapidly growing mania. Illegal drug addiction is also pervasive. First it was marijuana, then heroin, and then cocaine; soon meth (methamphetamine) dominated, and today illegal prescription drugs are lord and master of millions. Others get high daily on a cleaner, more socially acceptable "fix."

That fascination is politics. The news media focus on politics, especially presidential campaigns, nonstop with fanatical fervor. When candidates say anything controversial, pundits, commentators, and columnists feed on it like piranhas. For days, sometimes weeks, they analyze, condemn, or defend speaker and statement alike. When the feeding frenzy ends, they spit out the bones and seek their next victim. The pagan public loves this cannibalistic blood sport. But so do Christians.

Looking back, American evangelical Christians' foray into political hyperactivity and partisan bickering began with two truly alarming changes—the sexual revolution of the 1960s followed by the Supreme Court's landmark pro-abortion decision in 1973. It gradually morphed from a wise and justified church-based protest to an ill-advised, party-based movement to sanctify and control American politics. Millions of born-again believers enlisted in this new crusade to reform our society not by prayerful but by political action, a method not authorized by New Testament precept or precedent. The resurgent national pride of the Reagan era and American exceptionalism—the notion that America, if not superior, is exceptional and destined to spread democracy worldwide—combined to energize this holy war. For decades conservative Christian preachers and political action committees have striven for political dominance much as Roman popes clashed with medieval kings over national sovereignty, only with negative ads and political rallies instead of knights and swords. We now cling to a political vision of restoring America's greatness and preeminence among nations, blindly assuming God requires this of Christians before the Rapture. While thus captivated, we've neglected our primary duty of maintaining God's righteousness in our churches—and steadily sunk into lukewarmness, sin, and darkness. Shouldn't we be getting our own house in God's order rather than Congress'? (See 1 Corinthians 5:12–13.) Prophecy ensures the body of Christ's success but not America's preeminence. Shouldn't we be looking away? Looking forward?

Instead of blindly following political crusaders, shouldn't spiritually minded Christians discern their short-sightedness, step back, and reset our hearts on things above—the church's higher calling, God's higher methods, Jesus' soon appearing, and His enduring kingdom? Scripture commands, "Set your affection on things above, not on things on the earth" (Col. 3:2). Shouldn't we practice Christ's proven methods of changing societies by intercession, evangelism, missions, charity, our life witness, and our public protest against sin? Paul warned us of entangling distractions: "No man that warreth entangleth himself with the affairs of this life" (2 Tim. 2:4).

Shouldn't we disentangle ourselves from political hopes, however well intentioned, and refocus on the church's commission as light-bearer to all nations? If a cause isn't in our commission, it isn't our mission! Shouldn't we campaign to fulfill Christ's prayer for His church (John 17)? Shouldn't we be less bound to our country and more tethered to God's kingdom? Why? Every prince but Jesus will disappoint and every vision but His will fail.

American Christians don't have OCD, but we are dangerously addicted to politics. It's time we stop crusading for political power—while voting our conscience—and reset our hope on the things above. They cannot disappoint or fail us.

Then, when Jesus appears, He'll find us spiritually prepared, not politically obsessed!

Chapter 25

COURAGEOUS FAITH!

A VETERAN OF GOD'S testing, David urged us to have courageous faith: "Wait on the LORD; be of good courage..." (Ps.
27:14). But he didn't stop there.

David also promised if we'll have courage, we'll have encouragement:
"...and he [God] shall strengthen thine heart." God will faithfully send
anointings, insights, answers to prayer, favor, confirmations, open doors,
breakthroughs, and other spirit lifters, if only we'll "be of good courage."

Christian courage is the willingness to accept difficulty, hardship, or
danger in order to do God's will, rather than turn away in self-protecting
fear. Courageous faith is willing to face the very worst, blackest, most unrelieved contradictions to our faith rather than panic and abandon our
divinely appointed place, rebel against God, or compromise with unrighteousness. Christian courage is the final stage in the development of overcoming faith.

Overcoming faith begins with the belief of faith. After hearing God's
Word, with childlike trust we believe He's faithful and His Word true. The
confession of faith follows. We confirm our belief by confessing what we
believe to ourselves and others. Then comes the confidence of faith. As we
feed on Scripture daily, our certainty of God solidifies, for "faith [confi-
dence in God] cometh by hearing...the word of God" (Rom. 10:17). This
produces the hope of faith. We begin expecting to see biblical promises,
warnings, and prophecies—including Christ's return—fulfilled in their
season. Then we learn the patience of faith. When God delays answers to
prayer, we choose to continue seeking Him, discharging our duties, and patiently awaiting His help. Then we add endurance to our faith. When God's
delays wear long, we submissively decide to endure, or keep "the word of
my patience [endurance]" (Rev. 3:10). Finally we learn the courage of faith.
When these disciplines of faith lead to circumstances utterly contradicting
God's promises and allowing no hope of change, we bravely accept it as an
ultimate test of faith. Refusing to take offense, be discouraged, or panic, we
follow David's advice, choosing to be of good courage and keep trusting
God, His Word, and His ways until He rescues us! Whether we stand or

snap under this tension is crucial to our character development and usefulness to God. Many have stood in this ultimate crucible.

What courage David had to continue enduring King Saul's relentless persecution in the Judean wilderness when it seemed obvious he'd never rule Israel! What courage Elijah showed to endure months of intense, unrelieved loneliness by Cherith's brook without further reassurance from God! What nerve Elisha had when he calmly sat in his house, trusting God to deliver Samaria, while its people and king panicked—and turned on him! What valor Jeremiah demonstrated when he kept preaching God's despised but timely truth to Judah's leaders and people while they misjudged him a traitor and mistreated him cruelly! What daring the apostles had to continue ministering in Jerusalem despite a gag order by the Sanhedrin—that only days earlier had caused Jesus' execution! What courage Paul had to rise and exhort his storm-weary, discouraged shipmates, "Be of good cheer [courage], for I believe God, that it shall [yet] be even as it was told me" (Acts 27:25), after no signs of God's help were seen for many days!

What inner fortitude the reformers had to keep professing and living their biblical beliefs, though they contradicted their church-dominated European culture and caused clergy and citizens to reject them! How brave the English Separatists were when they risked life and liberty to preach and practice biblical Christianity secretly in their homes rather than join in false unity with the Roman or Anglican churches! What courage George Mueller had to trust God to provide for the growing needs of his orphanage and ministries by prayer alone, even when their supplies were often reduced to little!

We have the same faith these overcomers had, for "God hath dealt to every man the [same] measure of faith" (Rom. 12:3). But will we have their courage? Our tests will tell. When the endurance of your faith is exhausted, and fear and despair press you to capitulate, remember David's challenging counsel: If you'll have courage, you'll have encouragement! Or, "Be of good courage, and he shall strengthen thine heart" (Ps. 37:14). Who'll benefit?

You and many others. Your courageous faith will strengthen many weak, despondent Christians in these fearful last days. Oswald Chambers said:

> One strong moral man will form a nucleus around which others
> will gather; and spiritually, if we will put on the armor of God
> and stand true to Him, a whole army of weak-kneed Christians
> will be strengthened.[1]

God needs these nuclei now. Have courageous faith!

Chapter 26

UNMOVED BY SATAN'S SUBTLETY

*W*HEN THE CORRUPT Jewish religious leaders plotted to take Jesus "by subtlety" (Matt. 26:4), they weren't acting alone. Satan was inspiring and using them.

Subtlety is one of his favorite strategies—and oldest: "As the serpent beguiled Eve through his subtlety..." (2 Cor. 11:3, KJV). Anything *subtle* is cunning, wily, or crafty.[1] It's difficult to perceive; it's insidious, stealthy, beguiling. Satan rarely speaks frankly or works openly and directly. He prefers to cover his words and works with subtleness to hide his real intention from simple-minded people—and unspiritual Christians!—who tend not to think too long, deeply, or prayerfully about things. Thus Satan's servants often speak or act with hidden motives or agendas.

The Bible showcases numerous examples of serpentine subtlety.

Israel's corrupt chief priests claimed to oppose Jesus because He was a demonic Messianic pretender using false miracles to incite insurrection. The real reason, however, was they envied His powerful ministry and growing popularity which, if continued, threatened their control of Israel's religious life. Though pagan, Pilate was sharp enough to see through their subtlety: "He knew that for envy they had delivered him" (Matt. 27:18).

To Jesus' face the Pharisees and Herodians complimented Him effusively: "Master, we know that thou...teachest the way of God in truth" (Matt. 22:16). But behind His back their intention was to use their praises to induce Him to say something, anything they could use to arrest and execute Him. Wiser than the serpent in them, Jesus quickly discerned their craft: "But Jesus perceived their wickedness, and said, Why test me?" (v. 18).

Absalom undermined his father David's kingly authority, not by bold denunciations but by subtle innuendos, as he repeatedly insisted he cared for the people's causes—implying David didn't (2 Sam. 15:1–6)! Lacking discernment, the people were fooled by his act.

When Adonijah moved to again vie for Solomon's throne by requesting to marry Abishag,[2] Solomon quickly perceived his intent and executed him—while Bathsheba failed to see that Adonijah's request was not romantically but politically motivated (1 Kings 2:13–25). Why? Solomon was sharp

64

and Bathsheba simple: "The simple believeth every word, but the prudent [wise, thoughtful] man looketh well to his going" (Prov. 14:15). Will we be blind Bathshebas or seeing Solomons?

We better think long and hard about this, because our answer will determine whether we stand or fall before Satan's wiles. "Put on the whole armor of God, that ye may be able to stand against the wiles [subtle strategies, tricks] of the devil" (Eph. 6:11). Are we ready to face the enemy's subtle tricks?

Ready or not, discerning or dull, we're surrounded by Satan's subtle strategies and surrogates daily:

- Crafty flatterers sent to induce us to speak foolishly
- Clever politicians pursuing our vote but not our welfare
- Coy suitors who claim to love us but seek to use us
- Clean-cut "witnesses" and "elders" promoting false gospels with the truest zeal
- Silver-tongued spouses who vow faithfulness but live faithlessly
- Alluring investment offers that promise riches but deliver ruin
- Slick salesmen who promise a bargain but deliver a lemon
- New Christian fads, trends, and teachings that lead us backward while claiming to lead us onward

Genesis is spot-on: the serpent was, and still is, "more subtle" than all God's creatures.

With an enemy this cunning and active, we can't afford to be simple or naively blind to the subtleties of his untruthful, unethical messengers. Jesus challenged us to be not gullible but as sharp as our slithery enemies: "Behold, I send you forth as sheep in the midst of wolves; be ye, therefore, wise as serpents" (Matt. 10:16). How can we be "wise as serpents"?

Unfailing insight into Satan's subtleties comes from only one source: the Holy Spirit! He alone always discerns the craftiest wiles of Satan's agents. If we stay full of Jesus—His Word, prayer, worship, and the discipline of self-examination—we'll stay full of the Holy Spirit, and He'll faithfully alert us to Satan's wiles every time. Even the most inexperienced believers will perceive the enemy's shrewdest plots if they'll do this. And even the smartest, most insightful Christians, if they rely on their cleverness instead of their closeness to Christ, will be fooled by Satan's subtleties every time—and felled! Down they'll go, while those who rely on the Spirit stand firm and unmoved!

Whatever your IQ, be sharp, not simple! Ask for the Spirit's unfailing discernment. Depend on it: "Trust in the LORD with all thine heart, and lean not unto thine own understanding...and he shall direct thy paths" (Prov. 3:5–6). Then rest, rejoice, and stand, undeceived and unmoved by Satan's subtlety.

Chapter 27

GOD'S FLOOD MANAGEMENT PLAN

MERICA'S FEDERAL EMERGENCY Management Agency (FEMA) has flood management plans that it implements during floods and hurricanes. But they're not alone.

God has a flood management plan for believers described in Psalm 29. This inspired song glorifies God's power above that of nature, specifically the power of large thunderstorms and the flash floods they often cause. Figuratively, however, it describes the challenging spiritual storms and floods we face. These disturbances arise from demonic resistance.

Though unseen, these evil spirits are very real and resist true believers in many ways. They obey the "rulers of the darkness of this world" (Eph. 6:12), principal wicked spirits Satan has charged to block or minimize spiritual "light"—life- and hope-giving biblical truths, especially concerning Jesus, His salvation, and His redemptive plan—to keep the world, churches, and individuals in darkness. God's Word is and gives spiritual light: "Thy word is a lamp unto my feet, and a light unto my path" (Ps. 119:105). "The entrance of thy words giveth light" (v. 130). To prevent this light from spreading, demons stir, as Jesus said, the "tribulation or persecution" that "ariseth because of the word" (Matt. 13:21). While hating all believers, they specially target the brightest light-bearers: committed disciples, who study and obey God's Word consistently, and effective ministers, who dispense it regularly. Demons attack these truth-lamps most vigorously before, as, or after they obey the light or share it with others.

These attacks of trouble are spiritual storms and floods. Floods occur whenever our normalcy is overwhelmed by several large problems occurring simultaneously, often without warnings or easy solutions. These currents and waves of adversity may rush in suddenly like a flash flood or build gradually like an approaching hurricane, but their diabolical purpose is one—to offend us with Jesus, discourage our faith, uproot God's Word growing in our souls, and stop or slow our ministry of light. God, however, allows these floods for good purposes—to build our trust in Him, draw us closer, establish our obedience, mature our characters, and increase our effectiveness as light-bearers.

Jesus prophesied spiritual hurricanes and floods would severely test our houses of character (Matt. 7:24–27) yet gave only general instructions on managing them: "Do My sayings!" Psalm 29 reveals God's flood management plan in greater detail. Let's examine its chief insights and promises.

God assures us He sits upon, enthroned and fully controlling, every flood. "The LORD sitteth upon the flood" (v. 10). He affirms His voice is so powerful that, when reading Scripture, praying, or worshipping, we can still hear Him speaking even while waves of trouble roar and storm surges rise: "The voice of the LORD is upon ["heard over," NCV] the waters…the voice of the LORD is powerful" (vv. 3–4). His voice always brings timely comfort, wisdom, correction, or guidance. God promises two indispensable benefits in our floods, peace and strength: "The LORD will give strength unto his people; [and]…bless his people with peace" (v. 11). Using a thunderstorm and flash flood as symbols, He reveals that during even the worst storms He reigns by releasing His voice—or powerful Word in action—to answer our prayers and fulfill His promises. Omnipotent, His voice breaks unbreakably hard hearts (v. 5), divides impassable barriers (v. 7), exposes enemies' misdeeds hidden in forests of lies (vv. 8–9), and births new life in souls (v. 9). But this saving intervention isn't automatic.

We must activate it—or drown in our troubles! So Psalm 29 gives us four keys to activate God's plan.

First, we must believe this psalm's insights. Without faith, we'll flounder. Second, we should wait on God daily in our flood. His Word supernaturally strengthens us for the stress. Third, we must give God praise, worship, and thanksgiving, even when hurting, perplexed, and weary: "Give unto the LORD, O ye mighty, give unto the LORD glory…give…worship" (vv. 1–2). It's vital we understand releasing our voice in sweet praise releases God's voice in saving power (compare Ps. 29:1–3; Luke 6:38). Fourth, we must be holy, giving sin no place: "Worship the LORD in the beauty of holiness" (Ps. 29:2). When we sin, we sink; when we're righteous, we rise—and our house of character stands: "It fell not; for it was founded upon a rock" (Matt. 7:25). These keys will keep us close to God and His relief plan in force in every flood. If we reject them, we'll sink and fall short of God's purpose: "And it fell; and great was the fall of it" (v. 27).

It's no secret FEMA's plans sometimes fail. But God's plans don't! When your next flood comes, don't muddle your way through it. Manage it till deliverance comes. Believe and activate God's flood management plan.

Chapter 28

WHEN PROPHETS COME...

*A*FTER ANONYMOUS LAYMEN established a new church in Antioch, Christ sent prophets to help them: "In these days prophets came from Jerusalem" (Acts 11:27, NKJV). What are prophets? What do they do?

Prophets are believers specially gifted to deliver inspired messages that tell forth God's will or foretell future events to comfort, correct, and edify God's people. For this task the Holy Spirit gives them extraordinary spiritual vision and hearing.

Prophetic vision is deep, clear insight into God's Word, plan, and the condition and needs of His people, given to prepare them for things to come. Originally, prophets were called seers because of their keen spiritual perception and the way God often communicated with them "in visions...in dreams" (Num. 12:6, NIV). This extraordinary vision, not superior intellect, enabled them to interpret God's Word and plan, examine and correct His people, and foretell selected "things to come" (John 16:13).

Prophets also hear God's "still, small" voice with exceptional clarity and confidence (1 Kings 19:12). When others hope or believe, prophets *know* they've heard from God. And their clear communications help us greatly.

One of the prophets visiting Antioch, Agabus, predicted a great famine would visit (Acts 11:28). Later, in Caesarea, Agabus foretold Paul's arrest by the Jews (Acts 21:10–11). Both these Spirit-prompted warnings helped prepare believers for adversity: the Judeans for severe food shortages and Paul for persecution. Some of these traveling prophets remained, joining Antioch's leadership, and apparently became key leaders.

Luke mentions them before Antioch's teachers: "Now there were...at Antioch certain prophets and teachers" (Acts 13:1). No accident, this ordering agrees with Paul's inspired ministerial ranking (1 Cor. 12:28), suggesting God considers prophetic revelation just as vital to a church's survival and growth as teaching. Not either but both are necessary—teaching, constantly; prophecy, as needed. During God's "new thing" in Antioch, the written Word was faithfully and fully taught (Acts 11:26); when needed, the prophetic word was added (v. 28). This is ideal. Why?

Besides preparing us for future things, prophecy also covers the specificity gap between the Bible's general revelation and our specific needs. It addresses matters not directly addressed by Scripture—when to move, where to go, whom to befriend, whom to marry, what to buy, what our ministry is—yet never contradicts it. Agabus' prophecies disclosed two things not revealed in Scripture: a famine and a persecution. Antioch's prophets may have also unveiled another unwritten thing. Luke mentions prophets were present, then says the Spirit called Paul and Barnabas to their new mission, implying the Spirit spoke through the prophets (Acts 13:1–2). This further demonstrates the fullness of God's care.

Whatever our need, His grace is sufficient. If His wondrously sufficient Word is not specific enough in times of testing, He'll send prophets with the exact encouragement, warning, correction, or guidance we need! Agabus models these Christian seers.

Agabus' messages were perfectly accurate. Both his biblically recorded prophecies—the great famine and Paul's arrest—came to pass. Thus he symbolizes confirmed prophets, whose predictions come to pass (1 Sam. 3:19–20) and may therefore be trusted (1 Sam. 9:6). But not every prophet is an Agabus.

Some are Elymases (Acts 13:6–8). These false messengers may be unsaved angels of light or saved but ungifted pretenders (prophetic wannabes). Others are converted, churched, and called to prophesy but yet carnal, or spiritually immature and self-centered in thinking (Jonah). Still others are profiteering prophets, self-promoting prophets, sympathetic prophets (comforting but never correcting), sensational prophets (speaking only of shock, doom, or scandal), sorcerer prophets (delving in magical arts), or strange prophets (feigning super-spiritual demeanor). "From such turn away" (2 Tim. 3:5)—but not from true prophets or prophecy!

Superbly balanced, Scripture commands, "Despise not prophesyings" (1 Thess. 5:20), yet also requires we test prophecies, retaining and obeying whatever's of God: "Examine everything carefully; hold fast to that which is good" (1 Thess. 5:21, NAS). Mature Christian leaders must determine if prophecies are biblically aligned and inspired, separating the Spirit's words from the prophet's (1 Cor. 14:29, 32). Why consider this topic?

As Christ restores His church in these last days, He'll again send us prophets and teachers as He did Antioch. While teachers teach us, prophets will hear God's voice, see His plan, and tell us vital "things to come" (John 16:13). They'll minister to our specificity gap, correcting, guiding, warning, and encouraging us in our adversities with unerring, precise counsel. Like Agabus' messages, theirs will be biblical, sure, and spoken only as needed. Imposters, like Elymas, will surely arise, but we'll only grow stronger as we "test the spirits" (1 John 4:1), "hold fast" the truth, and discard the rest.

So be ready when prophets come...

Chapter 29

RESET THIS VISION BEFORE YOU

*W*HERE THERE IS no vision, the people perish" (Prov. 29:18). When we lose hope in the vision of God's plan, we begin losing our spiritual footing.

Disillusioned, we turn from God's hope-giving Word to selfishness, start indulging sin, and eventually bring judgment upon ourselves. But this perishing won't happen if we periodically reset God's vision before us. Psalm 67 does just that. It calls for and describes a wondrous divine visitation—a special time when God works not subtly and providentially but openly and miraculously to reveal His character and will—and urges us to set our hope on an approaching great harvest. While appropriate for any generation, this vision is especially timely for ours as we near the end of the Christian age. Let's consider Psalm 67's vision.

All visitations spring from God's merciful favor: "God be merciful unto us, and bless us, and cause his face [favor] to shine upon us" (v. 1). At His set time, in His own way, through His appointed servants, in His chosen "Upper Room," the living God releases His reviving Spirit into our spiritually dead churches. Suddenly the Messiah manifests His glorious greatness among and through His formerly inglorious people.

He reveals His ways to the nations: "That thy way[s] may be known…among all nations" (v. 2). Moses knew God's life disciplines and ways of working, Christ modeled them, the apostles lived them, the fathers taught them, the medieval church lost them, and the reformers began re-covering them. Today, sadly, we prefer our own ways of living and laboring for God, and too often they're worldly. The will of God must be done in the ways of God for the wonders of God to revisit us.

He makes known His compassionate, powerful healing to all nations: "Thy saving health among all nations" (v. 2). Malachi foresaw the "Sun of righteousness" arising "with healing in his wings" (Mal. 4:2). Matthew identified Him as Jesus and described His rising in Israel with beams of healing rays radiating from Him to the sick and oppressed: "Jesus went about…healing…all manner of disease among the people" (Matt. 4:23). In every visitation the Sun of righteousness rises, shines, and heals again by

His Spirit through His people. The world will see this stunning Son-rise one more time before this age ends.

He reveals His judgments to the nations: "For thou shalt judge the people" (Ps. 67:4). Visitations are marked not only by blessings but also by judgments. God puts down His hardened enemies who frustrate His plan and raises His friends to forward it. He had to remove Ananias and Sapphira so the revival in Jerusalem could flow on. Pentecostal purging marks every revival.

He fills nations with gladness and joy: "Oh, let the nations be glad and sing for joy" (v. 4). When Philip "preached Christ" with power in Samaria, "great joy" broke out (Acts 8:5, 8). When Christ visited the Jewish temple, He judged it and then used its courts to heal and teach—and the people sang for joy: "Hosanna to the Son of David" (Matt. 21:15). Every time He visits the temple of the church, He does the same—and Christians break out in song: "Then was our mouth filled with laughter, and our tongue with singing" (Ps. 126:2). Every visitation births new songs of praise and worship, and with a sermon and a song another generation is saved.

He'll reap His harvest: "Then shall the earth yield her increase" (Ps. 67:6). Since Pentecost every reformation, renewal, or revival has aimed to reap God's ultimate harvest. This "precious fruit of the earth" (James 5:7) is not wheat, barley, or corn but God's redeemed people—born again, Spirit baptized, Bible taught, life tested, established in Christ's ways, conformed to His image—caught away to be with Him forever. This rapturous heavenly ingathering will end God's work in the church. But not in the world.

After the Rapture the fear of the Lord will grip all nations: "All the ends of the earth shall fear him" (Ps. 67:7). Why? The impact of the Rapture! The undeniable harvest—the sudden, supernatural departure of overcoming believers worldwide—will stun the whole world. Then 144,000 single Jewish men will suddenly be utterly convinced Christians were right after all: Jesus is the Messiah! They'll evangelize Israel and Gentiles from all nations and await another stunning mid-Tribulation harvest to come (Rev. 7:9–17).

This isn't a popular, political, or prosperity vision, but it's a prophetic and biblical one, and it's God's. Whatever else may fail and disappoint, know this: this age will culminate with a great revival and harvest! Reset this vision before you.

Chapter 30

STRENGTHEN YOUR HULL

*D*UE TO DECISIONS and weather beyond his control, Paul suddenly found himself on a ship struggling to survive a fierce Mediterranean hurricane (Acts 27).

The "ship of Alexandria" (v. 6) was part of the Roman grain fleet that regularly transported wheat from Egypt's fertile fields to Rome's hungry citizens. It was large, probably 180 feet long, 45 feet wide, and 40 feet deep.[1] Such vessels were usually the fastest and safest way to sail from Palestine to Rome. But not this ship and not this trip!

As massive waves battered the heavily laden ship's bow, sides, and deck, the weight of the water put enormous stress on its hull. Recognizing this, the sailors took proactive measures. Rather than wait until the hull's timbers began separating and the ship flooding, they quickly began strengthening the hull.

"They used helps, undergirding the ship" (v. 17), or, "The sailors bound ropes around the hull of the ship to strengthen it" (NLT). By slipping ropes over the bow (or stern) of the vessel, sliding them down its length, and tying them off at regular intervals, the crew tightened the hull timbers. This prevented a watery invasion from slowly sinking the ship or causing catastrophic structural failure. No idle fear, even stronger modern ships have broken apart and sunk.

Robert Ballard's 1985 discovery of the *Titanic* wreck confirmed eyewitnesses' claims that, as it sank by the bow, the *Titanic*'s stern rose at a 45-degree angle, and, under stress, its hull snapped, sending the great liner spiraling to the ocean floor in two pieces.

In the Second World War, several original American Liberty ships cracked and sank in the North Atlantic. Flawed construction methods, overloading, stormy seas, and cold waters caused the cargo ships' steel hulls to become brittle and fail—until redesigned with stronger hulls.[2]

As ships need storm-worthy hulls, believers need test-ready souls. Our soul—essential nonmaterial self consisting of spirit, mind, emotions, and will—must be prepared to withstand the relentless stresses created by our stormy trials of faith, patience, and cross-bearing. When waves of anxiety, perplexity, sorrow, or despair persistently pound us, our core must be stronger than their weight. If not, they'll weaken our "hulls" (souls), rendering us spiritually frail, troubled in mind, emotionally conflicted, irresolute in will, and inconsistent in service. The waters of affliction will gradually fill us until we sink with discouragement or suddenly snap with an offended spirit, turning from Christ. Many have failed on the stormy seas of testing. Why? They didn't monitor and strengthen their "hull."

So watch your soul, especially in spiritually stormy weather. When your spirit becomes weak, your faith shaky, your heart cold, your prayers uninspired, your service ineffective, or your outlook discouraged, be proactive. Don't wait till you sink or snap; quickly strengthen your hull!

Turn from de-spiritualizing distractions. Get alone with God and be still (Ps. 46:10) so you can sense His reassuring presence and hear His saving instruction, correction, and guidance. Confess and forsake your sins. Give thanks, worship, and sing to the Lord. Pour out your needs in prayer. Read your Bible, slowly and thoughtfully. Reread writings that previously blessed you. Listen to edifying ministers teach and preach. Continue until you sense the ropes of Christ's faithful love tightening around you, drawing you close, stopping your spiritual leakage, and refilling you with the peaceful strength and inspiration of His Spirit.

It took many to strengthen Paul's ship: "*They* [the crew] used helps, undergirding…" (Acts 27:17). So ask others to strengthen you by intercession or other assistance, and do the same for them. Without this Paul's companions wouldn't have "all escaped safely to the land" (v. 44). Neither will we find relief, if we don't help each other.

In the storm Paul's faith- and hope-filled exhortation acted as a strong spiritual rope strengthening Luke's and Aristarchus' souls, which were leaking with grave doubts (v. 20). Jonathan's prophetic encouragement bolstered David's overstressed hull in the wilderness (1 Sam. 23:16–17). David strengthened his own spiritual core at Ziklag: "David encouraged himself in the Lord his God" (1 Sam. 30:6). Jesus strengthened His ministry-drained hull frequently by prayer: "Jesus Himself would often slip away to the wilderness and pray" (Luke 5:16, nas). When severely tested, George Mueller took additional time for Bible meditation. A. W. Tozer suggested drained Christians take a half-day off before their open Bibles. They were wise.

Are we? Though pagans, the sailors recognized their ship's hull needed extra support and quickly gave it. Are you giving way under the weight of relentless waves of trouble, sorrow, or affliction? Leaking? Listing? Lethargic? Be proactive.

Go strengthen your hull.

Chapter 31

SECRET BELIEVERS

OHN TELLS US the honorable Jewish counselor Joseph of Arimathea was Jesus' disciple. Then, lest we misunderstand, he adds, "but secretly" (John 19:38).

Apparently Joseph stood in awe of the Nazarene's works, believed His claims, anticipated His kingdom, pondered His teachings, and practiced them. But he never publicly confessed his faith. This suddenly changed, however, the day Joseph's fellow councilors collaborated with Pilate to crucify Jesus.

That day Joseph broke ranks with them to collaborate with Nicodemus, another godly Sanhedrinist, to remove Jesus' body from the cross and prepare it for burial. All four Gospels note the monumental moment Joseph's secret faith became saving faith: "Joseph...came, and went in boldly unto Pilate, and asked for the body of Jesus" (Mark 15:43). "Boldly" refers to the courage and daring of his act.[1] After long hiding his faith, he now heralded it. His actions provided plenty of evidence should his fellow councilors wish to try him as Christ's disciple: Pilate, his attendants, Nicodemus, and many others saw Joseph requesting Jesus' body or removing it to his newly carved tomb. How relieved Joseph must have been to finally come out for Christ.

And so boldly! It took great courage to so openly side with Jesus on the very day He had been so openly shamed by crucifixion—Roman execution reserved for the lowest criminals! The atmosphere was the opposite of that at Jesus' triumphal entry. The spirit of antichrist, not adoration, prevailed; Christ was hated, not hailed. By his actions Joseph risked censure, removal, or prosecution by the Sanhedrin; estrangement from his family, friends, and community; and rebuke or punishment from Pilate. But he no longer cared for these things, but only to be found loyal to Christ. As stated above, he didn't act alone.

"There came also Nicodemus" to Pilate's house (John 19:39). When visiting Jesus three years earlier, Nicodemus came by night to hide his budding faith. His mouth declared what his heart believed—"Rabbi, we know that thou art a teacher come from God" (John 3:2)—but privately, not publicly. Later he spoke up for Christ before his fellow Jewish leaders: "Doth our law judge any man, before it hear him?" (John 7:51). But this brought only rebuke: "Art thou

77

also of Galilee?" (v. 52). So like Joseph, Nicodemus believed, "but secretly"—until circumstances pressed him to boldly show his loyalty for his Lord. He implied other Jewish leaders also believed: "Rabbi, *we* know…" (John 3:2).

Indeed, "among the chief rulers," not some but "many believed on him" (John 12:42). (The most respected rabbi, Gamaliel, may have been one, as his later actions hint; see Acts 5:33–39.) But though they believed Jesus' claims, works, and words, they weren't yet converted. Why? "They did not [openly] confess him" (John 12:42). The apostle Paul insisted confession is required for salvation (Rom. 10:9–10). So secret faith is not saving faith. Why didn't these Jewish leaders confess? The consequences: "Lest they should be put out of the synagogue" (John 12:42). They also craved men's approval: "They loved the praise of men more than the praise of God" (v. 43).

These leaders, Joseph, and Nicodemus reveal three key facts.

1. As Matthew Henry wrote, "Christ has more secret disciples than we are aware of,"[2] and some in high places.

2. Secret believers, if true, will eventually come out, confessing their faith in unmistakably clear words and acts.

3. If they don't, they won't be saved (Luke 12:8–9; Rom. 10:9–10).

So if you're a secret believer, come out. Possessing Christ begins with professing Him: "With the mouth he confesses, resulting in salvation" (Rom. 10:10, NAS); or, "By declaring your faith you are saved" (GW). Tear down your walls of timidity, and shatter your shackles of fear: "Fear not the reproach of [mere] men" (Isa. 51:7). The antichrist spirit prevailed in Jerusalem, as it does today, but Joseph didn't fear it. Follow his example. Don't fear to confess your Lord and Savior; fear only not to.

Or God may be pressing you through circumstances to make other kinds of courageous decisions or statements, or take various stands or courses of action that please and show loyalty to Him, though doing so will displease certain people. These confessions save you not from hell but from the torment of fear, timidity, and a guilty conscience.

Or you may personally know secret believers. If so, remind them confessing their Savior is necessary for salvation, and afterward loyalty to Him is required for spiritual growth. Then pray for them faithfully. One day, as Joseph did, they'll speak up and stand up with those Jesus will soon take up. Why?

They're convinced He's not coming for secret believers.

Chapter 32

THE PROBING, PROMPTING QUESTIONS OF GOD

HE IMMORTAL NEVER asks mortals questions to gain information. Omniscient, He already knows the answer to every question He asks! Then why does He question us?

Not omniscient, we don't know all His reasons for questioning us. But here's one: He probes us to prompt positive changes in our lives. The heavenly Interrogator asks us questions so that, as we consider them, His Spirit may probe our minds and prompt us to realize vital truths about our souls or circumstances. He hopes this conviction will then move us to change our attitudes or courses of action to conform to His will. The probing, prompting questions of God come three ways.

First, the Holy Spirit's still, small voice speaks quietly to our consciences, which are divinely designed lamps God uses to search our innermost thoughts: "The spirit of man [conscience] is the lamp of the LORD, searching all the inward parts" (Prov. 20:27). Second, He speaks through the questions and opinions of godly elders, whether pastors, teachers, counselors, or mentors. Third, He sometimes speaks providentially, through the questions or statements of unsuspecting ordinary people in everyday conversations. (See 2 Kings 5:13.)

However they come, God's questions prompt us to:

- RECONSIDER AND STOP SHORT OF SIN. Jesus' question, "Friend, why art thou come?" (Matt. 26:50), was a last-minute plea to turn Judas from folly to faithfulness. How different it may have been if he had just considered why he was betraying Jesus—his love of money and hatred of correction—and stopped!

- CONFESS OUR SINS. After Cain murdered Abel, God asked, "Where is Abel, thy brother?" (Gen. 4:9), hoping to prompt Cain to confess and receive forgiveness. But proud Cain refused to reflect, confess, and be reconciled.

- REALIZE OUR SECRET FAULTS. "Cleanse thou me from secret faults" (Ps. 19:12). Jesus asked one sufferer, "Wilt thou be made well?" (John 5:6), hoping to expose his secret fault.

After years of sickness he had lost hope and no longer wanted healing. His will was now as infirm as his body!

- REALIZE WE'VE STRAYED FROM GOD. When God asked Adam, "Where art thou?" (Gen. 3:9), He knew exactly where Adam was. But He wanted Adam to realize where he was spiritually—separated from God by sin. Normally Adam drew near God in the "cool of the day" (v. 8), but now he drew back.

- ACKNOWLEDGE WE NEED HELP. When Philip asked the Ethiopian eunuch, "Understandest thou what thou readest?" (Acts 8:30), God wanted the eunuch to realize he needed a teacher to help him understand Scripture. He got the message—"How can I, except some man should guide me?" (v. 31)—and the Messiah! "I believe . . . Jesus Christ is the Son of God" (v. 37).

- ACKNOWLEDGE OFFENSE. Jesus asked two discouraged disciples, "What manner of communications are these that ye have . . . as ye walk, and are sad?" (Luke 24:17). He wanted them to see that they thought God failed them by permitting Jesus' crucifixion. Then they could acknowledge their offended spirit, He could answer their questions with His Word, and they could return to the rest of faith. Soon after His question, "their eyes were opened" (v. 31).

- CONFESS FAILURE IN SELF-CHOSEN WAYS. After His apostles' unsuccessful fishing trip, Jesus asked, "Children, have ye any food?" (John 21:5). Or, "Has your impulsive, selfish plan produced anything?" "No," was their humble confession—which opened a surprising new door to yet another miracle! "Cast the net on the right side . . . and ye shall find" (v. 6).

- CONFESS OUR FAITH FOR HEALING OR DELIVERANCE. "Without faith it is impossible to please him" (Heb. 11:6). The God of faith requires the people of faith to make confessions of faith before receiving the benefits of faith. Therefore Jesus asked two blind men, "Believe ye that I am able to do this?" (Matt. 9:28), so they would confess their faith and receive their healing. Soon "their eyes were opened" (v. 30).

- RECOGNIZE THE ROOTS OF OUR FAILURES. Often we recognize the fruits of our failures but not their roots, their consequences but not their causes. After Peter sank beneath Galilee's stormy waters, Jesus asked, "Why didst thou doubt?" (Matt. 14:31). After reflection, Peter realized why—he had shifted his focus from his faithful Lord to his fearful circumstances.

When the heavenly Interrogator probes and prompts you with His questions, whether quietly through conscience, audibly through elders' counsels, or providentially through unsuspecting people, don't insult Him by ignoring His probes. Cooperate with Him so He can cleanse your secret faults. Reflect on His question and, if convicted, confess, change, and grow!

And give thanks for the probing, prompting questions of God.

Chapter 33

Springs, Builders, Repairers, Restorers

*I*N Isaiah 58 God promises to make qualified believers His people's "springs," "builders," "repairers," and "restorers." Let's consider who these are and what they do.

Springs. "Thou shalt be...like a spring of water, whose waters fail not" (v. 11). As the source of natural life, water symbolizes spiritual life and its Giver, the Holy Spirit. Jesus compared the Spirit's presence in Spirit-baptized, trusting, obedient believers to "a well of water springing up into everlasting life" (John 4:14).

Because these stay very close to Jesus, the Spirit surges up daily to refresh them and flow out to touch and bless others—by their kindnesses, encouragements, intercessions, gifts, counsels, and teachings. Like the Spirit in them, they become a spring of spiritual life, so reliable that their waters don't fail. In even the most troubled, driest seasons of their lives, the precious water of life flows up and out to slake the thirst of those who want more of God.

For nearly forty years Charles Spurgeon was an unfailing fountain of eloquent heavenly truth in London. We're still drinking his stimulating messages.

Builders. "Thou shalt raise up [build] the foundations of many generations" (Isa. 58:12). The foundation of a true Christian is Christ's life within. "Other foundation can no man lay than that which is laid...Jesus Christ" (1 Cor. 3:11). When through evangelism this foundation is laid in us, we're saved. Then the building, or "raising" up, begins—the lengthy spiritual construction process of discipleship. For years pastors, teachers, and elders steadily build Bible teaching, life training, attitudinal correction, and spiritual guidance into us, until a spiritual temple of mature Christlikeness eventually emerges, a living, human sanctuary walking, working, and worshipping in perfect union with the living God.

Many well-laid foundations haven't yet become finished spiritual temples. God needs many builders to raise immature Christians to spiritual maturity.

Repairers. "Thou shalt be called the repairer of the breach" (Isa. 58:12). When Jerusalem fell to the Babylonians, war, weather, and time took their toll on its once-strong walls... until God sent Nehemiah to repair the breaches.

Sin, tests, and time have broken many Christians' walls, or unions, that once stood strong. Worldly thinking, values, sins, and lukewarmness have separated many Christians from Christ's presence and purpose. Denominations are divided by doctrinal error or pride. Leaders are separated by ministerial envy. Families are split in two by the grief and confusion of divorce. Siblings are divided by envious rivalry and strife. Oh, how we need repairers, or deeply cleansed believers committed to unity, to cleanse and reunify these breaches.

As these exhorters gifted in the art of reconciliation minister God's truth with wisdom, grace, and authority, a new, unified body of Christ will arise, truly "perfect in one" (John 17:23).

RESTORERS. "Thou shalt be called... the restorer of paths to dwell in" (Isa. 58:12). These "paths to dwell in" are the ways of God—daily spiritual life disciplines, or biblical methods of walking and working closely with God. He "made known his ways" to Moses (Ps. 103:7), who walked in and taught them. After briefly adopting God's ways, Israel abandoned them... until God sent Ezra, Nehemiah, John, and Jesus to restore His "paths to dwell in."

For twenty centuries Christians have known God's ways and sporadically lived in them. Our generation has largely abandoned them to adopt the more popular, sophisticated methods of our increasingly secular and confused culture. But God won't leave us wandering without "paths to dwell in." He'll send Ezras again to re-teach us His ways, Nehemiahs and Johns to urge us to walk in them, and Christlike leaders to demonstrate them.

How may we become one of these key servant-ministers? Of all the qualifiers cited in Isaiah 58, mercy is most prominent (vv. 6–7). So pursue mercy.

Fast and pray to deliver souls from the oppressive yokes of injustice, prejudice, fear, and personal sins. Feed the hungry with loaves of bread and lots of God's Word. Give to the poor by donating monies and materials, sharing God's rich truths and life principles, and modeling and teaching trust in His unfailing faithfulness. Use gentle, prayerful correction and generous restoration to cover the naked when their fleshly sins or unspiritual attitudes are exposed. (See Galatians 6:1–3.) And never hide from your own flesh, denying family members help when they request it.

If you practice these mercies, God will make you His minister. And

He'll send you, along with other qualified servant-ministers, to revive, re-build, repair, and restore the body of Christ in these last days before Jesus returns.

And when He appears, He'll commend and reward you for being one of His springs, builders, repairers, and restorers.

Chapter 34

LOOKING FOR A WAY OUT?

RANTIC THOUGH HE was to avoid rendering a decision in Jesus' case, Pilate couldn't find a way out. Or make one.

Perceiving the Jewish religious leaders bitterly envied Jesus (Matt. 27:18), Pilate knew they'd never withdraw their charges against Him. Shaken further by his wife's ominous warning that Jesus was "innocent" (v. 19, NIV), Pilate decided to take his case directly to the "jury"—the Jewish people gathered before his judgment seat. For goodwill the Romans released one prisoner every Passover. Knowing multitudes had enthusiastically received Jesus only days earlier (Matt. 21:1–11), Pilate hoped they would demand His release. To guarantee this, he gave them the option of choosing Barabbas, a notorious revolutionary, murderer, and robber. Surely the Jews would choose their Messiah over a murderer. Then Pilate could legally release Jesus, and himself, from the religious leaders' malicious strategy—to falsely charge their rival, Jesus, with insurrection so they could use Pilate to execute Him and claim not they but he did it! Pilate anxiously hoped the people would provide this escape.

But he overlooked the effectiveness of the Jewish leaders' "spin." As the nation's most respected religious leaders, the chief priests and elders easily and quickly turned the mob against Jesus. Within hours His public favor, which had recently peaked after Lazarus' stunning resurrection, plummeted. Soon the mad cry "Crucify Him" arose. Some scholars suggest these crazed criers were Judeans, not the Galileans who lauded Jesus when He entered the city. But it's just as likely many were former supporters who now rejected Jesus because, as a humbled prisoner, He looked shamefully weak, foolish, and un-kingly, and thus unfit to be the gloriously victorious Messiah-Deliverer of whom they had been taught from childhood. Meanwhile Barabbas, a known insurrectionist, had at least tried to rebel. He seemed more likely to throw off Rome's yoke than the soft-spoken, pacifist, defeated teacher from Nazareth! Whatever their "spin," the Jewish clergy cleverly manipulated the "jury"—and slammed shut Pilate's escape hatch! Determined, the governor kept looking for a way.

His next appeal was to King Herod, who, as Galilee's ruler, had jurisdiction over Jesus. Herod agreed that Jesus was innocent (Luke 23:15), but instead of freeing Him, he passed the buck, sending Jesus back to Pilate! Undaunted, Pilate continued evasive action.

After scourging Jesus, he brought Him before the people one last time, severely lacerated, crowned with thorns, and bleeding freely (John 19:1–6). Surely this spectacle would move them to change their minds. But to Pilate's dismay they remained implacable, shouting even more loudly, "Crucify him" (v. 15), and threatening to inform Caesar that Pilate had failed to punish a rival "king." Thus all Pilate's efforts to shirk his judicial duty failed.

No one would assume his responsibility. No rabbis stepped up to argue for truth. No Roman lawyers pleaded for justice. The religious leaders didn't withdraw their charges. The mob turned a deaf ear to reason and blind eye to Jesus' sufferings. Why? God wanted Pilate to make this decision. And he was very capable of it.

The Jews tried to deceive him, but he discerned their motives. They threatened him, but he still retained full authority over them. If they rioted, he had ample soldiers to subdue them. If they accused him before Caesar, he could have ably defended himself. Pilate needed only to say, "Jesus is innocent; release Him!" But he was unwilling to risk trouble for truth. Or justice. Or conscience. Or God! His is a classic example not to follow.

Like Pilate, you may occupy a position of authority—parent, business owner, elected official, administrator, doctor, coach, pastor, superintendent, teacher, principal, publisher, and so forth. When difficult decisions confront you, do you find yourself, like Pilate, looking anxiously for an out? If so, consider Pilate's folly and this application: God wants you to make the decision! Stop dreading and start accepting His will! Pilate couldn't have it both ways and please both sides. Nor can you.

So humbly trust God will lead you to the right decision: "The meek will he guide in judgment [the decision-making process]" (Ps. 25:9). Then after patient prayer, Bible meditation, and reflection, courageously render your decision. Trust also that, if trouble follows, the Lord who led you to your decision will defend you for it, as He did Daniel and friends (Dan. 1, 3, 6). His grace is sufficient to provide all the strength, protection, wisdom, and assistance you need. As a pagan, Pilate had no such grace.

As a Christian, you do. Stir yourself to walk in it. When dilemmas visit, don't evade them; embrace them! Don't be caught looking for a way out.

Chapter 35

THEY WATCHED HIM—AND WATCH US

GOOD FRIDAY WAS just another workday for Jerusalem's Roman execution squad. Their bloody deeds were habitual by now.

They shredded the condemned man's back with a scourge and walked alongside him as he carried a sign[1] around his neck and crossbeam on his shoulders to the execution site. There they offered him a painkilling drink, stripped his clothes, tied and nailed his wrists and feet to the crucifix, raised and dropped it into place, affixed the sign over his head, and calmly divided his personal effects among themselves. In high-profile cases, they remained to watch the victim's agony.

So, "sitting down they watched him [Jesus] there" (Matt. 27:36). The soldiers' deathwatch was an odd mixture of duty and pleasure. While most victims were abandoned to suffer for days whatever the elements, observers, and animals brought, Jesus was carefully guarded.

Perhaps His family would try saving Him, or His disciples, or the zealots who wanted to make Him king. Possibly Elijah, whom many Jews were expecting to return, would come save Him (vv. 47–49). Or Jesus may work a wonder. A renowned miracle worker, He had recently resurrected Lazarus after four days of entombment! As some taunted, He may use His supernatural powers to come down from His cross! Thus the guards remained vigilant.

Some soldiers may have gazed with curiosity, others with sadistic pleasure. Many Romans enjoyed various kinds of socially acceptable violence, such as gladiatorial games, violent dramas (in which actors, usually criminals, were actually killed), chariot races, or boxing matches. To the average legionnaire crucifixion was just another blood sport. So while Jesus suffered, they spectated.

Jesus' callous crucifiers weren't the only witnesses of His expiration. From His immediate family, Mary was present. The apostle John, His student and friend, stood by. Numerous anonymous bystanders, "they that passed by," gazed and gabbed (v. 39). Hostile Jewish leaders observed, gloated, and mocked. Two thieves crucified beside Jesus watched, and one added insults. Such was Jesus' "cloud of witnesses" on Calvary (Heb. 12:1).

As He faithfully endured to the end, some observers remained un-moved. Others were convicted and converted.

Chief among them was the commanding officer. A seasoned centurion, he had probably seen many victims crying out with vengeance, remorse, panic, or madness as they left this world. But when he saw and heard Jesus' calm demeanor, clear mind, thoughtful conversations and prayers, stunning forgiveness of His executors, and total absence of bitterness, he was convinced Jesus' claims must be true. Convinced of the Savior and convicted of his sins, he confessed, "Truly this man was the Son of God" (Mark 15:39). Amazingly, one of the two thieves also trusted in Christ—a defeated, dying King!—and His prophecies: "Lord, remember me when thou comest into thy kingdom" (Luke 23:42). As Mary beheld the strangely darkened sky shrouding the cross, she too saw the light and afterward joined His disciples in the Upper Room (Acts 1:14). Simon of Cyrene, who carried Jesus' cross, also witnessed these extraordinary events and likely received life as he watched Jesus release His; then, Mark implies, he led his two sons, Alexander and Rufus, who were known to Mark's readers, to the faith (Mark 15:21).

These effects sprang from one cause: Jesus submissively obeyed His Father's will in crucifixion. Will we, by grace, be as faithful and fruitful on our crosses?

Whenever Christ asks us to suffer injustices, make sacrifices, or ac-cept stressful duties or callings that cross our natural desire, we're being crucified. If we continue trusting and obeying Him, we reenact His cruci-fixion by willingly suffering to do God's will. As Jesus was watched, we too will have a "cloud of witnesses." Our persecutors will look on, mocking. Uncommitted, lukewarm Christians will gaze indifferently at our adversi-ties, as Joseph's brothers did his (Gen. 37:23–25). Curious friends will si-lently observe our losses and wounds. Unconverted family members will watch, weep, and wonder. Neighbors, who pass by daily, will stare, gossip, and stand back. Only one question will remain relevant: Will we maintain our close fellowship with God and faithfully fulfill our work or ministry to the end? If so, our witness on our cross, like our Lord's, will change curious ones into converts and watchers into worshippers of God. If we won't stay faithful, many will walk away from our Golgotha unconvinced and uncon-verted. Don't let that happen.

Follow Jesus' example. Pray for more grace in your Gethsemane. Humbly trust and obey God until He sends a "Simon" to help carry your load. Then endure, knowing, "Everyone who endures to the end will be saved" (Matt. 10:22, NLT), and save others. Why?

They watched Him—and watch us.

Chapter 36

ABANDONED, YET STRONGER!

*E*VER MALICIOUS, SATAN loves trying to trouble us with fears. One of his fiery arrows is the dread that those close to us may fail us in hard times. What will we do if they abandon or betray us? How will we get by?

God will stand by, faithfully loving and providing for us. When people abandon His faithful servants, He faithfully visits and raises them, eventually making them stronger, not weaker! More fruitful, not less! Victorious, not vanquished! Consider Paul and Joseph.

Near the end of his ministry the apostle Paul reported bad news: "All they who are in Asia turned away from me" (2 Tim. 1:15). Surprisingly "they" were not Paul's foes but his friends; not unbelievers but believers; not strangers but close associates. But here's the good news: their departure wasn't his demise. After they left, the Lord lifted Paul. When they drew back, Jesus drew near and gave him new conviction and strength to declare His Word without assistants: "At my first defense no man stood with me, but all men forsook me....Notwithstanding, the Lord stood with me and strengthened me, that by me the preaching might be fully known" (2 Tim. 4:16–17). Amazingly Paul was stronger without his associates than with them! Why? Human help is effective, but God's is more effective. There was also another reason Paul grew stronger.

God sent him new friends and assistants. "Onesiphorus," Paul testified, "often refreshed me, and was not ashamed of my chain, but...in Rome, he sought me out very diligently, and found me" (2 Tim. 1:16–17). And Mark, who failed Paul years earlier, now assisted him admirably: "He is profitable to me for the ministry" (2 Tim. 4:11). God did the same with Joseph.

Without warning Joseph's brothers betrayed him and dropped him, stunned and weak, into a pit of slavery. Jacob described their painful, demonically inspired treachery: "The [demonic] archers have harassed him [Joseph], and shot at him, and hated him" (Gen. 49:23). But God lifted His abandoned servant to new heights of spiritual fruitfulness by increasing his gifts, insights, and strength in slavery and prison: "But his bow abode in strength" (v. 24). When God gave Joseph favor with Pharaoh, he suddenly grew much stronger. Jacob recalled fondly, "The arms of his hands were made [even] strong[er] by the hands of the mighty God of Jacob" (v. 24). Summarizing, Jacob declared, "Joseph is a fruitful bough" (v. 22). But his fruitfulness wasn't automatic.

Human choice was a big part of Joseph's and Paul's empowerments. Suddenly abandoned, they may have momentarily felt offended or even briefly considered giving up hope and abandoning God. But not these two. Wholly committed, they chose to keep trusting, seeking, and serving. When they drew near God, He drew near and strengthened them by sending new helpers, wisdom, favor, and strength. So ultimately abandonment advanced them, as it does us. How?

Abandonment enables us to see God's hand working in our lives in new ways. The extraordinary pressures of desertions and betrayals force us to depend on God extraordinarily. Instead of leaning on Him occasionally, we now do so constantly. Forsaking all remnants of pride, we now receive any help God sends any way He sends it. This increased dependency and humility create a much closer union with Him, from which springs a deeper knowledge of His character and ways and a more consistent walk with Him. As we see God continuing to help us by His Word, presence, and people, we grow increasingly confident that Jesus never forsakes us—"I will never leave thee, nor forsake thee" (Heb. 13:5)—and always provides in His time and way. So abandonment advances our fellowship with God, knowledge of Him, and faith.

Have you been abandoned or betrayed? By a Christian friend? "Yea, mine own familiar friend, in whom I trusted…hath lifted up his heel against me" (Ps. 41:9). By a spouse? Child? Parent? "When my father and my mother forsake me, then the LORD will take me up" (Ps. 27:10). Pastor, have you been wrongly dismissed by your congregation or superintendent? Church, has your pastor abruptly resigned? Jesus warned us to expect human failures, abandonments, estrangements, or betrayals: "Ye shall be betrayed both by parents, and brethren, and kinsfolk, and friends" (Luke 21:16). So don't take offense at these offenses.

Rather see your crisis as an opportunity and follow Paul and Joseph. When deserted by men, don't desert God. Choose to stay close and faithful to Jesus so abandonment will advance you! Don't fear becoming weaker; believe to be stronger. Don't dread accomplishing less; anticipate doing more. Don't conclude failure is inevitable; expect success in God's plan.

Then you too will be abandoned yet stronger!

Chapter 37

CARING FOR CHRIST'S BODY

HE ACCOUNT OF Joseph of Arimathea reveals God gives special favor and honor to those who care for the body of Christ (Matt. 27:57–61).

Soon after Jesus expired, Joseph went to Pilate and "begged the body of Jesus" (v. 58) so he could remove it from the cross and prepare it for burial. He did this not only because it was the preparation but also to spare Jesus' terribly battered body—which was stripped, scourged, pierced, plucked, beaten, bruised, nailed, broken, and swollen beyond recognition ("so disfigured he seemed hardly human," Isa. 52:14, NLT)—further abuse from passers-by or animals and birds, who sometimes fed on crucifixion victims! Once he obtained Christ's body, he spiced and wrapped it in "clean linen cloth" and placed it in his own newly excavated cave, sealing it with a large stone door to prevent robbers. Thus Joseph honored and blessed Christ's severely dishonored and broken body. God's response was twofold.

First, He blessed Joseph's efforts by granting him special favor with Pilate, who was livid with the Jews for pressuring him at Jesus' trial and protesting his sign declaring Jesus "KING OF THE JEWS" (John 19:19–22). Second, He honored Joseph by recording his noble deed in all four Gospels!

Today we can't honor Christ's physical body, since it's glorified and in heaven. But we can honor His spiritual or mystical body, comprised of born-again believers worldwide. Joseph demonstrated his love for Jesus by caring for His physical body. Jesus taught us to show love for Him by caring for His spiritual body: "Lovest thou me?...Feed my sheep" (John 21:15). This includes all its members, even those seemingly "least" important: "As ye have done it unto one of the least of these my brethren, ye have done it unto me" (Matt. 25:40). The apostle Paul took this seriously.

Passionately and persistently he made caring for Christ's body his first priority. He prayed, preached, and endured many adversities—shipwreck, slander, scourging, stoning, incarceration, betrayal, loneliness—all for one purpose: to help nurture, guide, and protect Christ's people. But the more he cared for Christians, the less they sometimes cared for him: "I will very gladly spend and be spent for you; though the more abundantly I love you, the less I be loved" (2 Cor. 12:15). Undaunted, he urged other ministers to follow his selfless example: "Take heed…to feed the church of God" (Acts 20:28). And he commended those who did: "I trust…to send Timothy shortly unto you…for I have no [other] man likeminded, who will naturally care for your state. For all [others] seek their own" (Phil. 2:19–21).

Today Jesus' church body mirrors His crucified body. In hostile cultures some of its members have been cruelly stripped of their rights, scourged by slander, and pierced by hatred. Some have been nailed with injustices, plucked of dignity, or punctured by thorny crowns of mockery. Others have been bruised by betrayals, weakened with sickness, or beaten down by oppression. Consequently their hope has been broken by abounding iniquity. In friendlier cultures Christians have been bled of their first love from within—by greed, lust, pride, heresy, or worldly distractions. These satanically and self-inflicted injuries have left Christ's church broken and as unrecognizable as His corpse. The world examines us but finds little resemblance to the wondrous image of Jesus' truth, compassion, and power so evident in the early church.

It's time we follow Joseph's example. How can we care for Christ's broken body?

We can determine to help believers daily in every way—praying, instructing, exhorting, befriending, giving, comforting—especially when they're suffering, realizing, "Ye are the body of Christ, and members in particular" (1 Cor. 12:27). Whenever we help one member, we help Christ's entire body and mirror Joseph's loving care for Jesus' body. Such care begins with, well, caring.

Do we truly care about Christ's body? Whether its members are weak or strong, sick or well, near or far from God? Spiritually well fed or starved, fully developed or immature, divinely guided or misled? Or do we think only of our personal needs and desires? It's easy to be so absorbed in the kingdom of self that we overlook the kingdom of Christ in and among believers. Don't be careless.

Be careful. Like Joseph, minister to Christ's body in every way possible. Joseph "begged" Christ's body from Pilate and then prepared it for burial. Let's prayerfully "beg" blessings for the church from God and then help prepare it for Christ's return. Pleased, God will give us favor and honor, as He did Joseph, so we may increase our caring for Christ's body.

Chapter 38

HEAVEN'S HUMBLE MESSENGERS

*T*HOUGH BRIEF, IT was the greatest message ever delivered: "He is risen" (Mark 16:6). Whom did God choose to first share this monumental message with the world?

Surprisingly He didn't select His most honorable apostles Peter, James, and John, though they were His inner circle. He didn't tap the other apostles, though He had called and trained them three years. He didn't pick His close friend and the church's first celebrity, Lazarus, whose stunning resurrection had recently been well documented and widely publicized. He didn't even send the shining angel that opened Christ's tomb and stunned its guards. Instead He chose three humble women, Mary Magdalene, the "other Mary" (mother of James the less), and Salome (v. 1). They were the first to arrive on the scene, hear Jesus had risen, see His empty tomb, and carry the uplifting news to His crestfallen disciples—though their patriarchal culture often ignored what women thought or said. Paradoxically, then, God sent heaven's highest message through earth's lowest messengers. The reaction of Jesus' apostles confirms their gender bias.

They initially ignored the women God sent. These women, however, weren't selected randomly. They had been very faithful to Jesus for three years. Disciples themselves, they had followed Jesus with His other disciples and hung on His every Word and miracle. They had supported His ministry financially. They remained faithful to Him during His trial. They followed Him to His crucifixion. They watched as Joseph and Nicodemus prepared and entombed His body. And they had returned very early the third day to further care for His body—when, suddenly, an angel appeared and commissioned them to go and tell of Jesus' resurrection. But when they told their male counterparts the heavenly message, the apostles "believed them not," dismissing their inspired words "as idle tales" (Luke 24:11). Their haughty rejection of heaven's humble messengers displeased Christ.

He was so displeased that He appeared that very night and, in a rare display of anger, "upbraided [sternly rebuked] them... because they believed not those who had seen him after he had risen" (Mark 16:14). Why? They were rejecting the Father's chosen messengers and one of His long-established ways. The Father sent many humble messengers to Israel.

He sent Moses to the Hebrews from the backside of a desert, not a respected elder from one of their leading tribes or families. He sent Elisha from a farm, not from one of the schools of the prophets in Ramah, Jericho, Gilgal, or Bethel. He sent Jesus from a carpenter's shop in tiny, lowly Nazareth, in Gentile-bordering Galilee, not a prophet, scribe, or priest from the Jewish heartland of Judea. And He sent John the Baptist from the Judean wilderness, not from one of the prestigious rabbinical schools of Hillel or Shammai. Though from humble origins or circumstances, all these spokesmen brought heavenly communications.

In his memorable prose Luke emphasizes how God surprisingly passed over many high and mighty leaders to prepare and send the humble and unpretentious John the Baptist to Israel:

> Now in the fifteenth year of the reign of Tiberius Caesar, Pontius Pilate being governor of Judaea, and Herod being tetrarch of Galilee, and his brother, Philip, tetrarch of Ituraea...and Lysanias, the tetrarch of Abilene, Annas and Caiaphas being the high priests, the word of God came unto John...in the wilderness. And he came into all the country about the Jordan, preaching...
>
> —LUKE 3:1–3

God's surprising choices to send John, and later Mary and her friends, are a subtle warning: be prepared for the unexpected! God may send anyone He chooses to speak to you, your church, or your nation, not only typical but also atypical couriers. Are we ready to recognize and receive our unconventional "Johns" or "Marys"?

Will we receive their timely messages, insights, warnings, corrections, and guidance from the risen One? Even if they're laymen? Pastors of small churches? Unlettered but edifying Bible teachers? Young but inspired evangelists? Missionaries from poor or non-Christian nations? Ministers from new or unfamiliar church groups? Preachers from despised ethnic or racial groups? Unknown but faithful disciples? Godly housewives? Praying grandmothers? Young, meek-spirited prophetesses? Or any other of God's "hidden ones"? When Christ sends them, you may find yourself initially rejecting them.

But if their message is biblically sound, timely, and confirmed by the Spirit's witness, and you're hesitating only because they're not the kind of minister you expected, remember how God chose Mary to report Jesus' resurrection, and don't repeat the apostles' error. Rely on the Spirit's witness, not your carnal reasoning. Then humbly do three things: Receive the messenger. Receive their message. Respond to it.

And afterward stay ready for heaven's humble messengers.

Chapter 39

HE MEETS US AS WE GO

*W*HEN AN ANGEL ordered the three women to go quickly and tell the apostles Jesus had risen (Matt. 28:7), they obeyed quickly and joyfully! "They departed quickly from the sepulcher with fear and great joy, and did run to bring his disciples word" (v. 8). As they went, these already blessed women received more blessing.

"Behold, Jesus met them" (v. 9). The wondrous sight, sound, and touch of Jesus alive and active again were a great relief! It confirmed the angel's report: Jesus had indeed risen! And Jesus verified the angel's instructions for the apostles to meet Jesus in Galilee: "Go tell my brethren that they go into Galilee, and there shall they see me" (v. 10). So as the women went forward in obedience, Jesus met them with the blessings of relief and confirmation. Something similar happened to the apostles.

After initially ignoring the women's message from Jesus, the apostles repented and obeyed: "The eleven disciples went away into Galilee, into a mountain where Jesus had appointed them" (v. 16). As they went, these already blessed men suddenly became more blessed: "And...they saw him [Jesus]" (v. 17). Their rendezvous with the Messiah was remarkable! Jesus gave them a great revelation: "All authority is given unto me in heaven and in earth" (v. 18). He gave them a great commission to go, baptize, and teach all nations everything He had taught them (vv. 19–20). He gave them great security: "And, lo [as you go], I am with you always, even unto the end" (v. 20). These new, rich blessings—revelation, commission, security—were theirs for one reason: they trustingly obeyed Jesus' orders to go into Galilee. What do these examples say to us?

They declare Jesus meets and blesses every Christian who moves forward in obedience. And, conversely, He doesn't meet us with blessings, assistance, or encouragements if we neglect or refuse to move. Why?

Lovingly inclusive and passionately social, God wants our earthly lives to be a continuous partnership with Him. He wants us to walk not alone but with Him, and work not alone but with Him. He yearns to accomplish His will with, not without, our assistance. So every time He asks us to act, He hopes we'll respond so He can meet us with blessings as He did the three women and the apostles. Such blessings—answers to prayers, hearts' desires, delights exceeding our prayers or imaginations—are meant to prompt still more cooperation. He hopes to elicit from us responses such as these:

- Increased thanksgiving
- More time alone with Him
- New willingness to make sacrifices to do His will
- Closer, quicker self-examination
- Steadier execution of duties or ministries
- A humbler attitude
- More kindness to others, especially nearby
- Stronger confidence in God's faithfulness
- Brighter hope in God's promises and prophecies
- Quicker responses to His guidance

Every time He meets us and we respond, we strengthen our loving, trusting, fruitful, Master-disciple cooperation. The New Testament gives us examples of this collaboration with Christ.

For instance, as ten lepers obeyed Jesus' command to go show the Jewish priests they were clean, Jesus met them by manifesting the healing for which they had asked and believed. When in obedience to Jesus' orders the apostles tarried in the Upper Room, Jesus met them by releasing a mighty outpouring of His Spirit. Peter recognized, "He hath shed forth this, which ye now see and hear" (Acts 2:33). When they obeyed His orders to go and teach, He met them by powerfully converting and healing thousands and turning whole cities and regions to Him. Mark says, "They went forth, and preached everywhere, the Lord working with them, and confirming the word with signs following" (Mark 16:20). Unchanged, Jesus still meets us as we go. Are you going?

Or have you left undone something He told you to do? Have you let pride, fear of man, reasoning, greed, pleasure, or other selfish motives keep you from responding to Him—from giving a discouraged soul a word or message of hope, from seeking Him more often in your secluded "Galilee," from giving yourself wholly to preparation for the ministry, or from any other obedience to His voice? He won't meet you with further blessings— outpourings, healings, confirmations, revelations, commissions—and establish you in a fruitful cycle of cooperation with Him until you respond. Scripture repeatedly confirms this.

"Thou meetest him who rejoiceth and worketh righteousness" (Isa. 64:5). "Thou dost meet him with the blessings of goodness" (Ps. 21:3). So follow the three women's example. Go in obedience, quickly and joyfully, confident that He meets us as we go.

Chapter 40

WALKING ALONE TO ASSOS

*W*HILE THE APOSTLE Paul's companions sailed from Troas to Assos, he traveled there on foot—and alone (Acts 20:13). Why this longer, lonely overland route?

Several reasons are possible. Paul may have made the twenty-mile walk for some exercise. He later famously advised Timothy, "Bodily exercise profits a little" (1 Tim. 4:8, NKJV). He may have wished to view the region's beautiful trees and plants, as spring was gorgeously underway. Though Luke doesn't say, Paul may have been thinking of his persistently watchful and deadly enemies, as only weeks earlier he had discovered their plan to assassinate him while sailing to Syria, forcing him to travel by land to Macedonia instead (Acts 20:3). At Troas he may have decided again to covertly walk to Assos while his associates conspicuously sailed there (vv. 4–5). Even economy could have prompted him, as trekking the Roman roads was less expensive than sailing the Aegean.[1] Any of these factors may explain Paul's actions.

From a spiritual perspective his motive may have been pastoral or personal. Passionately pastoral, Paul may have sent Luke and his other companions ahead by ship so he could linger and further exhort the exceptionally hungry Troas believers (Acts 20:11).[2] While their sail took a whole day, his twenty-mile walk, even if very leisurely, would have taken less time. Or Paul may have wanted to be alone with God.

If so, he was imitating the master Minister, who "often withdrew to the wilderness for prayer" and intimate fellowship with His Father (Luke 5:16, NLT). (See also Mark 1:35.) Surely Paul was spiritually drained after his amazing all-night sermon at Troas (Acts 20:7–11). And living day and night with eight men, however godly, may have stirred his desire to have some private time apart. Thus he probably sought personal spiritual refreshment, knowing, "They that wait upon the LORD shall renew their strength" (Isa. 40:31), and, "In thy presence is fullness of joy" (Ps. 16:11). Additionally he may have been seeking more confirmation or information about his upcoming trip to Rome, which truths Christ wanted him to share in his upcoming "minister's conference" with the Ephesian elders (Acts 20:17–38), or time to pray in the Spirit for these elders' and the Troas Christians' spiritual growth. These too were the master Minister's ways (Mark 6:45–46).

Every godly minister and disciple understands the benefits of getting alone with God, whether at set times daily, for entire days, or for more extended periods. Besides these spiritual reasons, there are others that may prompt us to walk "alone to Assos," or apart from the Christian crowds, for a season. Let's mention some.

Though rare, a special call of God may force us to walk alone, separated from our country, culture, or kin, as it did Abraham: "Look unto Abraham...I called him alone" (Isa. 51:2). Having a heart that's very hungry for more of God, His Word, and His ways may separate us from others lacking spiritual hunger. Extensive preparation for exceptionally fruitful ministry may separate us for an extended time. God isolated Moses for forty years to deeply sanctify him for forty years of amazing service (Acts 7:29–30). Persecution may force us to walk alone with God for a season. Paul was shut away two years in Caesarea's prison, Luther for ten months in Wartburg castle, and Tyndale for over a year in Vilvoorde castle's dungeon. Righteous indignation may cause us to walk a path apart. Many early Christians wouldn't attend Roman public events that began with sacrifices to the "divine emperor." Like Jeremiah they said, "I sat alone because of thy hand; for thou hast filled me with indignation" (Jer. 15:17).

We may also walk alone because others, misunderstanding our ardent devotion or extravagant sacrifices for Christ, criticize and abandon us, as Judas did Mary of Bethany (John 12:4–5). Or having insight ahead of our times may cause us, like pioneers, to experience truths or trials ahead of our Christian peers, since God has called us to pursue something they can't yet see or won't admit. William Carey's vision for foreign missions led him far from his English brothers to a lonely mission post in India. No matter how alone, or why, we're never far from Him who said, "I will never leave thee, nor forsake thee" (Heb. 13:5). He walked with Paul to Assos.

He's walking with us today too: "Jesus himself drew near, and went with them" (Luke 24:15). Paul's separation soon ended and he rejoined his brothers: "When he met with us at Assos, we took him in" (Acts 20:14). Our times apart also end.

So ponder these truths and be encouraged, whenever you find yourself walking alone to Assos.

Chapter 41

THE WAYLESS WILDERNESS

*I*F CALLED TO help lead God's people as a minister, teacher, or elder, you'll eventually experience the wayless wilderness. Psalm 107:40–43 describes this difficult but beneficial and transformative season of training.

"He poureth contempt upon princes [leaders]" (v. 40). Christian leadership is a princely, or noble, calling. Yet God's developing "princes" will be treated un-princely, as certain unbelievers and lukewarm Christians reject and reproach them for their walk or witness. Sometimes these adversaries will pour it on! "He poureth contempt." But God is still with His leaders. In fact, He's causing and controlling the "pouring." "He poureth...[he] causeth." Why this strange baptism of rejection? God's using critics to humble His leaders. To know Him fully and lead His people well, leaders must be humbled. To lead very well, they must be very humble. "Before honor is humility" (Prov. 18:12).

"And causeth them to wander in the wilderness, where there is no [apparent] way [out]" (Ps. 107:40). Our "wilderness" is the spiritual desert. It's marked by a drought of favor and prosperity, by persisting misrepresentations and misjudgments that bring rejection and opposition. These adversities hinder God's vision for our lives and create a sense of failure, despair, and loneliness—relentless pressures that drive us to seek comfort in God more consistently. The *wild*erness is "wild," or seemingly uncontrolled, and marked by periodic assaults by spiritual beasts or bandits. Jesus faced Satan himself in His "wild-erness" (Luke 4:1–14); in ours Satan tries to rob and offend us spiritually through difficult people he prompts or controls. But our greatest challenge is this: there's no discernible way out! "Where there is no way [out]." Search as we may, we see no escape route, no way around our hinderers to fulfill our God-given work or vision. In every direction we see only roadblocks, barrenness, and hopelessness. So we wander, faithfully abiding in and serving Christ but longing and looking for help...until we realize only Christ can release us. Why does Jesus put us through this?

He uses this spiritual tension—our faith resting on His faithfulness to deliver us[1] while our reason wonders uneasily when, where, and how—to exercise, educate, and enlarge our trust in Him. "Thou hast enlarged me when I was in distress" (Ps. 4:1). This "enlarging" of our faith is necessary if we're to lead others into large faith. And lead we will.

God never abandons His princely leaders, even in the wilderness. His rich, satisfying rewards await. In His time God delivers them, opening His way out: "Yet setteth he the poor on high from affliction" (Ps. 107:41). By setting them "on high," or in higher service, He honors them. He increases their works and blessings, growing their personal and church families into larger flocks: "And maketh their families like a flock" (v. 41). Other Christians, identifying with them, rejoice at their victory: "The righteous shall see it, and rejoice" (v. 42). And God defends them by pouring shame on those who poured contempt on them. Stunned and speechless, "all iniquity shall stop her mouth" (v. 42). It's a perfect end to God's princely training. He's done this for many long-tried "princes."

For thirteen years Joseph "wandered" in Potiphar's estate and prison, not knowing how he would rise from his low status to the high service God foretold. But God made a way. For forty years Moses surveyed his future but saw no way to return to Egypt and liberate his oppressed brethren. But God made a way. For years David wandered Judah's wilderness, seeing only more "wild-ness"—King Saul's attacks, Nabal's reproach, the Keilahites' betrayal, Ziklag raided, his family kidnapped!—and waylessness, but no path to his prophesied kingship. But God made a way. When for years God delayed Paul's apostolic ministry, he didn't know how God would raise him from making tents in Tarsus to making disciples in churches. But God made a way. He makes a way for all His leaders.

Has He put you in a wilderness of reproach, delay, failure, separation, or prolonged "nothing"? Is there no way out? Rather than pout or panic, ponder.

Ponder this psalm's message and believe God's using your adversaries and hardships to humble you. Forsake your pride, forgive them, and think meekly. Worship God, believing He's enlarging your faith and ability to strengthen and lead His people effectively. And "wander" well!

Walk with God closely, wondering at His deep ways daily. Work with Him faithfully, discharging your duties large and small. Watch for Him confidently, sure He'll make a way where there's no way. Wait for Him patiently, until the day He releases you, tested, transformed, and prepared to lead, from your wayless wilderness.

Chapter 42

DON'T KEEP JESUS IN A TOMB!

*E*VEN AFTER CRUCIFYING Jesus, the Jewish leaders worried. "The deceiver," a proven miracle worker and resurrector, could revive after three days, as He promised, and resume His Messianic claims (Matt. 27:62–66). This prospect haunted and harried them.

Then they acted. To prevent the unthinkable, the chief priests thought up yet another plan against Jesus: Seal Him in the tomb! Secure the stone door with a seal—a cord stretched across it anchored at both ends in clay or wax pressed by an (uncopiable) official Roman seal to expose any tampering![1] Post Roman guards, four-man squads changed periodically to ensure alertness, to keep Jesus' followers away till the crucial third day passed. That would keep Jesus' body, and promise, dead. But there was more than a corpse in that tomb.

Unwittingly these unbelieving Jewish theologians were trying to restrain not a dead man but a living God. Today some Christian theologians are repeating their folly.

Liberal theologians deny the Bible's inspiration and inerrancy and consider Christ's miracles Christian mythology. Clearly they've concluded Jesus belongs in a tomb of incredibleness, safely wrapped in linens of rationalism and unbelief. But the sad news is they're not alone in advocating a dead Christ. Some evangelical scholars are also conspiring to keep Jesus safely entombed.

Cessationist theologians insist that when the last book of the New Testament (Revelation) was written and the last apostle (John) passed, the miraculous gifts and operations of the Spirit ceased.[2] Today God no longer inspires prophecies, tongues, visions, or works supernaturally. He did so in the first century only to authorize the apostles and establish the church. (Yet these same scholars affirm correctly the stupendously supernatural miracles that end this age, the resurrection and Rapture of Christians worldwide![3]) The Pharisees remembered Jesus' words, but cessationists ignore His key posthumous revelation, "Jesus Christ, the same yesterday, and today, and forever" (Heb. 13:8). They're not Christ's only current tomb keepers.

Any of us may be equally guilty. Even an apostle succumbed to stubborn doubts. Despite Jesus' promise to rise and believers' confirming testimonies, Thomas refused to believe Jesus' supernatural resurrection without natural proof. His trust in Jesus' faithful Word and character was hindered—sealed in a tomb of doubt—by his reasoning. His stony heart of unbelief restrained the enjoyment of Jesus' power in his life. Kindly Jesus liberated him with a word: "Because thou hast seen me, thou hast believed; blessed are they that have not seen, and yet have believed" (John 20:29). There are many other errors and sins that keep "Christ in you, the hope of glory" entombed (Col. 1:27).

Consider these:

- Loving or trusting money
- Practicing immorality
- Harboring pride or prejudice
- Idolatry (loving anything or anyone more than God)
- Disobeying God's guidance
- Not spending time with God
- Selfishness (asserting our wills over God's)
- Unforgiveness
- Loving this world's ways and values
- Envying (sinners or saints)
- Complaining
- Judgmentalism

Any persisting sin prevents Jesus' life and power from being released so He can freely live and move and minister in our lives. Like armed guards and wax seals, disobedience keeps Him dormant in our cold, stony hearts. Meanwhile we follow not the Bible's best examples but its worst!

The ancient Israelites first donned the mantle of hindering God. Their persisting idolatry and unbelief frequently restrained Jehovah's power. Repeatedly "they turned back and tested God, and limited the Holy One of Israel" (Ps. 78:41). The first-century Nazarenes continued this sad legacy: "Because of their unbelief," Jesus "couldn't do any miracles among them" (Mark 6:5, NLT). Many Christians and churches have worn this mantle down the centuries. But we don't have to.

Thankfully God won't let Christ's supernatural life and power be entombed very long. Despite our worst unbelief, Jesus' best—His compassionate, healing, delivering life and power—periodically breaks out working wonders among us and giving hope to a hopeless world and hindered church. We call these special times "visitations" or "revivals." We don't have to wait for them. We can have more of Jesus now, if we stop restraining Him.

He longs to be fully released in our hearts to fully bless us and others through us. On the resurrection morning God's angel removed the stone and broke its seal to show the world "He is risen!" Will you remove, break, or abandon whatever errant doctrines or sin issues have kept Jesus entombed in lukewarmness and non-expectation in your soul? If you'll release Him, He'll reward you—loving, laboring, and ministering freely in your heart, family, church, city, and nation. So act now!

Don't keep Jesus in a tomb!

Chapter 43

PREPARE TO BE TAKEN UP

OT ONCE BUT seven times the Bible describes individuals or groups being caught up bodily to heaven.

After Enoch "walked with God" and gave "testimony" to his pre-Flood peers sufficiently, God delightedly "took him" (Gen. 5:24; Heb. 11:5). After Elijah prophesied to Israel and trained Elisha, chariots of fire appeared and Elijah suddenly "went up by a whirlwind into heaven" (2 Kings 2:11). After Jesus witnessed and ministered to Israel and thoroughly trained His apostles "he was taken up...into heaven" (Acts 1:1–2, 9, 11). Like Christ, when the body of Christ's earthly members finish our witness and work, we'll be suddenly "caught up" to heaven (1 Thess. 4:17). After our ministerial successors—144,000 Jewish evangelists—finish their witness to Israel and the nations during the Tribulation, they and the great multitude saved through their labors will be caught up to God's throne (Rev. 7:9–17; 14:1–5). After God's "two witnesses" of the Great Tribulation "have finished their testimony" against the Antichrist, and are killed and resurrected, they'll also "ascend up to heaven," as their stunned enemies watch (Rev. 11:7–12). The pattern here is clear.

After faithfully finishing their work and witness on earth, God's servants are taken up to heaven. But bodily promotion is not the only kind. We may also be elevated figuratively to higher planes of life or labor in this world.

For example, God may raise us to a higher:

- COMPANY OF FRIENDS AND COMPANIONS. After leaving his tax booth to follow Christ, Matthew was taken up into a new circle of friends. Instead of socializing with unethical, worldly minded, emperor- and money-serving publicans, he now spent his time with upright, spiritually minded, Christ- and kingdom-serving disciples hungry to discover, discuss, and live Jesus' teachings daily.

- BIBLICAL INSIGHT. "If ye continue in my word..." (John 8:31). As we continue learning and living God's Word, the Spirit raises our biblical understanding. Doing God's truth increases our discernment of it: "If any man will do his will, he shall know of the doctrine" (John 7:17). We see fresh principles and patterns in old, familiar passages, and our biblical insight soars to new heights.

- SPIRITUAL WALK. "Lord, what wilt thou have me to do?" (Acts 9:6). If, as Paul did, we humbly leave others to God and focus on what Jesus wants us to do, we'll steadily ascend Mount Obedience. The more consistently we obey, the more consistently we enjoy a higher spiritual walk—sensing Jesus' presence more regularly, hearing His voice more distinctly, and discerning His hand more clearly.

- PLANE OF DIVINE TESTING. After passing His tests in Nazareth, Jesus rose to a higher plane of testing: forty days in the wilderness with Satan! But the Spirit gave Him the wisdom to see and strength to avoid every subtle trap. After overcoming our initial spiritual tests, we too are taken up to face higher challenges, more subtle, persistent, and fierce than any we've faced. But as our way grows harder, God's grace grows stronger. "My grace is [always] sufficient for thee" (2 Cor. 12:9).

- REVELATION OF GOD'S PLAN. Because John remained faithful while suffering intense loneliness on the isle of Patmos, Jesus gave him a higher revelation of His divine plan—a fuller, more detailed knowledge of things to come: "Come up here [beside Me], and I will show thee things [from My perspective]" (Rev. 4:1). If we're faithful in our long, lonely trials, Christ will elevate us to share His perspective. We'll see heaven's plan for our times—"things which must be hereafter" (v. 1)—with greater clarity, order, fullness, and certainty.

- PLACE OF SERVICE OR MINISTRY. God faithfully raises His faithful servants to higher service. He lifted Joseph from slavery to stewardship to national rulership to international ministry. He raised Paul from tent making to teaching to apostolic missions. If we're faithful in small duties, He'll call us to larger ones—"Friend, go up higher" (Luke 14:10)—and suddenly we'll find ourselves in more desirable and fruitful jobs, duties, or ministries.

- QUALITY OF EARTHLY REWARDS. Our benevolent heavenly Father loves to give us "richly all things to enjoy" (1 Tim.

6:17). If we don't crave worldly blessings or let them interfere with our calling, He may bless us richly for our enjoyment and His honor. To Joshua, David, and Solomon He gave a city, kingship, and fame respectively.

So get busy! Faithfully finish your work and witness on your present plane of life and labor. Then Father will take you up spiritually; and one day, bodily: "caught up...to meet the Lord" (1 Thess. 4:17). Tired of living low? It's time to go higher.

Prepare to be taken up.

Chapter 44

REVIVAL, THE SIMPLE WAY

*W*HEN PETER INFORMED the Sanhedrin that God gives the Holy Spirit to "them that obey him" (Acts 5:32), he revealed the simplest way to a fresh anointing of the Spirit: obey God!

This doesn't deny the necessity of God's grace or diminish the part played by personal prayer and faith. To receive spiritual refreshment, we must ask, we must believe, and God must graciously give to us. But here God's Word declares that obedience is also necessary. Without it showers of blessing won't fall.

At Pentecost the Spirit fell on 120 people who were, above all else, obeying Jesus. Before ascending, Jesus ordered them to "tarry" in Jerusalem until He sent "power from on high" (Luke 24:49) and "baptized" them with the "Holy Spirit" (Acts 1:5). How did they respond? They gathered, walked in loving unity, and prayed steadily for this Spirit baptism ten days. Then heaven rained life and power on their dry, weary souls! The church's second revival followed this pattern.

When the apostles obeyed Jesus' commission in Jerusalem, persecution soon followed. But instead of desisting, they persisted, choosing to move steadily forward in obedience despite ominous threats (Acts 4:18, 21). Why? Jesus taught and showed them courageous perseverance. Their daring prayer for boldness brought them another fresh anointing: "When they had prayed...they were all [re-]filled with the Holy Spirit" (v. 31). So again the Spirit filled obedient ones.

Every other time the Holy Spirit fell on or was received by believers, His visitation was ushered in by someone's obedience.

When the Samaritans were filled with the Spirit through Peter's and John's prayers, they had already obeyed the gospel by receiving Christ. At the time Saul of Tarsus received the Spirit through Ananias' prayer, he had obediently followed Jesus' instructions on the Damascus road. The Spirit fell on Cornelius' family and friends after he obeyed God's command to invite Peter and they obeyed God's invitation through Cornelius. Before twelve of John the Baptist's disciples in Ephesus received the Spirit, they complied with Paul's instructions to believe the gospel and be water baptized. Thus Acts repeatedly shows Christ pouring His Spirit upon the compliant, not the obstinate; the cooperative, not the contentious; the surrendered, not the defiant. Clearly those Peter addressed did not qualify.

The Sanhedrin obstinately rejected the heavenly origin of the many miracles and conversions that were filling Jerusalem daily with more followers of the Way. Everywhere they saw luscious spiritual fruit hanging from the church's branches—changed hearts, corrected lives, mended relationships, Jesus' very love and works flowing through His people—and marveled at it. Yet they stubbornly refused to admit the vine it sprang from was divine and their desire to uproot it despicable! This mulish disobedience disqualified them for spiritual refreshment.

But not us. As in Acts, our spiritual fillings and refillings always follow obedience.[1] Before receiving our first taste of the Spirit in new birth, we obeyed Christ's call to repent, believe, and receive Him. Before being baptized with the Spirit, we obeyed Christ's call to ask for the Spirit's fullness (Luke 11:9–13) and chose to follow the examples of this blessing recorded and recommended in Acts. Every time we've been refilled with the Spirit, it's been because we've submissively and trustingly obeyed some divine duty, guidance, call, or correction.

For instance, we've:

- Drawn near God more consistently to pray, feed on His Word, or worship
- Denied our will to obey God's Word in a life test
- Accepted a flesh-mortifying cross to spread the gospel, bless God's people, and grow our character
- Responded to Christ's challenge to launch out to live or minister by faith
- Taken steps to prepare for or advance the ministry God has appointed us
- Resolutely rejected sin or exhorted others to do so

Because we've "loved righteousness" and "hated iniquity" in these or other ways, God has "anointed" us "with the oil of gladness" (Heb. 1:9). Besides being righteous, this principle is reasonable.

Consider this logic. Why should Jesus give new supplies of the Spirit's wondrous inspiration, strength, comfort, and abilities to those who consistently refuse to obey Him? Should He refresh and empower us to disobey? Resist? Rebel? This truth is so simple.

Wisely Peter kept it simple, assuring his nation's religious leaders that God gives His Spirit to "them that obey him." Want the Spirit to refresh you personally or revive your church or ministry? Simply follow Peter's lead. Bring your and your congregation's obedience up to speed—where your conscience says it should be—while praying confidently for more of the Spirit.

Soon by grace, faith, and prayer you'll have revival, the simple way.

Chapter 45

RECEIVING CHRIST'S CONSOLATIONS

*A*LL THEIR LIVES the apostles had longed for Israel's restored kingdom. So after Jesus promised they'd help rule it "upon twelve thrones" (Matt. 19:28) and, after His resurrection, taught them many truths "pertaining to the kingdom" (Acts 1:3), they asked, "Wilt thou at this time restore again the kingdom to Israel?" (v. 6). Oh, how they wanted to hear, "Yes, now's the time!"

His response was soon and sad—"It is not for you to know the times" (v. 7)—but not short. There was more.

Rather than leave them down and disappointed with His no, Jesus added something to lift and heal their wounded hearts: "But ye shall receive power, after the Holy Spirit is come upon you; and ye shall be witnesses unto me...unto the uttermost part of the earth" (v. 8). This wasn't what they wanted. They yearned for confirmation that Israel's visible kingdom would appear immediately. But it was exactly what they needed—insight into God's present, perfect plan for their lives. He would launch not His political but His spiritual kingdom through them "not many days from now" (v. 5). This wasn't their choice. They preferred political power and national autonomy. But it was what Jesus wisely and lovingly chose for them—new, dynamic spiritual power and growing, meaningful international ministry.

We find here a threefold pattern of action:

1. Passionate prayer

2. Disappointing denial

3. Comforting consolation

The apostles asked their heart's desire, Jesus denied it, and then He gave them another blessing to console them. This prayer-denial-consolation pattern is seen throughout the Bible.

When Abraham pleaded for God to make His covenant with Ishmael, God refused but granted Abraham two other blessings. First, He revealed the name, mother, and year of birth of his heir, Isaac. Second, He promised to bless Ishmael since he was also Abraham's son (Gen. 17:18–22).

When Moses asked permission to lead Israel into Canaan, God denied him yet mercifully let Moses view Canaan from Mount Nebo and train his successor, Joshua, to lead the long-awaited invasion (Deut. 3:23–28).

When Paul asked release from his torturous "thorn," the Lord declined yet gave him a new understanding of its purpose—to keep him humble, receiving ever more insights for the church, and to perfect God's strength and grace in him (2 Cor. 12:7–10).

For years Hannah prayed for a son, but strangely God shut her womb. Meanwhile He gave her husband Elkanah's second wife, Peninnah, many sons (1 Sam. 1:1–10). Bitter as this was, God's hand released two sweet comforts for Hannah. First, He caused Elkanah to love her more than Peninnah, though it looked the opposite. Second, He prompted Elkanah to give Hannah a love-gift, a "worthy" (double) portion of the sacrifices at the annual festival meals. Because Hannah ignored her consolations and continued envying Peninnah, she remained tormented with discontent—though chosen to birth the great prophet Samuel! Though God subsequently answered Hannah's prayer, He denied it for many years. Why?

God's no means: (a) our request is not His will or in His plan for us; (b) it's not His way or the method He wishes to work; or (c) it's not His time, thus He hasn't finished preparing for it. The apostles and other petitioners cited above were denied for one of these reasons. Yet God gave them all rich consolations—generous, comforting gifts. Understanding this, overcoming Christians accept God's denials.

Whether God's no means "never," "not that way," or "not now," overcomers realize it's God's sovereign decision and His choices are better than ours. His plans, methods, and timing are always best, and resisting them is always futile, self-opposing, harmful to others, and disruptive to God's kingdom work. So they quickly accept His denials—and eagerly await His consolations! When they come, they give thanks and rest, joyfully content in the blessings He has given. Besides, after denying us one prayer request, our Father may grant us the next. Let's follow their example, knowing Christ's disappointing denials are always followed by His compassionate consolations.

Has the Lord denied your heart's desire? Are you frankly disappointed? Don't be! Look expectantly for your consolation! "Not many days from now" Jesus may refill and refresh you with the Spirit's power. He may send you as His authorized witness to the "uttermost part of the earth." Or He may open to you "worthy portions" of inspiring insight from His Word that nourish your heart and inspire others. Your church may help convert, train, and send a "Samuel"—inspired spokesman—to the body of Christ! Or He may give you other blessings to sweeten your cup.

So get ready to recognize and receive Christ's consolations.

Chapter 46

COMPLETE YOUR SPIRITUAL RÉSUMÉ

*I*N ACTS 15:36–41 two of Christ's best messengers had their worst disagreement over someone's spiritual résumé—or record of Christian service.

Paul and Barnabas agreed on the proposed mission "to go again and visit our brethren in every city...and see how they do" (v. 36). But they clashed when selecting an assistant. Barnabas "determined to take...Mark" (v. 37), but Paul "thought it not good to take him" (v. 38). Paul's rationale is stated.

However sympathetically he read Mark's résumé, Paul just didn't feel comfortable with it. On Mark's only previous mission, he "departed from them...and went not with them to the work" (v. 38; see Acts 13:13). From this Paul could draw only one conclusion: Mark hadn't yet proven himself faithful. This much he knew. Whether Mark would fail again or be faithful he didn't know. For these reasons Paul was resolved. Barnabas' reasons aren't given.

Maybe family ties influenced him, since Mark was his nephew. Or since Barnabas frequently encouraged disheartened Christians (Acts 4:36), perhaps he saw this mission as Mark's chance to redeem himself. Whatever his reasons, he too was resolved not to yield.

Apparently Paul, a prophet, sensed this mission would be a formidable task and wanted a proven assistant, not one on probation. They faced many dangers on their first mission: sorcerers, slander, plots, expulsions, arduous treks, harassments, and a brutal stoning. Paul couldn't forget this persecution or the scars it left on his body. He also recalled that Mark abandoned them just after their initial opposition arose, the defiance of the Jewish sorcerer Elymas (Acts 13:6–11). Were Mark's nerves too weak for spiritual war? The second mission confirmed Paul's forethought.

Like the first mission, the second was extraordinarily challenging. As Paul spread the light of God's Word, the rulers of darkness opposed him viciously with false convictions, shameful public whippings, imprisonments, riots, attacks on his meetings, slander, legal action, and other adversities (Acts 16:1–18:22). Sensing such trials looming, Paul searched Antioch's files for an assistant minister with a strong spiritual résumé.

When "Paul chose Silas" (Acts 15:40), he found one up to the task. No less than James, president of the Jerusalem church, characterized Silas as a "chosen" and "chief" Christian minister (v. 22). When Paul read this, he stamped Silas' résumé in bold red letters, "FAITHFUL," and immediately gave him Mark's position. Paul held no animosity toward Mark. His was strictly a ministry not a personal decision. Scripture also may have influenced Paul's decision.

Well versed in the Jewish writings,[1] Paul knew the proverb, "Confidence in an unfaithful man in time of trouble is like a broken tooth, and a foot out of joint" (Prov. 25:19). Both a "broken tooth" and a "foot out of joint" are unusable and painful. To Paul that may have described Mark at the moment—an unreliable servant likely to bring distress rather than rest! But the story didn't end here.

Mark went on to prove himself faithful. He became Peter's protégé and aide, a Gospel writer, and, ironically, one of Paul's valued assistants (2 Tim. 4:11). Some feel this proves Paul's earlier decision to reject Mark was wrong. Others believe, as I do, it proves Paul's decision was effective discipline, prompting Mark to humbly reevaluate his service, resolutely change, and diligently complete his spiritual résumé! Have we completed ours?

Can our record of Christian service be stamped, "Faithful"? "Proven"? "Ready"? Or are we like broken teeth and disjointed feet—painful and unusable applicants to leaders needing sure help in trying times? Every duty, mission, or ministry, however small, affords us an opportunity to prove ourselves faithful. If we discharge them faithfully, our spiritual résumés will be filled with positive entries:

- "Worked long and hard for his church with little pay or recognition..."
- "Gave sacrificially to the ministry God called her to support..."
- "Loyally helped a struggling inner-city mission..."
- "Faithfully assisted an embattled pastor..."
- "Diligently fasted and prayed for her church's leaders..."
- "Completed small tasks and errands whenever asked..."
- "Taught the Bible excellently for years with little recognition..."
- "Faithfully led worship in a small church..."

With such comments posted to your service record, you have the one indispensible requirement for ministry: faithfulness! "He that is faithful in that which is least is faithful also in much" (Luke 16:10). Like Silas, you'll be ready for any call. And you'll be "chosen."

Remember, Paul didn't reject Mark because he was sure Mark was unfaithful, but because he was unsure he was faithful. Enable leaders to say of you, "He's faithful! She's faithful! I'm sure!" Complete your spiritual résumé.

Chapter 47

READY TO RISE?

s PETER PASSED through all quarters" of Israel, he stopped to minister to the Christians in Lydda (Acts 9:32–35). There he found a man ready to rise.

Aeneas, whose name means "praise," was afflicted with palsy, or paralysis (v. 33). Having "kept his bed eight years," his condition was chronic and incurable. He was probably a quadriplegic, able to turn and raise his head and receive nourishment, but nothing else. His bedridden condition implies severe bedsores and perhaps depression, since, from a natural perspective, he was incurable and his outlook hopeless. But something beyond the natural was coming.

When Peter met Aeneas and by the Spirit declared, "Jesus Christ maketh thee well" (v. 34), instantly Aeneas arose, completely restored. Supernatural, sudden, by the Spirit, in Jesus' name, Aeneas' healing was a miracle. It defied human understanding and explanation—but not recognition.

Peter attributed the miracle to Christ, declaring, "Jesus Christ," not Peter the apostle, "maketh thee well." Occurring about a decade after Jesus' crucifixion, this incident proves that Jesus hadn't changed. As during His Galilean ministry, He still desired to make people whole, or normal and without physical deficiency. He does the same today by His Spirit working through the members of His body. Once healed by, "Jesus Christ, the same, yesterday, today, and forever" (Heb. 13:8), Aeneas was ready to turn from idleness to industriousness.

So Peter promptly put him to work: "Arise, and make thy bed" (Acts 9:34). Get up?! Roll up his bed mat?! These were humble duties! But Aeneas responded quickly: "He arose [and made his bed] immediately" (v. 34). More productive activities followed, causing many to take note.

As Aeneas continued humbly obeying God, his fame grew. Eventually, "all that dwelt at Lydda and Sharon saw him [walking and working]" (v. 35). Like Lazarus, he became a genuine Christian celebrity—one to whom people are drawn not because of worldly fame, fortune, or achievements, but because of what Jesus has done in, for, or through him. The attraction was so strong multitudes throughout the region of Sharon[1] praised,

and many surrendered to, Aeneas' Healer-Lord: "all…turned to the Lord"
(v. 35). Caligula still ruled Rome, but a new King held sway over many in
Lydda—because He found a man ready to rise.

Whether Aeneas was or was not a Christian before his healing, he's
an example to us. Why? Any Christian may suffer spiritual "palsy." Let me
explain.

After beginning our faith walk with Jesus, we may become offended,
distracted, or "weary in well doing" (Gal. 6:9) and stop walking closely with
Him. Once "palsied"—rendered spiritually inactive—we stop seeking God,
searching His Word, or listening for His voice. We stop responding when
He calls, yielding when He warns, and repenting when He chastens. Thus,
to Christ, whatever our religious profession, we're as paralyzed as Aeneas,
spiritually bedridden with lukewarmness and utterly useless in His kingdom work.

Selfishness and sin cause the onset of this spiritual paralysis. Every
time we say no to God and yes to self-will or sin, we weaken "Christ in
you, the hope of glory" (Col. 1:27) until, eventually, we become spiritually
paralyzed.

Some common cripplers are:

- Offense at God, due to many, harsh, or long tests
- Self-pity
- Fear, of reproach, rejection, or failure
- Unmercifulness, especially unforgiveness and the lust to
  judge or condemn others
- Besetting sins to which we stubbornly cling
- Unbelief, or doubting God's faithfulness
- Crosses we refuse to carry for Jesus' sake

When these things trouble us chronically, say, for "eight years," we feel
incurable. Thinking about our condition depresses us. We feel utterly hopeless, naturally speaking. But something beyond the natural is near.

Our loving, living, supernatural Healer-Lord can restore our spiritual
health and activity as quickly as He did Aeneas'. He's promised to release us
from spiritual paralysis: "The truth shall make you free…ye shall be free indeed" (John 8:32, 36). He wants to make our walk with Him "whole," or "perfect and entire, lacking nothing" (James 1:4). He wants us working joyfully

for His kingdom. He's ready to use the news of our personal spiritual revival to draw many to praise and walk with Him—if we're ready to rise.

His still, small voice is calling: "Rise, Jesus Christ is ready, willing, and able to make you whole today!" Are you willing to accept whatever correction, initiate whatever changes, make whatever sacrifices, surrender whatever comforts, and face whatever challenges so Christ can heal your spiritual lethargy? He'll lift you from your spiritually inactive, unproductive past to a refreshingly meaningful, fruitful walk with Him if you're willing. Aeneas was willing.

Are you ready to rise?

Chapter 48

STAND UP, SPEAK UP!

$\mathcal{W}$ HEN THE TIME for wise waiting and silence ends, the time for bold stands and speech begins. Pentecost was such a moment.

Once the required tarrying period elapsed, it was time to stand up and speak up. So "Peter, standing up...lifted up his voice...Ye men of Judaea" (Acts 2:14). When Peter, prompted by the Spirit, rose in response to God's initiative, took a firm stand before his audience, and began speaking God's Word into men's hearts, wondrous things followed. We too will see God work when we stand up and speak up.

We stand up by taking firm positions on key issues. Our moral stands occur when we courageously oppose open sin or fundamental error in our churches. We graciously but resolutely stand against sinning or erring Christians for love's sake, to turn them back to truth and obedience. If they stubbornly reject biblical truth and godly leadership, we should break fellowship (1 Cor. 5:9–13). When Satan attacks, tempts, or deceives fellow believers, loved ones, leaders, or churches, we should also take spiritual stands. We do so by committing ourselves to diligently pray and fast for them, as Paul urged: "Withstand...stand...praying always with all prayer and supplication in the Spirit...for all saints" (Eph. 6:13–18). We speak up by voicing our convictions and counsels in such controversies clearly and without apologies. Mordecai, Esther, and Moses show us the way.

Ironically Mordecai first stood up by *refusing* to stand at attention to honor proud, wicked Haman (Esther 5:9, 13). Later, when he saw Esther refusing to take a stand for her people, he took his—against her! He also spoke up by sternly warning Esther of the consequences of refusing to help her people in a deadly crisis. Stirred by Mordecai's stand and speech, Esther stood up, entered Xerxes' court uninvited, and two days later boldly spoke up for her people, exposing Haman's malicious plot before Xerxes.

After forty years of divinely led silence, Moses stood up by pursuing his destiny to deliver his people and spoke up by informing their elders of all the words God spoke to him (Exod. 4:29–31). He also stood firm against Pharaoh while he defied God's demands and refused to waver when Pharaoh responded with cruel reprisals. Furthermore Moses spoke up by faithfully warning Pharaoh of judgment, despite his insulting retorts, and by speaking reassuring, hopeful messages to his weary brethren despite their worsening conditions. Our lesson doesn't end here.

We must also learn the opposite—when to stand down and quietly say no more. Jesus illustrates this.

In Gethsemane Jesus humbly stood down by not resisting arrest despite the cruelty of Judas' betrayal and the injustice of the Jews' charges. Why? He realized these sufferings were part of His Father's plan; also, that if He didn't stand up to resist His enemies, His Father would (Rom. 12:17–21)! During His trial Jesus quietly said "nothing" (Mark 15:3) as bitter men hurled false accusations at Him. Why? He realized if He was quiet, His Father would speak for Him. And He did, through Pilate, who publicly declared Jesus innocent three times! Are we cultivating Jesus' spiritual sensitivity or bungling opportunities?

Too often we stand up when we should stand down. We take zealous stands in issues Christ wants us to leave alone. Sons of crusaders, we fight the wrong war or the wrong way. We resist personal injustice or persecution when Christ wants us to quietly accept it as a test, trust Him to turn it for good, and move on, offering the sacrifice of praise: "Give thanks in all circumstances, for this is God's will for you" (1 Thess. 5:18, NIV). Or we speak up when we should be quiet. We evangelize people whose hearts aren't prepared, begin preaching before we've studied sufficiently, or share precious spiritual truths ("pearls") with uninterested sinners ("swine"). Thus our works clumsily block God's and our words hinder His.

At other times we sit down when we should stand up. We passively ignore issues on which God wants us to take bold action. Or we're quiet when we should cry out. We sit in self-protecting silence when God wants us to "give an answer to every man that asketh you" with biblical wisdom, conviction, and grace (1 Pet. 3:15). Awkward as we are, how can we cultivate Jesus' sensitivity?

By prayer and practice. Ask the Lord to increase your discretion. Then grow it by practice, as Peter did, remembering there's "a time to every purpose" (Eccles. 3:1). Prayerfully examine your present circumstances.

Have you humbly and wisely tarried, letting God speak and work? Maybe it's time now to stand up, speak up!

Chapter 49

PERFECTING THE PRAYER OF FAITH

HE PRAYER OF faith is believing, successful, fruitful prayer that blesses Christ's people and builds His kingdom.

Jesus taught it succinctly in these words: "Whatever things ye desire, when ye pray, believe that ye receive them, and ye shall have them" (Mark 11:24). The apostle John clarified that these prayers filled with "confidence...in him" should be made "according to his will" (1 John 5:14). In his epistle James ordered elders to practice "the prayer of faith" and suggested Elijah as a model petitioner (James 5:15, 17). Let's examine one of Elijah's confident prayers.

First Kings 18:41–46 describes Elijah's response to a test that perfected—fully developed, matured, and completed—his prayer of faith.

There the great prophet prayed:

- ACCORDING TO PROMISE. Elijah's house of confident prayer rested on a firm foundation: When sending him to Ahab, God promised: "I will send rain" (v. 1). We can't pray confidently unless we're sure our requests are God's will. His plan is revealed generally in the Bible and specifically (for us personally) by the Spirit's witness and confirmation (Acts 16:10).

- IN MEEKNESS. Elijah "cast himself down" on the ground to pray (1 Kings 18:42). His physical posture reflected his heart attitude. Like Daniel he was broken, not brazen; humble, not haughty; a confessor, not a denier of his sins. Are we meek and mannerly or rude and demanding in God's presence? We are to come boldly but never brashly.

- WITH DETERMINATION. Elijah "put his face between his knees" (v. 42) so the things seen wouldn't distract him. He knew God could create a way out of no way and was determined to focus on Him, not temporary contradictory evidence. Are we focused on shifting events or God's unchanging promise? Our fickle feelings or the Spirit's consistent witness? Our fallible reasonings or our Father's perfect wisdom?

124

- LOOKING FOR AN ANSWER. He told his servant, "Go...look toward the sea" (v. 43), since rain clouds usually came from the Mediterranean. No trifler, Elijah expected God to respond in His time and way to every petition he offered in His will. Are we looking for something or nothing? Expecting answers or disappointments? "Unto them that look for him shall he appear" (Heb. 9:28).

- PERSISTING...DESPITE LACK OF EVIDENCE. Repeatedly the servant found no evidence confirming Elijah's confidence: "There is nothing" (1 Kings 18:43). This spiritual tension—Elijah's intellectual doubts pulling against his implicit trust— was necessary. It exercised and increased Elijah's faith, just as barbells resist weightlifters' muscles and increase their strength. The more discouraging evidence we face and dispatch without discouragement, the stronger our faith—and the more effective our prayer of faith. So lift your weights! "Cast thy burden on the LORD....Trust in him...pour out your heart before him" (Ps. 55:22; 62:8).

- PERSISTING...DESPITE UNEXPLAINED DELAYS. After six reports of "nothing," Elijah was baffled! Everything was in place: He was asking the right thing at the right time in the right way— in humble, persistent faith in God. But still nothing! And God offered no explanation! Though this discipline was very hard, Elijah submitted to it. As he kept praying resolutely, refusing to doubt God's faithfulness, God used the tension to increase his confidence in Him. (See John 11:15.) At the "seventh time," God's perfect or appointed time, when Elijah's faith was perfectly focused and persistent, God released the visible answer, "a little cloud out of the sea, like a man's hand" (1 Kings 18:44). Does this explain your unexplained delays?

Spiritual maturity in action, Elijah discerned God's mighty hand in minuscule signs. When Elijah's servant finally reported the "little cloud" (v. 44), he thought it was of little importance. But Elijah instantly detected a large message: "great rain," God's restored blessing on His chastened people, was imminent! It resembled a "man's hand" because God's hand (power) was in it coming on Elijah to lead the national revival (v. 46). So we see Elijah used the prayer of faith not for selfish ends but to bring blessings on God's suffering, discouraged people in a desperate hour—just like ours.

Many Christians today are as dry as Elijah's parched land. Overstressed, under-blessed, and out of options, they're ready to give up on the prayer and God of faith. We desperately need "great rains" of the Spirit. Are you undergoing hard spiritual discipline, praying humbly, determinedly, and watchfully according to God's promises, yet with nothing to show but baffling contradictions and unexplained delays? Don't give up!

Get up to the top of your "Carmel," or place of prayer. Perfect the focus and persistence of your faith. Your intercession may bring in a latter rain greater than Elijah's—if you perfect the prayer of faith.

Chapter 50

TRANSFORMATIVE TEACHING

*T*HE NEW TESTAMENT presents Christ's Great Commission in three parts.

Mark remembers Jesus mandating evangelism: "Go ye into all the world, and preach the gospel" (Mark 16:15). Luke says He commissioned all Christians to be witnesses: "Ye shall be witnesses unto me" (Acts 1:8). Matthew recalls Jesus solemnly charging we "teach all nations" everything He's taught us (Matt. 28:19). Let's study this teacher's commission.

To "teach" is literally to *make disciples or followers*.[1] Primarily, churches should be teaching centers producing disciples of Christ. There born-again believers are informed of Christ's life, ministry, and teachings; trained in His ways of living; and transformed into His likeness.

For this, pastors and teachers must:

- PRAY. Intercession is the indispensable accompaniment of effective instruction. Prayerless teaching is powerless talk, even if it's biblical, scholarly, and spiritual. Teachers' prayers enable the Spirit's power to quicken and deeply embed the truths they teach. Intercession inspires students to do whatever they must to grow: seek, pray, study, worship, give, love, suffer. Jesus prayed for His disciples constantly, especially during severe tests like their Galilee crossings (Matt. 14:23) and Peter's sifting: "I have prayed for thee, that thy faith fail not" (Luke 22:31–32). Paul did the same, confiding to Timothy, "without ceasing I have remembrance of thee in my prayers night and day" (2 Tim. 1:3).

- INSTRUCT. Knowing students need precise knowledge, Christ's instructors teach in detail, defining key words and illustrating biblical principles with biblical, historical, and current examples. Orderly informers, they describe their subject's history from beginning to end and explain its simplest concepts to its most advanced. And since their studies, experiences, reflections, and prayers enable them to recognize what's most and least important, their emphases are accurate (Matt. 22:35–40; 23:23).

- EXHORT. Besides informing, New Testament teachers exhort, urging students to live right and avoid sin. They're passionate professors, not lethargic lecturers. For three years Paul warned the Ephesians constantly "with tears" (Acts 20:31).

- OBSERVE. Christlike teachers caringly watch their students' responses. Are they alert or asleep? Understanding or confused? Receiving or rejecting? This benevolent observation guides their correction and counseling work.

- CORRECT. Besides implanting seeds, teachers must uproot weeds. They identify their students' faults—wrong attitudes, values, speech, and habits. Then they show them how to replace them with Christ's ways—biblical attitudes, spiritual habits, and godly reactions to situations. They constantly prescribe scriptures to heal their students' weaknesses, knowing, "All scripture is inspired by God and is useful for…correcting error, for re-setting the direction of a man's life and training him in good living" (2 Tim. 3:16, PHILLIPS). Teachers who neglect correction fail their students; those who practice it love and mature them: "As many as I love, I rebuke and chasten" (Rev. 3:19).

- COUNSEL. Knowledge is information; wisdom is the good judgment to know when to use information. We may be well informed yet unwise. Daily God arranges situational tests to give us opportunities to apply biblical knowledge we've learned to life situations. Christlike teachers stand by, ready to help us recognize which scriptural principles apply to our current problems. As we humbly ask for help, our hearts are laid bare, ready to receive wisdom. As our teachers probe us with questions and give counsel, wisdom is imparted and we become wiser.

As teachers, pastors, mentors, and counselors pursue these duties, a wondrous miracle gradually unfolds in every teachable student under their instruction.

Steady teaching, combined with the student's steady obedience, renews (reforms) the latter's thinking (Rom. 12:1–2). No longer "conformed to this world," his (or her) attitudes and character become increasingly "conformed to the image of his [God's] Son" (Rom. 8:29). He entered his training as one kind of person, a saved but immature believer, but now emerges as another—one who increasingly thinks, loves, works, prays, gives, waits, sacrifices, and reacts like Jesus! Others notice the change, as the Sanhedrin did: "They marveled; and...took knowledge of them [the apostles], that they had been with Jesus" (Acts 4:13). Thereafter the disciple "proves what is that good, and acceptable, and perfect, will of God" (Rom. 12:2), or demonstrates in his daily living God's good and perfect will. Specifically, he reflects God's wise plan to use transformative teaching to change baby Christians into mature, Christlike disciples. Thus spiritual reproduction occurs: Christ reproduces His character in teachers, and they reproduce it in others.

Are you seeking this teaching that intercedes, instructs, exhorts, observes, corrects, and counsels? Pastor, teacher, are you rendering it? It's time we fulfill the Teacher's commission. Let's begin by asking the Teacher's help: "Lord, help us make our churches discipleship training centers, schools of Christ filled with transformative teaching."

Chapter 51

CALLING CHRISTIAN ARMOR-BEARERS!

HEN HOSTILE JEWS arrived in Berea seeking to harm Paul, the Berean Christians wisely sent him off to Athens with an escort (Acts 17:14). "They that conducted Paul" (v. 15) served as spiritual armor-bearers.

In ancient times armor-bearers were military combat assistants, young men who accompanied kings or military officers into battle to render aid. Their primary duties were to carry into combat armor and weapons—shields, bucklers, swords, spears, javelins, bows, arrows, axes—dispensing them to their masters as needed. But their service didn't stop there.

Armor-bearers also fought. Typically they followed behind their masters rendering death blows (*coups de grace*) to those they wounded or knocked down: "Jonathan struck down the Philistines. His armor-bearer, who was behind him, finished killing them" (1 Sam. 14:13, GW). This rear-guard action was defensive, insuring the wounded would not rise again to harm their masters.

To more fully understand armor-bearers' characteristics and ways, let's look to Scripture. It reveals:

- THEY ARE COURAGEOUS IN BATTLE. King Saul made David his armor-bearer not because of his musical skills but because, though young, David was reputed as "a mighty, val-iant...man of war" (1 Sam. 16:18, 21).

- THEY FEAR GOD. When Saul, mortally wounded, asked his armor-bearer (David's successor) to slay him, "he would not; for he was very much afraid" (1 Sam. 31:3–4). His trepidation evinced a holy dread of harming the Lord's "anointed" (Ps. 105:15).

- THEY DON'T ASSIST SELF-OPPOSITION. Saul's armor-bearer also refused Saul's request because it was self-opposing.

- THEY ARE UTTERLY LOYAL. Saul's armor-bearer also demon-strated total loyalty by choosing to die with Saul rather than flee when it became clear defeat was inevitable (1 Sam. 31:3, 6).

130

- THEY EXHORT THEIR MASTERS TO PERSEVERE. When Jonathan announced he would boldly assault the Philistine garrison, his armor-bearer, a man of faith, urged him on in God's will despite the impossible odds, promising to support him: "Do all that is in thine heart...I am with thee according to thine heart [plans]" (1 Sam. 14:7).

- THEY CLOSELY FOLLOW THEIR MASTERS' WAYS. Jonathan instructed his armor-bearer to stay close and follow his footsteps: "Come up after me [following closely]" (v. 12).

- THEY ARE HONORED WITH THEIR MASTERS. Scripture describes Jonathan's victory as a "slaughter, which Jonathan and his armor-bearer made" (v. 14).

- THEY DEFLECT BLOWS. Goliath's armor-bearer is described as "one bearing a shield" who "went before him" hoping to deflect enemy blows (1 Sam. 17:7).

- THEY RENDER SAVING AID. Years later, when David "grew faint" in battle, a Philistine rushed to kill him. Though not an armor-bearer but a "mighty man," Abishai nevertheless intervened like an armor-bearer to save David from certain death: "Ishbibenob...thought of slaying David. But Abishai...came to his aid" (2 Sam. 21:16–17).

All these natural traits and duties parallel those of Christian armor-bearers—believers called, gifted, and trained to assist spiritual leaders in the ongoing conflicts they endure to minister the light of God's Word in this sin-darkened world.

Christian armor-bearers stay close by their spiritual leaders in daily contact and support. They follow their godly ways and spread their teachings and vision, as Timothy did Paul's: "Timothy...shall bring you into remembrance of my ways which are in Christ" (1 Cor. 4:17). They faithfully encourage them to press on with God's will despite difficulties, even impossibilities—yet wisely and graciously disagree if their leaders fall into self-opposing moods of unbelief, self-pity, or despair. While adversaries think nothing of slandering their spiritual leaders, armor-bearers fear God and refuse to say or do anything that would harm the reputation of the "Lord's anointed" or hinder their ministry to God's people. Courageously and loyally they stand by their faithful leaders in the hottest battles—including church controversies and splits—even when their cause, for the moment, appears lost. Some go before their leaders to meet the enemy, as Daniel Nash did for Charles Finney, giving themselves to intercessions and fasts before approaching meetings, missions, or crises. Others step in to render saving assistance when their leaders are exhausted or broken due to over- work or long trials. Thus they wield mighty spiritual swords to assist their masters. But not literal swords!

A young, zealous John Knox once guarded the Scotch reformer, George Wishart, while he preached, clutching a huge two-handed sword to dissuade would-be assailants.[1] We need Knox's spiritual equivalent: faithful assistant pastors, attentive personal aides, godly board members, spiritually minded elders, helpful travel companions, committed intercessors, support- ive congregants, and anyone else willing to help[2] spiritual leaders rise above Satan's workers, weapons, and wiles. Leaders, ministries, and churches need them.

So listen and respond: Jesus is calling Christian armor-bearers!

Chapter 52

CHRIST OUR SECURITY

FTER CHARGING His disciples with their mission, the Great Commissioner added a few words: "And, lo, I am with you always" (Matt. 28:20). Though small, it was a powerful addendum. Paraphrasing, He said, "I am going with you." Or, "I will securitize you—My presence will make you safe wherever you go." He implied, "I am your companion to keep you company and your coworker to assist you." Mark says Jesus kept His promise: "They went forth and preached everywhere, *the Lord working with them...*" (Mark 16:20). So Christ Himself became His original disciples' security.

More elusive today than ever, security is the restful sense of being protected from harm, injury, loss, or lack. It is confidence that an impenetrable barrier exists between us and danger. The Commissioner still gives His servants this restful sense of safety through certain benefits.

They are:

- PROTECTION. "Hedged" by angels (Job 1:10), we're safe from all unauthorized Satanic attacks—on our health, family, finances, property, or works. If God lets him breach this barrier, it's always for His higher purposes: to confirm our righteousness or fruitfulness, to qualify us to rule with Jesus and fellowship with cross bearers, to give us compassion for sufferers and deeper knowledge of God, to increase our spiritual power and fruit, or to conform us to the image of the "man of sorrows" who was "rejected of men" (Isa. 53:3). Whether kept from or in such troubles, if we don't rebel, we're safe. Why? Our fellowship with Jesus is sure, sweet, and untouchable.

- STRENGTH. Our Reinvigorator, Jesus gives us strength of mind, will, and body when our powers are spent. Abandoned by his coworkers, Paul wrote, "Notwithstanding, the Lord stood with me and strengthened me, that by me the preaching might be fully known" (2 Tim. 4:17).

133

- WISDOM. Christ taught His missioners to be "wise as serpents, and harmless as doves" (Matt. 10:16). When Paul stood before Jewish leaders anxious to murder him as they had Stephen, Jesus gave him a word of wisdom that divided his enemies (Acts 23:6–10). Suddenly their plan collapsed, and Paul, thanks to Christ's wisdom, stood safe and secure.

- GUIDANCE. After fishing unsuccessfully all night at their initiative, the apostles were humbled and ready for Jesus' leading. So He gave it: "Cast the net on the right side of the boat, and ye shall find" (John 21:6). Obeying, they were filled with fish—and renewed confidence!

- COMFORT. Jailed in Jerusalem, Paul received a personal visit from Jesus, who comforted him with news that a greater work lay ahead: "Be of good cheer…as thou hast testified of me in Jerusalem, so must thou bear witness also at Rome" (Acts 23:11).

- CONTENTMENT. Jesus gives us contentment—satisfaction with what one has—through fellowship with Him. Wherever we are, we can be content because "He hath said, I will never leave thee" (Heb. 13:5). He also satisfies us through fellowship with other disciples. On his long, arduous journey to Rome, Paul found fresh satisfaction when he "found brethren" in Puteoli and visited with them seven days (Acts 28:13–15).

- ASSISTANCE. Imperfect and limited, we need help often. So Christ gives us favor with believers and unbelievers so they'll assist us. He inclined Julius to treat Paul courteously (Acts 27:1–3). He also prompted Mark to assist Paul: "He is profitable [helpful] to me for the ministry" (2 Tim. 4:11).

- MIRACLES. As needed, Christ gives miracles. He gave a "sign" on Malta. By enabling Paul to survive an accidental snakebite, Jesus erected a figurative billboard, reading: "This is My messenger, and his message is true."

This wonderful security given by Christ's protection, strength, wisdom, guidance, comfort, contentment, assistance, and miracles is unceasing and unfailing: "I am with you *always*." In every circumstance, city, and country, Christ our security is on the job. No other security—homeland, airport, auto, home, or computer—is failsafe. Truly, "It is better to trust in the LORD than to put confidence in man" (Ps. 118:8). But not everyone enjoys Christ's security.

Its original recipients were not casual or carnal but committed Christians. Their successors today are committed disciples of Christ, called of God, Spirit led, true worshippers, faithful in duty, and lovers and doers of God's Word. These alone enjoy the full, deep peace of Christ's security, as Abraham did long ago: "Fear not, Abram: I am thy shield" (Gen. 15:1). Others may search for this elusive treasure, but only fully committed ones find it.

Today Christ is recommissioning believers for the church's final revival and harvest. Prepare to receive your commission—and live, labor, and rest in Christ our security.

Chapter 53

HOLDING JESUS—TIGHTLY!

*A*FTER HEARING JESUS had risen, Mary Magdalene and the "other Mary" ran to tell His disciples. When they suddenly met Jesus, they fell down and "held him by the feet," worshipping (Matt. 28:9).

"Held" is translated from a Greek word (*krateō*) meaning, "to be strong, mighty, powerful,"[1] thus implying a strong, firm, or determined action. Other renderings are "took hold of" (NAS) and "laid hold of" (YLT). So theirs was a tight grip, like that of a man adrift clinging to a lifeline! For three agonizingly tense and gloomy days they had feared they would never see Jesus again. Now, with Him back, they were determined to never again let Him go. Ever!

This *holding tightly to Jesus* is a key component of a devout Christian's life. Devout believers are *devoted*—wholly dedicated or given to seeking, worshipping, and serving Jesus. Spiritually concentrated, they nourish and protect their relationship to Him at all costs. The Bible showcases them.

Luke describes the three thousand converts at Pentecost as "devout men" (Acts 2:5). So they were neither careless nor casual but serious about their relationship to Jehovah, men who held tightly to Him. Their presence at the festival proved that.

Many of these proselytes "out of every nation" (v. 5) had made a long, arduous, expensive, and dangerous journey to obey God's command to attend the major annual feasts, in this case Pentecost. Others, who were Jews of the Diaspora,[2] demonstrated equal devotion. Though foreign born and raised, these Jews had sold everything to relocate and live their final years in the Promised Land. They wanted to worship in God's temple, fellowship with His people, experience His culture, walk His hills, work His earth, and excavate their tombs from His rocks. Barnabas understood this complete devotion to God.

Barnabas exhorted Antioch's new converts, "that with purpose of heart they would cling unto the Lord" (Acts 11:23). His was not the light talk of a lukewarm Christian but the weighty words of an experienced, wise man of God. He knew they needed to hold Jesus tightly in order to take deep root in Him. Then, when storms of afflictions struck, they wouldn't be shaken loose from Him. David agreed, writing, "I have set the LORD always before me; because he is at my right hand, I shall not be moved" (Ps. 16:8). Paul also agreed and complied. He clung to Jesus so tightly he wasn't moved from Him by even the worst adversities: long delays in his ministry, injustice, slander, incarceration, hurricanes, shipwrecks, snake bites, whippings, stonings! We too must hold Jesus tightly.

Satan's constantly trying to steal or ruin everything God gives us. He wants to spoil our blessings, make us lose our rewards, discourage us from praying, uproot the biblical truth we receive, all in order to sever our devotional lifeline—daily fellowship with Jesus in prayer, worship, and Bible meditation—which is the key to our fruit-bearing. Realizing this, Paul warns us six times in his epistles to "stand fast" (1 Cor. 16:13; Gal. 5:1; Phil. 1:27; 4:1; 1 Thess. 3:8; 2 Thess. 2:15). John added, "Hold that fast which thou hast, that no man take thy crown [reward]" (Rev. 3:11). And Jesus warned us every time we receive God's Word, "Satan cometh immediately" (Mark 4:15) to steal it, and our devotion and fruitfulness. Our reaction to this continuing struggle is crucial. If we hold our devotional lifeline to Jesus tightly, we win and bear fruit; if loosely, we lose, and the fruit of the Spirit and His blessing of others through us wither. Not everyone is willing to hold the Lord close.

The needy but worldly crowds pressed hard to touch Jesus but stopped there. After His inspiring touch they returned to their uninspired interests and ways. But Jesus' disciples weren't satisfied with a touch. They bound themselves closely to the living Word. Are we close or just touched?

Is Jesus our religious hobby or real lifeline? Are we careful to reconnect with Him every morning and hold Him close all day—by not only our devotional time with Him but also self-examination, confession of sins, giving thanks, singing praises, obeying His voice, and watching for answers to prayer? Or are we casually content to briefly touch and hear Him twice a week in church meetings? Mary and company held Jesus tightly—and He upheld them.

If we hold Him firmly, He'll uphold us: "My soul followeth close behind thee; thy right hand upholdeth me" (Ps. 63:8). Or, paraphrasing, "I hold on to you for dear life, and you hold me steady as a post" (THE MESSAGE). Get busy holding Jesus—tightly!

Chapter 54

READY FOR LAUNCH?

THE CHURCH'S BEGINNING was neither mundane nor methodical. It was meteoric—a spiritual rocket launch!

After the Spirit fell and Peter spoke, three thousand were added on the first day alone (Acts 2:41). After launch the church continued steadily rising, as "the Lord added to the church daily" (v. 47). Soon the number swelled to ten to fifteen to twenty thousand! (The "five thousand" figure in Acts 4:4 included men only.) Thus the Spirit suddenly supercharged the believers with explosive power and, like a NASA rocket booster, blasted them into spiritual "orbit"—worshipful, prayerful union with Jesus in "heavenly places" (Eph. 1:3)—and a dynamic walk and work with Him on earth.

How did they rate this astronomical growth? Most pastors would donate an arm, leg, or organ to discover their secret. Well, keep your body parts, Reverend.

The apostles' secret is out: they humbly obeyed Jesus! This is the underrated theme of Acts 1 that we typically overlook in our holy haste to study and seek the wonders of Acts 2. After the believers honored Jesus with humble obedience, He honored them with a heavenly outpouring, accompanied by all His wondrous manifestations, works, gifts, and graces. Peter confirmed, "This Jesus...he hath shed forth this, which ye now see and hear" (Acts 2:32–33).

Pastor, hear and hold these facts. The apostles used no gimmicks to draw the thousands! There were no new methods used—no Philistine carts. There were no visiting celebrities—no famous Roman senators, philosophers, or orators. There were no exciting athletic events staged—no Ben Hur-esque chariot races or gladiatorial exhibitions. There were no creature comforts offered—no hot Roman baths or oiled massages. There were no materialistic appeals—no Phoenician merchandise, Indian spikenard, or Egyptian linen raffled as door prizes. There was no superstitious baiting with religious relics—no piece of Jesus' cross or tassel from His garment with purported healing powers. No, the wonder of Pentecost was that it was a purely divine intervention, sent in God's time, executed by His Son, energized by His Spirit, and facilitated by His people's humble obedience.

While the apostles wanted to please Jesus and bear fruit unto Him, their Vine, they no more expected their ranks to suddenly go from 120 to 3,120 than they did to hear a tornadic wind, see tongues of fire, or be used by God to speak to others in unknown languages! Their instant mega-church was a mega-shock! While this huge congregation was instant, its leaders were not.

The apostles were slowly, deeply, fully prepared men of God. Students, they had been personally taught by Jesus for three years. Humble, they had served as His ministerial understudies and assistants. Teachable, they had allowed Him to repeatedly correct their pride, ambition, and prejudices. Experienced, they had served a spiritual apprenticeship, or period of practice ministry. Spiritual, they had learned Jesus' way of sustained private communion with the heavenly Father and walked in it. Proven, they had overcome stormy (Mark 4), strange (John 11), and shocking (crucifixion) tests of faith and now trusted Christ's faithfulness at all times! Tempered, they had passed through all the vicissitudes of ministry—excitement, dullness, acclaim, rejection, loyalty, betrayal—they would experience leading Jesus' followers. Thus they were a deeply laid "foundation" for this new, large spiritual temple, the church. Paul acknowledges it was "built upon the foundation of the apostles" (Eph. 2:20), and John adds their names are inscribed on the foundations of the church's eternal home, New Jerusalem (Rev. 21:14). Let every spiritual leader listen.

Bishop, pastor, elder, deacon, and missionary, have we learned from the apostles' example? Are we, by humble obedience, building ecclesiastical foundations? Spiritual launching pads? Peter tells us, "Humble yourselves...under the mighty hand of God, that he may exalt you in due time" (1 Pet. 5:6). The Word promises blessings for all who comply: "If my people, who are called by my name, shall humble themselves...I...will heal their land" (2 Chron. 7:14). Let's stop seeking crowds and start seeking righteousness. Let's stop examining the nation and start examining our churches. Let's stop condemning unenlightened sinners and start confessing our sins and faults one to another. Let's stop trying to change government policies and start changing our practices. Let's stop murmuring about others' pride and start humbly obeying God's Word and guidance ourselves. We'll emerge deeply trained leaders—well-laid foundations and launching pads—ready for a visitation of the Spirit and explosive growth. Don't delay!

It's time for new leaders, a new Pentecost, and a new round of local church "launches" worldwide. Wait, I hear a sound from heaven! "T-minus ten seconds and counting...nine, eight, seven..." Ready for launch?

Chapter 55

OFFERING PRAYER WITH WORSHIP

FTER PENTECOST BELIEVERS began assembling in the Jewish temple courts to pray at the appointed "hour[s] of prayer" (Acts 3:1). These times coincided with the morning (9:00 a.m.) and evening (3:00 p.m.) offerings. So the first Christians prayed while worship—in their case, the burnt offering—was being offered. It was a powerful combination!

One day, as Peter and John entered the temple at the afternoon hour of prayer (Acts 3:1), their prayer healed a crippled beggar. Lame from birth over forty years earlier, this man's legs and feet were severely withered. Yet he instantly received vibrant health, athletic use of his legs, and exuberant joy! "He, leaping up, stood...walking, and leaping, and praising God" (v. 8). Everyone in the temple courts recognized him, because for years he sat daily by the prominent, brass-covered Beautiful Gate that opened into the heavily trafficked Court of the Women. "Overcome with wonder and sheer astonishment at what had happened to him" (v. 10, PHILLIPS), they quickly gathered in Solomon's Porch, seeking an explanation, which Peter duly gave.

The early Christians' habit of prayer and worship was not the only example we have. Other Bible characters also learned to offer their petitions to God with praise and worship—and powerful results.

After twenty years of backsliding and with war on their doorstep, Israel thirsted again after God. So Samuel "cried unto the LORD for Israel" while simultaneously "offering up the burnt offering," and God responded by routing Israel's enemies and restoring the chosen nation to full favor and blessing (1 Sam. 7:9–10).

One day King Jehoshaphat awoke to find Jerusalem surrounded by large enemy armies. When he offered humble prayers for deliverance followed by high praises to God, whose "mercy endureth forever," God suddenly intervened, giving a stunning victory (2 Chron. 20:5–13, 18–22).

Desperate for her daughter's deliverance, a Syrophoenician woman fell at Jesus' feet. As she worshipped and begged His help, He responded, and moments later her pitifully bound daughter was powerfully freed (Matt. 15:25–28).

In Philippi Paul and Silas found themselves illegally beaten, jailed, and in desperate need. But as they "prayed, and sang praises unto God," He suddenly shook the prison and released them to finish their mission (Acts 16:25–26).

During the Great Tribulation angels will offer the "smoke of the incense" of worship before God with "the prayers of the saints," and God will respond by releasing awesome judgments on the Antichrist-worshipping world (Rev. 8:2–6).

These powerful divine responses show us that prayer offered with worship pleases the Lord greatly and moves His hand powerfully. Shouldn't we too offer our prayers with praise or worship? Here are some suggestions.

Begin your private prayer times with a few minutes of pure worship, lifting, adoring, and lauding the Lord. Recount what He's done for you, especially recently. Or quietly offer the "sacrifice of praise...our lips giving thanks to his name" (Heb. 13:15). Don't rush through this love session to get to your petitions! Take time to be sure Jesus gets His blessing and comfort first before asking Him to bless and comfort you with answers. Conduct prayer meetings the same way. Begin with praise and worship, as you typically do on Sunday mornings, and then petition the Lord for His help. Always finish your petitioning "with thanksgiving" (Phil. 4:6–7) to demonstrate your confidence He's heard you and you have received everything you've asked for in His name and will. This agrees with Christ's explicit instructions.

Jesus taught us to begin prayer with praise and worship: "Our Father...Hallowed be thy name" (Matt. 6:9). In Scripture God's name is synonymous with His character. To hallow His name is not only to set apart His personal designator from and above all others but also to worship and praise His flawlessly beautiful character. So to hallow God's name is to worship. It's love talk, our extravagant expressions of passionate delight in our unfailingly faithful Father God. After this, says Jesus, we should begin petitioning: "Give us this day our daily bread...forgive us...lead us not...deliver us" (vv. 11–13). Everything else being in place, this combination will be powerful!

Awesome answers will follow, "exceedingly abundantly above all that we ask or think" (Eph. 3:20). When we see these open responses to our private prayers regularly, we'll be filled with a faith, joy, and zeal we've never known (John 16:24). Peter's and John's petition resulted in an astounding, city-quaking, false-religion-shaking, church-enlarging miracle, a wonder that won thousands to Christ in a day. Neither they nor their churches were ever the same! What wonders, encouragements, and joy will result if we follow their example?

Let's find out! Begin daily offering prayer with worship.

Chapter 56

TRIUMPHANT TWOSOMES!

*T*HE LORD ORDAINED dual leadership in the early church. Luke notes Peter and John went together to lead the believers' afternoon prayer meeting in the temple courts (Acts 3:1). Jesus had prepared them for this—together.

Before meeting Jesus, Peter and John had worked together for years in Zebedee's fishing business. Throughout Jesus' three-year ministry they were in His inner circle, witnessing together the raising of Jairus' daughter, the Transfiguration, and Jesus' agony in Gethsemane. At the end both were present when Jesus was tried at the high priest's home. Jesus also assigned both special responsibilities: John, to care for His mother, and Peter, to feed His sheep. After Jesus rose, Peter and John ran together to His tomb to verify He had risen (John 20:4). Before ascending, Jesus restored Peter to leadership but checked his impulsive fishing trip and nosiness about John's future so he would lead humbly with John assisting. Thus prepared, they became tandem leaders—two closely linked shepherds leading God's flock. This was, and still is, God's way: "Two are better than one" (Eccles. 4:9). The Old Testament era gives many examples of dual leadership, discipleship, ministry, or missions.

It tells of Moses and Aaron, Joshua and Caleb, Deborah and Barak, Naomi and Ruth, Hezekiah and Isaiah, Elijah and Elisha, Joshua and Zerubbabel, Haggai and Zechariah. Even the infernal imitator, Satan, knows two are better than one. He trained and sent many pernicious pairs, such as Korah and Dathan, Hophni and Phinehas, Ahab and Jezebel, Sanballat and Tobiah, and Herod (Antipas) and Herodias, to do his bidding! Leadership by twosome continues in the New Testament.

Jesus sent His disciples "by two and two" (Mark 6:7) on training missions (vv. 12–13), to prepare cities for His ministry (Luke 10:1), to find mounts (Matt. 21:1–2), and to prepare banquets (Mark 14:13). He continued this as Head of the church.

Repeatedly Acts says "Peter and John" did this or that:

- "The lame man...held Peter and John" (Acts 3:11).
- "When they saw the boldness of Peter and John" (Acts 4:13).

- "Peter and John answered and said" (Acts 4:19).
- "They sent unto them Peter and John, who...prayed for them" (Acts 8:14–15).

So not one but both apostles led the fledgling church together. The trend persisted.

The Spirit sent Barnabas and Paul on the first foreign mission and Paul and Silas on the next. Paul and Apollos fed the growing Corinthian church, assisted by the husband and wife team of Aquila and Priscilla. Paul and Timothy were also an effective twosome. Tradition says Peter and Mark were another. Revelation says the last chosen pair will be the "two witnesses" of the Great Tribulation (Rev. 11:3). Church history continues the story.

God sent powerful pairs to lead every reformation, revival, and domestic or foreign mission. Luther and Melanchthon, Whitefield and Wesley, Catherine and William Booth, Adoniram and Ann Judson, Moody and Sankey, Seymour and Parham, and more recently, Graham and Roberts—these dynamic duos either ministered together or simultaneously with lasting effect on their generations.

Why are two better than one? Ecclesiastes 4:9–12 enlightens us. Two make more work possible; some jobs require two people. Two share burdens, decreasing their weariness. They share honors, reducing the risk of pride. They share rewards, so greed is less likely indulged. Two can earn a "good [better] reward" (v. 9); their joint labors create more income for each of them than they can earn individually. If one stumbles into a pit of sin or discouragement, the other "will lift up his fellow," but alone, they may not recover (v. 10). Through regular, edifying fellowship two produce more spiritual heat—devotional warmth, faith, soul comfort, brotherly love, and righteous zeal—than they can generate alone (v. 11). Two possess more spiritual fighting ability to "withstand" (v. 12) Satan's relentless attacks on their minds, bodies, families, and ministries. And for Christians, two are actually three! Wherever Christ links two believers, He's also present: "Where two...are gathered together in my name, there am I" (Matt. 18:20). The Spirit braids them, like strands of hemp fiber, into a threefold spiritual rope so strong it won't snap however heavy its load of ministry or adversity: "A threefold cord is not quickly broken" (Eccles. 4:12).

Summing up, two are far more likely to be spiritually victorious in life and labor. Every powerful pair cited above prevailed, fully accomplishing

God's will in their leadership, ministries, or missions. Do you want to be part of a triumphant twosome?

If so, pray for a divinely chosen partner—in discipleship, marriage, vocation, ministry, or missions! "Lord, lead me to the other half of my triumphant twosome."

Chapter 57

DO YOU SEE YOUR OPPORTUNITY?

$\mathcal{W}$HEN GOD GAVE Peter an opportunity to speak, he quickly recognized and made the most of it. It happened near the Beautiful Gate of Herod's temple.

After Peter's and John's prayer miraculously raised a lame beggar, a huge crowd quickly gathered, hushed, thoughtful, and prayerful. Immediately Peter "saw his opportunity" (Acts 3:12, NLT) and evangelized them. As a result, thousands converted to Christ. The Bible describes others who used their "door of utterance" excellently (Col. 4:3).

When Philip saw an Ethiopian official traversing the Gaza desert, he quickly saw his opportunity and ran to share Jesus with him (Acts 8:30). When the men of Sychar came asking Jesus to remain in their city, He saw His opportunity and spent two days ministering there. When the Philippian jailer fell down and asked Paul, "What must I do to be saved?" Paul saw his opportunity and "spoke unto him the word of the Lord, and to all that were in his house" (Acts 16:30, 32). When informed that Tyrannus' lecture hall was available, Paul saw his opportunity and used the facility to teach God's Word in Ephesus, so much that "all they who dwelt in Asia [Minor] heard the word of the Lord" (Acts 19:9–10). Such "doors of utterance," or opportunities to speak for God, are not the only kind of "doors" God opens.

Other "doors" are, for example, opportunities to:

- Work out a biblical truth in daily living
- Show kindness to a needy one—and grow in mercy
- Overcome evil with good—and grow in God's love
- Accept and pursue a hidden work God has given us—and grow in humility
- Have more time for fellowship with Jesus in Bible study, worship, and prayer—and know Him better
- Sit under an excellent, anointed Bible teacher
- Be discipled by a Spirit-taught man or woman of God

- Join a Christ-centered, Word-rich, Spirit-led, kingdom-minded church
- Find a good job in the field of our gifting and training
- Have a "way to escape" (1 Cor. 10:13) from distressing hindrance, oppression, or persecution
- Receive wise counsel from a caring pastor or elder
- Go on a mission to help Christ's people abroad
- Give financial support to worthy ministries, churches, or missionaries—so they can respond to open doors
- Forge edifying friendships with other faithful, spiritually minded Christians
- Share quiet times or joyful activities with a hurting, troubled child
- Listen to and pray for a distressed fellow Christian

Jesus opens these prospects for spiritual growth, mercy, ministry, or blessing for us just as surely as He opens chances to share the gospel or teach His Word: "Behold, I have set before thee an open door" (Rev. 3:8). But we must realize that He also sometimes closes doors.

"These things saith he that…shutteth, and no man openeth" (v. 7). When He does so, we should accept it and watch for another opportunity. Paul wisely accepted it when Jesus closed the door to minister in Asia. Why was this desirable ministry opportunity denied him? Macedonia needed Paul's ministry more immediately: "Come over into Macedonia [now], and help us" (Acts 16:9). Second, Asia Minor in general and Ephesus in particular were apparently not ready for Paul's potent ministry. Later they were, and Jesus opened a wide-open door there, through which Paul sowed and reaped a huge harvest over three years. He wrote: "There is a wide-open door for a great work here" (1 Cor. 16:9, NLT). Do we fully accept it when Jesus closes doors—realizing He may open them later? Or that someone else may be better suited for that work? Or presently He has another meaningful work for us in our "Macedonia"? If so, we'll help forward His plan. If not, we'll hinder it, our spiritual development, and others' blessing.

When Jesus opened Peter a door in the temple courts, he saw his opportunity and maximized it. Can you see your opportunities? Doors for speaking? Windows of charity? Ways to lift the oppressed? Chances to render hidden, humble service? Openings for broader, more fruitful ministry?

It's one thing to pray for doors, another to see our opportunities, and another to maximize them—abiding, praying, and preparing so that we take full advantage of them for Christ and His kingdom. Elisha prayed for his servant, "LORD, I pray thee, open his eyes, that he may see" (2 Kings 6:17). May God answer His prayer in our lives by helping us see and maximize our opportunities.

Look up; do you see your opportunity?

Chapter 58

THE RICH REWARDS OF REPENTANCE

EPENT...and be converted" (Acts 3:19, NKJV), cried Peter as God used him to call first-century Jews to New Testament repentance.

Not mere mental assent, the repentance God desired was deep, real, and twofold—in thought and deed. *Repent* meant reverse and reset your innermost intentions. *Be converted* implies reverse and reform your habitual actions. Or, "Repent...and reform your lives" (WEY). Such an inspired about-face is firm, not fickle; lasting, not passing.

For repentance of this kind the Spirit through Peter promised four rich rewards: forgiveness, revival, more of Jesus, and restitution. Let's examine these blessings in context and see what they mean to us today.

FORGIVENESS. "That your sins may be blotted out" (Acts 3:19, NKJV). Peter promised repentant Jews forgiveness—for any and all sins, even their heinous crime of crucifying Jesus!

To us today this pledges full spiritual cleansing by Jesus' blood the instant we confess and forsake our sins. New and Old Testament references promise this: "If we confess our sins, he is faithful and just to forgive us our sins, and to cleanse us from all unrighteousness" (1 John 1:9). "He that covereth his sins shall not prosper, but whoso confesseth and forsaketh them shall have mercy" (Prov. 28:13). Immediately the depressing burdens of guilt, shame, and fear lift, and a deep, abiding sense of relief—the wondrous, permeating peace of God's acceptance—fills us.

REVIVAL. "So that times of refreshing may come from the presence of the Lord" (Acts 3:19, NKJV). Peter pledged that, if the Jews converted, they would receive the very same supernatural, reviving "living waters" Christ's disciples drank in at Pentecost. Prophetically this promises the end-time Jewish remnant that they too will be spiritually reborn and refreshed the moment they turn and embrace Messiah Jesus.

But for us in the Church Age God has mercifully appointed "times of refreshing from the presence of the Lord." These are divinely scheduled seasons in which God sovereignly sends fresh rains of His Spirit to graciously revive and restore His people, the body of Christ. To receive these showers of blessing, we must have humble and contrite hearts: "Repent…so that times of refreshing may come." Pride and hardness perpetuate dryness.

MORE OF JESUS. "And that He may send Jesus Christ" (Acts 3:20, NKJV). Peter vowed that, if his Jewish audience would repent, Messiah Jesus would come to them personally to establish His loving reign in and among them. Since Jesus had only recently visited their nation, this would be a second visit—or more of Jesus!

When we're first converted, Jesus enters our hearts, giving us a rich, new personal relationship with Him. When as Christians we sin, our fellowship with Him is broken. But if we repent, Christ visits us again, spiritually speaking, to cleanse us, restore our fellowship, and resume growing our faith and knowledge of Him. Thus we receive more of Jesus in our souls— more appreciation for His amazing grace and enduring love, more awareness of His presence, more assurance in prayer, more willingness to make difficult sacrifices for Him, more endurance for demanding duties, more insight into God's Word, more trust in His unfailing faithfulness, more confidence in His supernatural power, more infusions of His reviving Spirit, more wisdom for life decisions, more compassion and power for ministry.

RESTITUTION. "[Jesus] whom heaven must receive until the times of restoration of all things, which God has spoken" (Acts 3:21, NKJV). To the Jews this "restitution," or reordering of things, meant the restoration of Israel's autonomy and beginning of its worldwide Messianic kingdom. Despite the nation's heinous Christ-killing, repentance en masse would have indeed—and amazingly—"[restored] again the kingdom to Israel" (Acts 1:6). (See Acts 3:26.)

Our times of restitution are periods of God's amazingly gracious restoration. In response to our contrite confessions and changed ways, God restores the blessings we've lost, wasted, or allowed to fall into disarray due to our sins and foolish decisions. Then He helps us reorder our disorder— His way! As He enabled David to recover his family, Nehemiah to repair Jerusalem's walls, Zerubbabel to rebuild Israel's temple, and Hezekiah to recover his health, so God kindly permits us to recover the blessings, provisions, worship, and health the "locusts" have eaten.

Have you broken God's Word? Disobeyed His guidance? Failed His righteousness? Neglected His call? Ignored His warnings? Stopped seeking Him? Then Peter's call and promises to the first-century Jews are yours. The moment you begin to earnestly "repent and reform your lives," forgiveness, revival, more of Jesus, and restoration will be yours. So don't wait.

Today experience for yourself the rich rewards of repentance.

Chapter 59

CONTENT IN HIS COURTS

*W*E SHALL BE satisfied with the goodness of thy house" (Ps. 65:4), exclaimed a thoughtful, thankful David as he pondered the rich blessings of Levites and other God-seekers. Psalm 65 records his inspired, praiseful musings.

The Levites generally and Aaron's sons particularly were divinely chosen to "approach" and "dwell" in God's temple courts daily (v. 4). Since God's presence indwelt the temple and pervaded its courts, Levites enjoyed special access to His presence. Devout Jews could approach and dwell in the temple courts but not the holy place. And their visits would be seasonal, at the festivals, not daily, like those of the priests laboring at the altar or offering incense in the holy place. Thus the Levites lived nearer to God and visited Him more often than other Jews.

Though not a Levite, David was an avid seeker and worshipper of God. As he pondered the Levites' advantages, he realized the more he and other worshippers sought God, the more they would enjoy the same blessings. Overjoyed, he gratefully declared these blessings were enough to satisfy him: "We [Levites and God-seekers] shall be satisfied with the goodness [good blessings] of thy house!"

Multifaceted, the "goodness" of God's house includes:

- THE JOY OF GOD'S PRESENCE. In David's day this was the Shekinah, or visible cloud of God's glory. Today it is the indescribable yet sure sense that Jesus is near. To all who obey His Word He promised, "I will…manifest myself to him" (John 14:21). "Manifest" is rendered "show" (NIV), "reveal" (NLT), and "make myself known" (PHILLIPS). No joy compares with the Spirit-induced awareness that Jesus is present: "In thy presence is fullness of joy" (Ps. 16:11).

- THE SECURITY OF GOD'S PROTECTION. Angels' "chariots of fire" surrounded Elisha with unbreachable supernatural security (2 Kings 6:17). Today angels still protect God's faithful ones: "He shall give his angels charge over thee, to keep thee in all thy ways" (Ps. 91:11). Human security is fallible; heaven's is failsafe, even with terrorism everywhere.

- THE CONFIDENCE OF HIS PROMISES. Ancient Jews affirmed, "God is not a man, that he should lie" (Num. 23:19). Today we confess, "God is faithful" to His every Word (1 Cor. 1:9). We're confident that whatever He promises, He performs in His time and way. If "it is written," it is trustworthy, whether historical, revelatory, poetic, parabolic, or prophetic!

- THE HOPE OF GOD'S PROPHECIES. In David's time God gave seers visions of a greater King and kingdom. Today the King's Spirit shows us "things to come" (John 16:13)—first, His world plan in biblical prophecy; second, His plan for us personally. Today He's pointing us to Christ's bright appearing so we won't despair as sin and darkness increase. When tsunami waves of fearful, confusing news wash over us, "I will come again, and receive you" (John 14:3) is our high, stable refuge of hope.

- THE SWEET FELLOWSHIP OF GOD'S PEOPLE. Devout Jews' sweetest fellowship occurred during their three main annual festivals. Today most Christians fellowship twice weekly, or more, in the "courts" of our churches and "exhort one another daily" (Heb. 3:13) for mutual edification. No human companionship is sweeter than our fellowship with other committed believers. "Behold, how good and how pleasant it is for brethren to dwell together in unity" (Ps. 133:1).

- THE UNFAILING PROVISIONS OF GOD'S HOUSE. David's phrase "the goodness of thy house" (Ps. 65:4) referred primarily to the bounty of the temple, which was well stocked with the Jews' tithes and gifts. Today it speaks of God richly providing our earthly needs by His inexhaustible heavenly wealth. To all believers who faithfully give to churches and ministries the apostle vows, "My God shall supply all your need according to his riches in glory" (Phil. 4:19). And this pledge is unfailing—sure in even the most unsure times.

As New Testament believer-priests, every born-again Christian has a levitical, or priestly, calling: "Ye also…are…an holy priesthood" (1 Pet. 2:5).

Today God is calling all Christians to approach and dwell in His presence. Not seasonally, but daily. Not in the Old Testament way of Jewish festivals and temple worship, but in the "new and living way" of daily, personal fellowship with Jesus that He opened by His blood (Heb. 10:19–20). He's calling you: "Come unto me" (Matt. 11:28).

If you answer, drawing near Christ regularly, you'll experience the goodness of His house. It will so deeply and strongly satisfy you that you'll be able to be content whatever your circumstances. With David you'll testify, "I shall be satisfied with the goodness of thy house." So don't just consider His call.

Answer it, enjoy His goodness, and be content in His courts.

Chapter 60

PENTECOSTAL PERIL

THE ACCOUNT OF Ananias and Sapphira showcases Pentecostal peril—the danger of willfully practicing sin in a Spirit-filled church (Acts 5:1–11).

Only weeks after Pentecost, the Lord refilled His bold, young church with the Holy Spirit (Acts 4:31). Reenergized, they produced even more fruit with "great power" and "great grace" (v. 33)—and great judgment! Why the judgment?

Filled anew with God's love, believers were selling properties to support their poor Judean brethren and help foreign believers who remained in Jerusalem after Pentecost to sit under the apostles' teaching (vv. 32–35). Barnabas made a particularly large donation (vv. 36–37). Envying him and other donors, Ananias and Sapphira imitated their generosity by selling land and giving part of the proceeds—while claiming to give all (Acts 5:1–2, 8)!

Their sin was sevenfold:

1. LYING to God's Spirit, leaders, and people

2. TESTING GOD (Would He detect their secret sin?)

3. ENVY (of Barnabas' generosity)

4. GREED (craving money)

5. HYPOCRISY (pretending generosity)

6. PRESUMPTION (expecting no punishment)

7. CONSPIRACY (agreeing in these sins)

For this, God suddenly, shockingly struck them in a rare miracle of judgment (vv. 5, 10). Why?

Their continuing, bold sin offended the Holy Spirit, whose presence filled the assembly. It hindered His work in the ongoing revival. Holy power is checked when unchecked sin is present. Their sin would have spread throughout the church. Never stagnant, sin grows like leaven, and "a little leaven leaveneth the whole lump" (1 Cor. 5:6). Furthermore, judgment brought the fear of the Lord—a new, deep respect for God's awesome holiness, presence, power, and warnings. It was also an example of God's righteous judgment in His house. So to stop offending God's holiness, continue the powerful revival, prevent sin from growing, induce the fear of God, and give an example of Christ's judgment for the ages, Ananias and Sapphira were summarily executed before God and His people. Though unexpected, this wasn't unprecedented.

Centuries earlier Nadab and Abihu were suddenly judged "before the LORD" (Lev. 10:2). After God's glory filled the tabernacle, Nadab and Abihu entered it presumptuously, offering "strange" (unauthorized) fire. Immediately they received God's shocking response: fiery judgment! (vv. 1–2). God explained, "I will be sanctified [held holy] in them that come near me" (v. 3). This reveals they took God lightly and didn't fear Him. This disrespect for God's authority explains why they entered the sanctuary contrary to His Word (which authorized only Aaron), without God's permission, with self-appointed worship (strange fire), in pride (imitating their father, who had ministered with authorization—and miraculous effects, v. 24), and possibly drunk (vv. 8–9). Thus God judged them by a sudden miracle of judgment. And Israel never forgot it.

Nor have Christians forgotten Ananias and Sapphira. To this day their folly teaches us to never test but ever fear God and never take His warnings lightly. It also illustrates the fullness of sin. God often waits till sin is "full," or fully developed and established, before punishing it.

Ananias' and Sapphira's sins were full. Peter said, "Why hath Satan filled thine heart to lie?" (Acts 5:3), or "taken such possession of your heart?"[1] This implies for a long time Satan had been putting evil thoughts and plans in their hearts—envy, pride, greed, malice, deception—and they had been acting on them without fear of divine chastisement. Their sin had become habitual and their hearts hardened. They were taking God lightly. Being sin-filled Christians in a Spirit-filled church, one of two things had to happen: repentance or removal. God's judgment—ever perfect and always His last resort—proves they refused to repent.

It also shows that while all sin is dangerous, sinning "before the Lord," or in an assembly filled with His Spirit, is especially so. If we stubbornly persist in sinful actions or attitudes before the Lord, we'll eventually be chastened. Or worse.

Naturally we all prefer to ponder the pleasant aspects of Spirit-filled churches: their power, unity, love, prayers, devotion, conversions, miracles, etc. The early church showcases all these desirables. But let's also remember this undesirable—Pentecostal peril—and fear God, obey His correction, and never again take Him or sin lightly.

Then we'll grasp what the first Christians learned: The Spirit in our midst is not just our helper, comforter, or teacher. He's our *God*—holy, sovereign, awesome, and irresistible. He can revive or remove us, commend or chasten us. If we take Him lightly, the consequences will be heavy. Just ask Ananias and Sapphira. So the choice is ours.

We can choose humble, submissive obedience to Christ, or we can choose to test His gracious, longsuffering patience. One choice leads to Pentecostal power, the other to Pentecostal peril.

Chapter 61

A FEW THOUGHTS ON SELF-PITY

*O*VERWHELMED AND UNDONE, Job cried, "Have pity upon me, O ye my friends" (Job 19:21). His present problems were twofold: his awesome troubles and awful self-pity. Let's give some thought to the latter.

An unhealthy, obsessive sorrow for oneself arising from a selfish viewpoint of one's troubles, self-pity afflicts us all. Whenever it arises, anger, unthankfulness, and unmercifulness are also present. We're inwardly angry because of unfair treatment, real or imagined, from people—and God, who, in our view, isn't helping us sufficiently! We're unthankful because we're failing to appreciate our past and present blessings. We're merciless because we're ignoring or minimizing others' sufferings that equal or surpass ours. For the moment we see no one but ourselves and nothing but our troubles. There's nothing innocent or benign about self-pity.

It isn't a natural transition, unavoidable letdown, or harmless passing mood. It's satanic! When Jesus announced He was going to the cross, Peter responded, "Be it far from thee, Lord" (Matt. 16:22). By suggesting Jesus reject His divinely chosen hardship, Peter was urging Him to pity Himself: "Be kind to thyself, sir" (YLT), or "Spare thyself,"[1] or "Pity thyself."[2] Jesus' response exposed the real spirit behind Peter's suggestion: "Get thee behind me Satan!" (v. 23). Let's learn more.

Self-pity arises as a faulty reaction to adversity—offenses, injustices, indignities, injuries, or crosses that come because we're doing God's will or obeying or ministering His Word. It may also be triggered by disappointment over unrealized hopes; sinful attitudes, such as envy (1 Sam. 22:8); severe or prolonged sicknesses, as Job's; God's correction; poverty; bereavement; or other hardships or losses.

Self-pity resides in our sin nature, which the Bible refers to as our "old man" (Rom. 6:6) or "flesh" (Rom. 8:12). It's one of the attitudes, or fixed patterns of thinking, that make up our unrenewed, unspiritual "carnal mind" (v. 7).

Self-pity captivates us when we fail to recognize and cast down our self-sympathizing thoughts (2 Cor. 10:3–5). Or it may be suggested through the overly sympathetic words of friends, family, or fellow Christians who, though they mean well, lack a spiritual (biblical) viewpoint toward our problems. (See Acts 21:12.)

Self-pity's effects are powerful. It traps us in a revolving door of spiritual stagnation that keeps us from finishing the race set before us. It renders us weak and unfaithful in duty and encourages self-indulgence (excessive self-comfort). It moves us to slander our adversaries. It distorts our view of others, events, and ourselves. Ultimately, it destroys us. It also makes our companions stumble by causing them to misjudge and condemn those we complain about and question God for seeming to neglect us. Highly contagious, it infects them. After talking with us, they lose their positive outlook and start pitying themselves!

Many overcome self-pity and finish their courses. The apostle John rose above his lonely exile and received rich spiritual rewards: a vision of Jesus, an open door in heaven, and a revelation like no other! John the Baptist forsook self-pity in prison and received high praise from Jesus (Luke 7:23–28). In her widowhood Ruth threw off self-pity, and God tossed rich blessings her way: a husband, home, child, and honorable family line. But others succumb.

King Saul indulged his self-pity until his soul was barren, his spiritual walk halted, his anointing lost, and his destiny aborted. We must eliminate, not indulge, self-pity.

We remove self-pity by:

- Confessing our self-pity to God (1 John 1:9) and others (James 5:16)
- Commanding Satan, "Be gone!"
- Believing we can do all things, including mastering self-pity, through Christ (Phil. 4:13)
- Developing a spiritual mind by seeing our troubles through the wide viewfinder of Scripture, not the narrow spyglass of self-sympathy
- Accepting that all difficulties come from our Father's hand for good (Rom. 8:28)
- Thanking and praising God in our adversities and for them, since only by mastering them can we become like Jesus

- Rising to minister to others' needs, which breaks the chains of selfishness and frees us to live and serve joyfully

- Looking around us and considering how others are suffering as bad as we are, or worse!

If persisted in, these simple measures will eliminate self-pity and make us the rarest of wonders, overcomers—mature Christians who, no matter what happens to them, are able to continue walking closely with Jesus, worshipping Him, faithfully serving others, and giving thanks for what they have. If we don't eliminate self-pity, it will eliminate our usefulness to God. So examine yourself.

Are you pitying yourself over anything present? Past? About to happen? If so, ponder and practice these few thoughts on self-pity.

Chapter 62

SHADOWED BY THE SAVIOR

FTER GOD REMOVED Ananias and Sapphira, the river of the Spirit surged through the church with unprecedented power (Acts 5:12–16). No longer requiring laying on of hands, the Holy Spirit now healed everyone merely touching Peter's "shadow" (v. 15).

We know a shadow is a dark profile cast when our presence intercepts a beam of light. But figuratively it speaks of the memory of someone's character traits or distinctive mannerisms. For example, "The founder, though retired, still cast a long shadow over the business." Also, to "shadow" is to follow someone closely: "The CIA's best man shadowed the terrorist." One source adds, "Ancient people thought that one's shadow was attached to oneself; in Jewish law, if one's shadow touched a corpse one was as unclean as one who physically touched the corpse."[1] What, then, was Peter's "shadow"?

Over the previous three years sustained closeness to Jesus had remade Peter, conforming him to Jesus' character image or profile (Rom. 8:29). This former fisherman was now, like his Master, a fisher of men. His character was now like Jesus' character. The distinctive traits of Jesus' heart, words, manners, and ministry, including His love, truthfulness, graciousness, and boldness, were real and growing in Peter and showing themselves daily. Everywhere Peter went, this image, or "shadow" of Jesus' character, followed. Because he had humbly submitted to Christ's teachings, tests, and corrections, Peter's shadow was refined, or cleansed from the distortions caused by his errors, sins, and folly. It was also well defined, revealing Jesus' profile sharply.

Whenever Peter preached or witnessed, the light of divine truth shined brightly in his every word—and Jesus' shadow was seen standing in that light! The Sanhedrin saw it: "Now when they saw the boldness of Peter and John…they took knowledge of them, that they had been with Jesus" (Acts 4:13). When Peter quietly went about his daily activities, "walk[ing] in the light, as he is in the light" (1 John 1:7), the same shadow was cast by his works. So, in a sense, wherever Peter went, he was shadowed—followed closely as by a friend or bodyguard—by Jesus! Mark said as much when summarizing the church's early years: "The Lord [Himself] working with [and accompanying] them [the apostles], confirming the word with signs following" (Mark 16:20).

Therefore Peter's shadow was more than his bodily profile cast on Jerusalem's streets, walls, and houses. It was more than Christ's distinctive character traits evident in Peter's speech and behavior. It was nothing less than the presence of Christ Himself shadowing Peter, following close by or behind and attached, touching the sick and freeing the oppressed as in the days of His Galilean ministry. This is the core message of Acts.

More than a record of the apostles' labors and the church's early history, Acts inscribes Christ's post-resurrection ministry through the human members of His mystical body by the power of the Holy Spirit. The language Luke uses in Acts 5:16 could easily fit into the Gospels (cp. Mark 6:56; Luke 4:40). The context (Acts 5) describes the church ministering in the same manner (healing sick and afflicted multitudes, verse 16), time (early in the morning, verse 21), and places (temple courts, verse 42) Jesus had ministered just months earlier. Why? Jesus was ministering again through them. The Savior's posthumous ministry was not lost on the crowds. They sensed Jesus was still among His followers, shadowing them. He still is.

After twenty centuries, Jesus is still shadowing—closely following or attached to—all His true disciples. If we "walk in the light, as he is in the light" (1 John 1:7), or humbly submit to the biblical teaching, testing, and correction Jesus sends, our characters are being remade in His image, just as Peter's was. Our shadow is being increasingly refined and defined, enabling others to see the profile of Christ's love, truth, and faithfulness ever more sharply in our "acts." Consequently, wherever we go, Jesus goes, shadowing us by the Holy Spirit who indwells us and pervades the fringes of our presence. As we live in His Word, walk in His love, and "pray without ceasing" (1 Thess. 5:17) for everyone we meet, whenever we pass by, Jesus comes behind us—bringing conviction, turning hearts, lifting oppression, healing bodies, mending relationships, judging injustice, giving hope to the hopeless, and awakening apathetic Christians to become His ardent disciples. Why? So He may re-form their characters, shadow them, and touch others through them! David believed this.

He proclaimed the Good Shepherd's goodness and mercy would "follow me all the days of my life" (Ps. 23:6). With David, believe and confess you're being shadowed by the Savior.

Chapter 63

DETERMINED DISCIPLES OF JESUS

SALM 84 DESCRIBES dedicated Jews making long, trying pilgrimages to worship and serve God at the annual festivals in their beloved meeting place, the temple in Jerusalem. For Christians, it conveys another message.

This song describes the life story of determined disciples of Jesus embarking on an arduous, lifelong pilgrimage through this troubled and trying world—our "valley of Baca [weeping]" (v. 6)—to live with, worship, and serve God forever in perpetual festival in our "Zion," New Jerusalem (v. 7). Let's examine this spiritual trail.

After receiving Jesus' amazing forgiveness and tasting His tender compassion, we're forever mastered and motivated by His love. It inspires a driving, insatiable desire to "be with him" (Mark 3:14). "My soul longeth, yea, even fainteth for the courts [presence] of the LORD; my heart and my flesh cry out for the [presence of the] living God" (Ps. 84:2).

Once we learn this special hidden fellowship with Jesus imparts new life to us, we seek Him early and often. As birds build and constantly return to their nests, so we establish and habitually revisit our spiritual "nest," or secret communion with Jesus in private prayer, Bible meditation, and worship: "The swallow hath found...a nest...even [near or within sight of] thine altars, O LORD.... [Similarly] Blessed are they who dwell [nest] in thy house [presence]" (vv. 3–4). In His presence God opens our eyes.

We soon discern nothing in this life is more important than preparing for eternity. So we determine to pursue a lifelong quest, a great spiritual pilgrimage, to prepare to live with and worship God forever in New Jerusalem: "What joy for those...who have set their minds on a pilgrimage to Jerusalem" (Ps. 84:5, NLT). (See Colossians 3:1–4.)

To prepare for perpetuity, we please and praise. We please Christ in this life by learning His ways—spiritual disciplines or biblical ways of living, working, and ministering. "In whose heart are the ways of them [Zion's pilgrims]" (Ps. 84:5). Having learned these ways, we determine to walk in them, including the way of thanking and praising God regularly in private and public worship: "They will be still praising thee" (v. 4), or "always

163

singing your praises" (NLT). Responding, God initiates His own plan to prepare us.

He leads His determined disciples through various "valleys of Baca [weeping]," humble times of testing that cause stress and sorrow yet also enable us to receive and learn to rely on the unfailing refreshment God gives us as we seek, trust, and obey Him in our trials: "When they walk through the Valley of Weeping, it will become a place of refreshing springs" (v. 6, NLT).

Every time we emerge from these adversities, He gives us large refillings of the Spirit. These plentiful "autumn rains" (v. 6, NLT) mark the changing of our seasons from adversity to blessing. They also restore our souls' deeply depleted inner reservoirs, or "pools" of strength: "The rain also [re]filleth the pools" (v. 6). (See Psalm 126:4.)

So each of these cycles of testing further exercises our spiritual "senses" (Heb. 5:14) and makes us stronger in spirit and endurance: "They will continue to grow stronger" (Ps. 84:7, NLT), or "go from [one level of] strength to [a new level of] strength."

Besides strength, our tests forge extraordinary character. We grow so deeply gratified with our "nesting," or sustained close fellowship with Jesus, that we become content in even the lowest positions and humblest tasks: "A single day in your courts is better than a thousand anywhere else! I would rather be a gatekeeper in the house of my God than live the good life in the homes of the wicked (v. 10, NLT). Just being near Jesus, in His will, pleasing to Him, and loved by Him compensates for any hardships we face. This blesses God greatly.

Delighted with us, He:

- Favors us with His "look" of approval (v. 9)
- "Suns," or warmly comforts, our hearts with deep peace daily (v. 11)
- "Shields," or protects, us from detractors, demons, and dangers (v. 11)
- Withholds "no good thing," releasing to us every good blessing we need, in His time and way, even in our longest, lowest "valleys" (v. 11)

One day, after our final cycle of testing, we'll experience the ultimate reward—appearing before Jesus in heaven to receive His personal review and rewards: "Every one of them appears before God in Zion" (v. 7, NAS). This rendezvous will be rapturous (1 Thess. 4:13–18)!

Disciple of Christ, Psalm 84 tells your story. Study it! It describes your life. Live it! It maps your pilgrimage. Follow it! It declares your destiny as a determined disciple of Jesus.

Chapter 64

HAS YOUR CITY FALLEN?

$\mathcal{U}$NFORTUNATELY, IF WE speed-read Acts 5:12–16, we probably won't grasp just how effective the early church was in Jerusalem. When pondered, the facts are stunning.

Thousands of deeply unified believers were gathering twice a day for prayer and teaching in the temple courts (v. 12). There were additional gatherings in houses all over the city day and night (v. 42). The apostles held street meetings in which miraculous healings and deliverances flowed like a river, drawing seekers from nearby cities who were also "healed every one" (vv. 15–16). These "signs and wonders" confirmed the apostles were God's true messengers (v. 12). As respect for the church grew, "multitudes" converted to "the Way," though others stayed away (vv. 13–14). Eventually Christianity's power, growth, and fame deeply shook Jerusalem's religious leaders.

Then a leading rabbi, Gamaliel, made a shocking admission: Jesus' way may be "of God" (v. 39). Many priests grew convinced it was (and later defected, Acts 6:7). What was happening?

Jerusalem and its environs were about to convert en masse to Christ! A spiritual coup was in progress, led not by clever politicians, public relations experts, or social activists, but by the heavenly Savior working through His earthly people by the simple but awesome power of His Spirit and Word. Jesus was taking the city by storm—the very city that only months earlier had brutally rejected Him and His ministry. That same ministry, now flowing through His followers, was overwhelming the invisible ramparts the powers of darkness erected around Jerusalem. The city's central citadel of dead religion—Christ-rejecting Judaism—was collapsing, in its own capital! Furious, the high priest unintentionally acknowledged the true extent of the apostles' work: "Ye have *filled* Jerusalem with your doctrine" (Acts 5:28). It wasn't the first time Jerusalem had fallen to hostile armies.

But it was a new way. Jerusalem was being sacked by a spiritual army with bold apostolic officers under the command of an all-wise, all-powerful General! This heavenly Joshua was battling Jerusalem as He had Jericho long ago, except His weapons were spiritual, not iron, and His warriors preachers, not soldiers. They were shooting arrows of truth that pierced the hardest hearts, using shields of faith that threats couldn't penetrate, and wielding swords of the Spirit that severed even the toughest strongholds of false doctrine and unbelief. Neighboring cities were also shaking as their citizens visited Jerusalem and surrendered to its Conqueror (v. 16). But Jerusalem refused to capitulate easily.

Its proud religious leaders "rose" to waylay the Way. Prompted by the "rulers of the darkness" (Eph. 6:12), they jailed, threatened to kill, and brutally flogged its leaders (Acts 5:17–18, 40). It was crass religious self-preservation at its worst: eliminate your rivals before they win all your people!

Despite the Jews' worst, God's best prevailed. The Spirit strengthened the church and its faith held, work continued, and message grew. Even more Judeans converted! Then Samaritans! And Syrians, Greeks, Romans! Soon the Way stretched round the world! But note this.

Overcomers, not compromisers, accomplished this work. The apostles were fervent and abandoned, not lukewarm and self-serving. They were ready to suffer rejection, even abuse and death, to fulfill their commission—and did so. They were so abandoned that they took cruel floggings, and later brutal persecutions, and kept on ministering without whimpering, retiring, or retaliating (vv. 40–42). And those they led were like them. Are we?

Make no mistake; it's not easy taking cities, provinces, or nations for Christ. The demonic bastions of secularism, atheism, and false religion don't capitulate to compromised, self-serving, self-protecting Christians. They fall only before fully committed disciples who are abandoned to Christ's call, led and empowered by His Spirit, and willing to continue living righteously, praying daily, witnessing boldly, evangelizing steadily, and training disciples faithfully while being rejected and persecuted. Whenever the Spirit fills cities with Acts-like works, such Christians are present.

As they stand, faithfully ministering and interceding, "Joshua" fights and conquers the rulers of darkness in their cities. An awesome miracle, a spiritual coup, follows, powered not by presidents, pollsters, or political parties, but by the Paraclete, the Prince of Peace, and His supernatural gospel. Despite this postmodern world's relativism, sophistication, technology, and innovation, the simple, eternal, absolute truth of the gospel, lived and spoken, is still "the power of God unto salvation" (Rom. 1:16). Though corrupt clerics, sinners, and secularists unite to fight it, no city can stand before it—and overcomers.

It took blood, toil, tears, and sweat for Churchill's England to overcome

Hitler's demons. It will take courage, determination, endurance, and suffering for us to overcome Satan's strongholds in our cities. Will you pay this price? Has your city fallen?

Chapter 65

THUS FAR, NO FARTHER!

ONG AGO GOD gave a reassuring message of hope to believers facing uprisings. It came through Jeremiah and Job. In Jeremiah's day the Judeans were in threefold rebellion to God: sinfully worshipping idols, stubbornly denying God's chastening (Babylonian siege), and wickedly persecuting His faithful messenger, Jeremiah. When they rose up against the Lord and those faithful to Him, He spoke.

God's message, addressed to the rebels, deeply comforted Jeremiah and the faithful remnant:

> Fear ye not me? saith the LORD. Will ye not tremble at my presence, who have placed the sand for the bound of the sea by a perpetual decree, that it cannot pass it; and though its waves toss themselves, yet can they not prevail; though they roar, yet can they not pass over it?
>
> —JEREMIAH 5:22

Let's examine the symbols God uses in this metaphorical statement.

The "sand" represents God's faithful ones, Abraham's loyal faith-children. God told Abraham his seed would be "as the sand" by the seashore. "I will multiply thy seed…as the sand which is upon the seashore" (Gen. 22:17).

"Sea," which typically represents the unredeemed populace (Rev. 13:1), here symbolizes God's apostate people. Their unbelief and rebellion link them spiritually with the vast sea of unbelievers and its stormy uprisings against God: "This [My apostate] people hath a revolting and a rebellious heart; they are revolted and gone [from Me]" (Jer. 5:23). These rebels have no peace: "The wicked are like the troubled sea, when it cannot rest" (Isa. 57:20).

The "waves" roaring and tossing themselves against the sandy shoreline represent these rebels' contentious words and actions against God's faithful ones.

The "bound" represents the boundary or time limit God sets on their uprising. It can't endure, but must one day end: "Thou hast set a bound that they may not pass over" (Ps. 104:9).

The "perpetual decree" is God's command that the sea not pass the shoreline. Similarly God's Word commands that surprising, stressful insurrections won't destroy us but must one day yield a "way to escape" (1 Cor. 10:13). This parallels nature.

Normally the sea doesn't pass the sandy shoreline but, submitting to God's decree, stays in its divinely ordained place. During hurricanes or tsunamis, however, it seems to get away with rebellion! The shocking storm surge or massive tidal wave swamps the shoreline, causing great destruction. The sand appears totally overcome, defeated, and its future hopeless. But only for a time. When God's boundary—of minutes or hours—is reached, the rebellious surging waters humbly retreat. No matter how viciously they have roared and tossed themselves, in the end God's decree prevails and they return to their place. What message does this convey?

God is pledging that rebels can't oppose or overcome His faithful people forever. They didn't in Jeremiah's day—Jerusalem fell!—and won't in ours either. They may roar, loudly and shamelessly arguing, accusing, threatening, slandering. They may toss themselves, opposing our every word and move in an attempt to ruin our family, church, ministry, or reputation. And, shockingly, they may win—but only for a time. God has set a limit on their "hurricane."

Job describes it:

> Thus far shalt thou come, but no farther; and here [God's appointed time and place] shall thy proud waves be stayed.
>
> —JOB 38:11

"Thus far shalt thou come"—this describes God's surprising yet wise permissive will. He decrees the rebellion will continue, but only temporarily, and only to test the faithful. When the defiant "sea" has its way against them, will they still trust Him? Wait patiently for His help? Endure their difficulties? Remain loyal to God's Word and will while other grains of "sand" compromise or desert? Will they reach faith's summit of total abandonment? Job reached it while viciously misjudged: "Though he slay me, yet will I trust in him" (Job 13:15). Abraham reached it on Moriah. Will we?

So spiritual hurricanes only serve God's higher purposes. Once they're accomplished, His decree takes hold: "No farther!" Suddenly, in His time, He subdues our adversaries: "Here [at God's limit] shall thy proud waves be stayed." So, like Jeremiah, Job assures the faithful we always triumph in the end.

Are you faithfully following and serving God, yet find yourself in the fight of your life, opposed and slandered by unreasonable unbelievers or backslidden Christians? Is your authority as a pastor, elder, husband, parent, teacher, employer, etc., being ruthlessly challenged by adamant rebels? Have they dealt you a stunning injustice? Left you defeated, overwhelmed, and hopeless? Don't rebel or run away.

Quietly remember God's decree. Your tsunami must go back in God's time. Wait patiently for Him to say to your overwhelming waters, "Thus far, no farther!"

Chapter 66

FOLLOW THE WISEST WISDOM

OVERCONFIDENT IN THEIR wisdom, Jewish religious leaders engaged Stephen in a lively public debate (Acts 6:9–10). But their best efforts failed to best him.

"They were not able to resist... [that] which he spoke" (v. 10). Clearly these wise men met a wiser one. Why was Stephen wiser? Three times Luke describes Stephen as a Spirit-filled man: "Stephen, a man full... of the Holy Spirit" (Acts 6:5; cp. Acts 6:3; 7:55). Stephen won the debate not because of superior intellect, exceptional education, or debating experience but because of "the wisdom and the Spirit with which he was speaking" (Acts 6:10, ESV), or because "the Spirit was helping him to speak with wisdom" (NCV). So his superior wisdom came from the Holy Spirit. This wasn't unprecedented.

The Spirit had long given humble, God-fearing believers wisdom—good judgment, excellent decision making, and knowledge perfectly applied to the spontaneous and fluid situations of life. And His wisdom always surpassed that of the wisest men!

When Daniel's enemies challenged him, their wisdom was to enact a law Daniel couldn't honor, entrap him, and request his execution (Dan. 6:4–8, 13–15). His wisdom, given by the Spirit in prayer, was to continue praying, worshipping, working, and serving God "continually" (v. 16) and request and expect God's help. Initially Daniel looked foolish and his enemies wise. But after he was released and promoted and they were arrested and executed, it was evident his wisdom was the wisest. It confirmed, "There is no wisdom, nor understanding, nor counsel against the [LORD's counsel]" (Prov. 21:30). Daniel's deliverance stunned everyone but him.

He had often observed the Spirit's wisdom in action, when:

- After three years of Spirit-blessed studies in Babylon's university, Daniel, still a teenager, emerged "ten times" wiser than Babylon's wisest sages (Dan. 1:17–20)

- Twice the Spirit gave Daniel interpretations of King Nebuchadnezzar's baffling dreams, while other renowned interpreters remained clueless (Dan. 2:27–28; 4:6–9)
- The Spirit enabled Daniel alone to decode the encrypted handwriting on King Belshazzar's wall (Dan. 5:10–16)

In all these crises the Spirit gave Daniel wisdom surpassing that of the world's brightest minds. Joseph also relied on the wisest wisdom.

When Pharaoh called his brightest advisers to interpret two troubling dreams, there was "none that could interpret them" (Gen. 41:8). But Joseph, gifted by the Spirit to interpret, not only explained the dreams (vv. 25–32) but also recommended a plan to prepare for the famine they foretold (vv. 32–36). Again the Spirit's wisdom proved wisest. It surrounds us daily.

His superior decisions are built into God's Spirit-breathed Word. Every time we obey biblical instructions, we obey the Spirit's wisdom! God's wisdom is behind His guidance. The paths He chooses for us are those He knows are the smartest and safest. The Spirit's wisdom is behind God's call. By following it, we engage in the vocation, profession, or ministry for which we're perfectly suited and gifted. The Spirit's wisdom is behind God's warnings. Every arresting "Stop!" or "Don't!" is consummate wisdom's loving decision, and we disobey it at our peril. The Spirit's wisdom devised God's ways—spiritual daily life habits, or biblical methods of living and ministering—for our good. Anything done God's way is done the best way, even if it initially seems foolishly simple or bound to fail. The Spirit's wisdom appoints God's times and seasons in our lives. "To every thing there is a season, and a time to every purpose under the heaven" (Eccles. 3:1), and everything is best, for God's honor and our joy, in God's wisely appointed times. The Spirit's wisdom is working when He convicts us of sin. Whenever He quietly makes us aware of our wrong attitudes, words, actions, or inactions, His assessments are always perfectly accurate, revealing just how deeply He knows us. "LORD, thou hast searched me, and known me...thou understandest my thought afar off" (Ps. 139:1–2). And the Spirit's wisdom is behind God's commands to commit every worrisome issue to Him in believing prayer (Phil. 4:6–7). Trusting God is always the wisest course of action. No one will be ashamed who relies on and waits for Him. So the choice is yours.

You can be wise, wiser, or wisest. The wise trust their own reasoning. The wiser, the world's findings. The wisest, the Spirit's decisions. Like

Daniel, Joseph, and Stephen, they obey the Bible, follow divine guidance, and pursue God's call. They yield to His warnings, practice His ways, and flow with His appointed seasons. When He convicts, they confess and grow. When He says, "Trust Me," they commit and rest. These wisest ones thrive in the Spirit's wisdom—a wisdom available to us all! Ready to thrive?

Follow the wisest wisdom.

Chapter 67

HANDS UP!

AVID VOWED, "I will lift up my hands in thy name" (Ps. 63:4). No passing whim, this practice of praying, worshipping, or praising God with raised hands is mentioned in numerous Davidic psalms and Bible references.

Consider these examples:

> Hear [my] voice...when I lift up my hands toward thy holy oracle.
> —PSALM 28:2

> I shall lift up my hands to Your commandments, which I love.
> —PSALM 119:48, NAS

> Accept...my upraised hands as an evening offering.
> —PSALM 141:2, NLT

> I stretch out my hands to you; my soul longs for you...
> —PSALM 143:6, NAS

> All the people...lifting up their hands...worshiped the LORD.
> —NEHEMIAH 8:6

> I will...that men pray everywhere, lifting up holy hands.
> —1 TIMOTHY 2:8

Since they're inspired, these references reveal divine thoughts. So not only these biblical writers but also God Himself desires us to praise, worship, or pray with raised hands. Let's consider what raised hands symbolize.

Raised hands mark joyous victories. Victorious at last over Pharaoh, the Israelites left Egypt with a "high hand" (Exod. 14:8). When we win athletic, political, business, legal, or other victories, we shout, pump our fists, and raise our hands. So by raising our hands to God, we celebrate His victory over Satan and those He gives us over temptations, adversaries, and adversities: "Lord, Your help always causes me to triumph."

Raised hands accompany solemn promises. When swearing to judge Israel's oppressors, God raised His hand: "I lift up my hand to heaven...if I whet my glittering sword...I will render vengeance" (Deut. 32:40–41). We too raise our hands when pledging (or affirming) to fulfill oaths or vows. So raised hands evoke thoughts of God's promises and ours: "Lord, I trust Your covenant promises—and I'll keep my vows and pledges."

Raised hands speak of impending judgment. When ready to execute judgment, God raises His hand: "Thine hand shall be lifted up…and all thine enemies shall be cut off" (Mic. 5:9). Thus His outstretched hand saves His people from enemies. As God's agent, Moses raised his hands (and rod) to release judgments on the Egyptians and Amalekites (Exod. 14:27; 17:11). Our raised hands express trust in, and request releases of, God's saving judgments: "Lord, You are my Defender; rescue me to continue serving You."

Outstretched hands imitate children reaching for their fathers. When a lost, hungry, or hurting little girl is reunited with her loving father, she instantly reaches for him. Why? She knows he'll mercifully help her. Our raised hands express childlike confidence that our heavenly Father will guide, feed, and heal us when we're spiritually lost, hungry, or hurting. "Lord, You're my perfect Parent, my unfailing Father in time of need."

Raised hands speak of Jesus' appearing. When reuniting after long separations, spouses stretch out their hands to embrace the love of their life. Christians are called to be Christ's bride, covenantal lovers of the King of glory (Ps. 45:10–11). Our raised arms testify, "Lord, You're the love of my life, my eternal spouse, my soul mate. I'll reach out and reunite with You when You appear."

Raised hands signify Christ's blessing. At His ascension Jesus our High Priest blessed His followers with raised hands: "He lifted up his hands, and blessed them" (Luke 24:50). Aaron, Israel's high priest and a type of Christ, did the same when blessing Israel (Lev. 9:22). Our raised hands symbolize our need and request for Jesus' blessing: "Jesus, my High Priest, as my hands are raised, so raise Yours and bless me now with Your protection, favor, mercy, and peace."

Raised hands express readiness to receive. When given gifts, we extend our hands to receive them. Our raised hands tell God we are ready to receive His natural or spiritual gifts—abilities, talents, insights, provisions, promotions, answers to prayer, spiritual gifts, anointings, ministries: "That which thou givest them they gather" (Ps. 104:28). We're expectant, humble, and trusting: "Lord, I'm ready to receive whatever You will give me today."

Raised hands signify surrender. Whenever combatants capitulate, their hands go up in a universal sign of submission. The battle is finished and issue settled. Our raised hands signal complete submission to God's will. The turbulent inner war between self and Christ is over. His enduring love has subdued our stubborn self-will. In Gethsemane Christ fully capitulated to His Father: "Not as I will, but as thou wilt" (Matt. 26:39). In the same spirit our lifted hands say, "Lord, I surrender freely and fully to Your will!"

All these demonstrative messages bless God's heart—deeply! If David and others sent them, shouldn't we? The next time you pray, praise, or worship, remember: Hands up!

Chapter 68

ARE YOU NESTING IN GOD?

*L*ONG AGO AN anonymous Jewish worship leader paused to inscribe his deep affection for the temple of God—and, even more, the God of the temple (Ps. 84:1–12).

He and other devout Jews weren't alone in loving and craving the wondrous divine presence that filled the inner temple and set apart its courts. Seeking and savoring God's presence, birds—particularly sparrows and swallows—came and nested in the various parts of the temple complex within sight of its altars: "Yea, the sparrow hath found an house, and the swallow a nest for herself, where she may lay her young, even thine altars, O LORD" (v. 3). Thus the psalmist uses birds nesting in God's temple as an example of worshippers abiding in His presence.

To understand what he meant, let's review some facts about birds and their nests.

Wherever located—in treetops or trunks, hanging from limbs, in barns, on cliffs, among rocks, in fields, in mud mounds, on rafts made from decaying plants, and even underground—bird nests are dwelling places associated with feeding, singing, warmth, rest, and refuge. There newly hatched chicks feed: "A nest...where she may lay her young" (v. 3). There songbirds sing. There fledglings are brooded as their parents cover and warm them with their wings. There parents and fledglings take rest. There they find refuge from many perils, including storms, cold, predatory animals, and hunters.

These facts reveal six spiritual truths helpful to every Christian who, like the psalmist, aspires to "nest" in God.

First, like birds, we should appoint a "nest," or place where we can fellowship with God daily. This is our "secret place of the Most High" (Ps. 91:1). It may be a bedroom, study, office, kitchen nook, attic, basement, shed, barn, closet, or any other place assuring privacy. Jesus instructed us to have such a room: "Enter into thy room ['[most] private room,' AMP]...shut thy door, [and] pray to thy Father, who is in secret" (Matt. 6:6).

Second, we should feed regularly on God's Word there, meditatively reading and studying the bread and honey of the Word that nourishes and sweetens Christ's life in us. "Christ in you, the hope of glory" (Col. 1:27) depends not on natural "bread alone," but on "every word of God" (Luke 4:4). The more of the written Word we digest, the more of the living Word we manifest.

Third, whether our voices are ordinary or operatic, we should sing to God in our nests. Every morning birds lift their voices in praise to their Creator. Overcomers imitate them: "They will be still praising thee" (Ps. 84:4). "With understanding" we should sing sweet melodies and thoughtful lyrics that express our growing love for Jesus (Ps. 47:7). The apostle Paul practiced and preached this: "[Sing] psalms and hymns and spiritual songs...making melody...to the Lord" (Eph. 5:19).

Fourth, we receive the comforting warmth of God's presence in our nests. As we feed, sing, and also pray, dwelling "under the shadow of the Almighty" (Ps. 91:1), our heavenly Father broods us. His invisible wings cover and hold us, and His Spirit permeates us with reassuring peace. This satisfying embrace deeply comforts and warms our hearts, even in the coldest spiritual winters of loneliness, defeat, or betrayal.

Fifth, we receive the rest of faith in our nests. As we feed, sing, pray, and soak in God's presence, our trust in God is strengthened: "Under his wings shalt thou trust [rest in faith]" (Ps. 91:4). When exhausted by labors or ministry, our minds are more easily harassed by doubts or worries. But our nesting times reinvigorate our faith, restore our weary souls, release us from worry, and inspire us to restfully rely on our Redeemer and even "mount up" on the Spirit's currents to boldly face new challenges (Isa. 40:31).

Sixth, if we don't rush them, our nesting times become an impenetrable refuge from powerful, persisting storms of adversity. Birds don't always rush in and out of nests. They often linger and abide, safe from storms and predators. No matter how fierce our enemies or unrelenting our troubles, if we learn to linger sufficiently in our nests daily, we'll always find enough strength, grace, and joy to see us through (Ps. 46:1–2; 2 Cor. 12:9). They're the perfect storm shelter!

After building their nests, birds revisit them regularly to maximize their benefits. Follow their wise ways.

Don't build your nest in worldly securities, pleasures, entertainment, or mere religious activities. Nest in nothing less than God's "temple" or presence: "My soul thirsteth for God, for the living God" (Ps. 42:2). And revisit your nest and its blessings often! Today, are you nesting in God?

Chapter 69

THE DIVINE DRAWING

MIRACULOUS AND SUDDEN as it is, spiritual rebirth doesn't just happen. It always follows a divine drawing. Jesus declared, "No man can come to me, except the Father... draw him" (John 6:44).

This drawing is a growing attraction, not to any religion, ritual, doctrine, group, or saint, but to Jesus: "No man can come to me... draw him [to me]" (v. 44). It's the Father's will: "Except the Father... draw him." It's universal: "No man [worldwide] can come." It's indispensable. Without it no spiritual rebirth occurs: "No man can come [to rebirth]... except [unless] the Father... draw." It's a sustained process: "the Father... draw [allure over time] him." It's the Holy Spirit's supernatural work, springing not from various random forces but from two redemption forces: (1) Jesus' cross, "I, if I be lifted up from the earth [on a cross], will draw all men unto me" (John 12:32); and (2) our prayers.

As we intercede for sinners, the Spirit creates in them interest in Jesus. Day by day He softens their hearts, prompts curiosity, and plants thoughts that incline their wills toward saving faith and faithful living. As we continue presenting their names—"Father, please draw George, Jim, Ann... to Jesus"—their fascination with Jesus grows. Why? This drawing is the Father's will. He's "not willing that any should perish, but that all should come to repentance" (2 Pet. 3:9). In time God shows faithful intercessors signs that He's openly answering their secret petitions.

Those we're praying for ask questions about Jesus, start reading the Bible, attend church, soften their attitudes, become dissatisfied with sin, grow disenchanted with false religion, abandon atheistic theories, and worry openly about death and eternity. Eventually a breakthrough occurs.

God sends a saving event, something that causes this gradual, invisible process of attraction to birth a sudden, visible conversion to Christ. Consider these salvation triggers:

- GOSPEL PREACHING. When evangelists verbally lift up Jesus and His sacrificial death on the cross, God's power draws

(John 12:32) sinners to fear God, confess sin, and receive Jesus as their personal Savior and Lord.

- BIBLE TEACHING. When anointed teachers explain Christ's words, they grip sinners' hearts and captivate them with God's convicting, converting grace (John 7:32, 45–46).

- TESTIMONIES. When Christians tell others who Jesus is or what He's done for them, goats become sheep and enter the Good Shepherd's fold (John 1:35–37).

- SAVED RELATIVES AND FRIENDS. Often when sinners' closest acquaintances, their family members or friends, turn from disbelief to discipleship, the Spirit suddenly lifts them from the floodwaters of sin into the ark of Christ. When Andrew converted, so did Peter (John 1:40–41).

- NOTABLE CONVERSIONS. When notorious sinners suddenly become humble Christians, many are impacted…suddenly! The woman at the well's about-face drew her entire city to the Savior (John 4:28–30, 39–41).

- LOVING, UNIFIED CHURCHES. When sinners who are disillusioned with un-Christlike churches see loving, unified congregations, they believe in their Unifier—just as He prayed and predicted (John 13:34–35; 17:21, 23). The early church's oneness won Jerusalem (Acts 2:44–47).

- EXPRESSIONS OF DIVINE LOVE. When sinners detect God's unselfish love in our actions, "the goodness of God" in us leads them straight to Him (Rom. 2:4). When the apostle Paul gave up his freedom to spare Philippi's jailer, the latter and his family converted (Acts 16:25–34).

- HEALINGS, SIGNS, WONDERS. Once reported, Christ's healings drew thousands to Him and His teaching (Matt. 4:23–5:2). The early church's "sign" miracles attested to Christ's resurrection, the apostles' authenticity, and their message's truthfulness—and thousands "wondered" and "ran together" to receive Christ (Acts 3:3–11).

- DELIVERED DEMONIACS. When all Decapolis heard Christ delivered a well-known demoniac from thousands of demons and restored his sanity, "all men did marvel" (Mark 5:20) and later receive his Deliverer.

- CHRISTIAN ENDURANCE. Because the Philadelphian Christians obeyed Jesus' command to patiently endure persecution, He converted their enemies and brought them into their church (Rev. 3:9–10). Our overcoming faith sometimes wins the hearts of our most persistent critics to Christ.

Other conversion prompters are punishments of adamant persecutors, which may break and draw them (Acts 18:12–17; 1 Cor. 1:1) or others (Acts 13:12); dreams or visions (Acts 10:1–6); or gifts of the Spirit (1 Cor. 14:23–25). Don't just ponder this divine drawing. Start praying for it.

Daily ask the Father to draw to Jesus every unsaved life you know—family members, friends, coworkers, neighbors, strangers you meet. When the signs of His drawing appear, keep praying. Pray "without ceasing" (1 Thess. 5:17). Pray "in the Spirit" (Eph. 6:18). Pray in faith, confident you'll see their drawing end and discipleship begin. And pray with joy. You're assisting in the divine drawing.

Chapter 70

THE BURNING BOOK

S STEPHEN TELLS it, God simply "appeared" in a burning bush, without saying or doing anything more to engage Moses' attention (Acts 7:30). He didn't call out Moses' name, invite him to draw near, or ask him to leave his flock to examine the bush. He just appeared in Moses' field of vision. The next move was Moses'.

When Moses noticed the strangely glowing shrub, he turned from shepherding to seeking: What was it? What, if anything, did it mean? His response was threefold.

First, he "saw" the wonder, initially noticing it (v. 31). This shows that, as a good shepherd, Moses was watchful, or alert and attentive to changes in conditions. Second, he "wondered" at it (v. 31). This reveals he was thoughtful, pausing to consider the significance of things around him. Third, he "drew near" the bush, or "went close to investigate" (v. 31, AMP). Thus he was curious. This holy curiosity—spiritual hunger to understand the things of God more accurately and fully so one can better know, serve, and please God—drew Moses up Mount Sinai for a closer examination. He didn't realize it, but his devotional research would do far more than answer his questions about an unusual thornbush.

His examination would lead to two huge blessings: an extraordinary life of unmatched intimacy with and usefulness for God, and his nation's joyous departure from long, bitter bondage. This patient, humble shepherd who had faithfully kept God's vision for forty years would for the next forty years see, speak to, and hear from God "face to face" daily (Deut. 34:10). And the point we must see is that all these wonders began the moment Moses responded. "Seeing" the burning bush and "wondering" about it wasn't enough. Moses had to "draw near" to prayerfully study it. Then "The voice of the Lord came unto him," revealing more about God and His plan (Acts 7:31). It's the same with us.

Today our "burning bush" is God's burning book, the Bible. In its "living words" (Acts 7:38, NIV), we "see" believers' exploits, sacrifices, and miracles glowing with red-hot devotion to God. We also see that, despite the Bible's fiery trials—critical scholars' and atheists' heated attacks on its credibility—its influence hasn't been consumed. People of every nation, race, and culture still fervently believe Scripture. And we "wonder" at its wealth of inspired revelatory, historical, and prophetic facts, especially regarding:

- Earth's and man's creation
- Abraham's life of faith
- Israel's history
- Jesus' life, teaching, and works
- Early church history
- The last days
- Christ's kingdom
- Eternity

But will it all end there? Will we only see and wonder?

Do we expect God to do more? To coax us with audible pleas? To win us with amazing miracles? To shock us with heavenly thunder, lightning, and trumpet blasts? Or will we in holy curiosity quietly make the next move?

This will mean drawing near to study God's glowing Book. For that we must climb the mount—not of Sinai, but of Scripture; not of higher elevation, but of divine revelation. Prayerful, diligent, Spirit-illuminated Bible examination, combined with obedience, is the great key. It unlocks for us what Moses' investigation of the burning bush brought him—a life of unimaginably satisfying intimacy with God and, if we continue seeking Him, a life of influence that helps release others from bondage to sin, self, and Satan. But the next move is ours.

If we never seek, God will never speak. If we never step away from distractions and draw near God, He'll never step out of the pages of His blazing Book to draw near us—and reveal Himself, bless us with life-changing fellowship in His presence, and unveil His purposes for us, our times, and His people. So don't just see God's blazing scroll and wonder.

Investigate it for yourself! "Study to show thyself approved unto God, a workman that needeth not to be ashamed, rightly dividing the word of truth" (2 Tim. 2:15). Then begin expecting.

Expect to hear God's voice speaking to you. Expect new intimacy with Him. Expect new influence for Him. Expect Him to let you help in the "exodus" of God's people from "Egypt"—the last-day church's departure from the controlling, oppressive bondage of "the things of the world" (1 John 2:15). And be persistent.

Persist in studying and obeying the burning Book until our physical "exodus" from this world occurs at Christ's appearing: "Till I come, give attendance to reading...doctrine...meditate upon these things; give thyself wholly to them" (1 Tim. 4:13, 15). It's time to study and be changed by the burning Book.

Chapter 71

LEARN FROM A LAME MAN

AME THOUGH HE was, the beggar by the Beautiful Gate possessed key traits of wise Christian disciples (Acts 3:1–11). Let's note them.

He discerned clearly, recognizing Peter and John as true ministers, not false prophets or hypocritical Pharisees. He "clung" (v. 11, ESV) to them closely for more instruction and counsel. He was faithful and courageous, "standing with them" even in dangerous persecution (Acts 4:14). He prayed in faith, "expecting to receive something" (Acts 3:5). His changed life won many to Christ, "greatly wondering" (v. 11). He "entered...into the temple [courts]" to fellowship with other believers (v. 8). And, most significantly, he obeyed his ministers' instruction quickly and enthusiastically. When Peter said, "Look on us," immediately the beggar "gave heed" (vv. 4–5). When Peter charged him to "rise up and walk," he "leaped up...and walked" without delay (vv. 6, 8). This outstanding obedience is typical of wise Christians.

In awe of God, wise believers are spiritually awake and thirsty for more of God's Word, Spirit, presence, and favor: "O God...my soul thirsteth for thee...my soul followeth close behind thee" (Ps. 63:1, 8). Their chief hallmark is consistent obedience not only to God's Word and the Spirit's guidance but also to their leaders' biblical instruction. But not all Christians are wise.

When taught God's will, we generally respond in four ways: swiftly, slowly, sporadically, or sadly.

Swift responders waste no time in applying the Word they learn to the life they live. Knowing that Christ the Obeyer lives in them, who said through the psalmist, "I delight to do thy will, O my God" (Ps. 40:8), they never doubt they can do whatever God's Word commands or His Spirit leads. Like the lame man, they respond at the first, not the final, opportunity.

Slow responders let their stubborn pride spoil their godly initiatives. Unsubmissive, they don't like any authority, even God, telling them what they should do. They know they'll have to obey eventually or lose God's favor, but they still drag their feet. While they take their sweet time, Satan steals their sweet joy, leaving them dry, dull, and as disappointed with Christ's lordship as He is with their servantship: "I am sorry that I ever made Saul king, for he…has refused to obey my command" (1 Sam. 15:11, NLT).

Sporadic responders obey, but only in favorable conditions. When God gives them prosperity, pleasure, or popularity, they give Him praise, respect, and compliance. But when adversity comes—a season of failure, loss, trouble, lack, reproach, or persecution—they feel excused to rebel and do so, if not outwardly, inwardly. They stop offering thanks and tithes and start making excuses and complaints…until conditions change. Then they obey again. God can't rely on these "on again, off again" Christians who are faithful on life's mountaintops but faithless in its valleys.

Sad responders are non-responders. Despite receiving excellent teaching, personal counsel, and much intercession, they never consistently obey God in good or bad seasons. They come to Christ just as they are and remain just as they were—worldly, carnal, self-centered, uncommitted, and uninterested in Jesus' Word and plan. Rather than accomplish God's will, they avoid it. Their earthly lives end not in triumph but in tragedy—for God, the church, and themselves. How will ours end?

Let's examine ourselves. Are we responding to the instruction of our "Peters" and "Johns" as wisely as the lame man, with discernment, closeness, faithfulness, courage, fellowship, a changed life, and consistently quick obedience? If our obedience is still slow, sporadic, or sad, there's a reason.

It may be doubt. We're uncertain of the Bible's certainty. It may be timidity. We're afraid to act when God calls us to new or difficult tasks. It may be ignorance. We've never learned with Christ's help we can do "all things" (Phil. 4:13). It may be self-will. We aren't ready to displease ourselves to please Jesus. It may be laziness. We're not willing to work hard, steadily, and long. It may be pride. We're rejecting the humble path, duties, and positions Christ has chosen for our training. It may be covetousness. We're craving the "things of the world" more than the truths of the Word (1 John 2:15–17). It may be carelessness. We're ignoring biblical instruction, making no serious effort to become "doers of the Word" (James 1:22). It may be procrastination. We're content to obey God later rather than sooner. These are just a few traits of foolishly disobedient Christians.

Though weak, the crippled man by the Beautiful Gate wasn't foolish. Wisely he obeyed godly teaching—and swiftly. Never again obey slowly, sporadically, or sadly. From this day forward be wise. Learn from a lame man.

Chapter 72

CHILD SACRIFICE, OUR WAY

URING HIS IMPROMPTU history lesson Stephen reminded the Sanhedrin of a sad period in Jewish history when their forefathers worshipped the Ammonite god Molech: "Ye took up...Molech" (Acts 7:43). Molech's cult practiced child sacrifice.

Causing children to "pass through the fire" was an abomination God ordered Jews to shun. Nevertheless some practiced it in the infamous Valley of Hinnom. Shockingly King Solomon, to appease his Ammonite wife, was first to "build an high place...for Molech" on a hill near Jerusalem (1 Kings 11:7). King Ahaz also "made his son to pass through the fire" (2 Kings 16:3). His grandson Manasseh followed his dark example. But Manasseh's grandson, the reformer-king Josiah, destroyed Solomon's altar to Molech. Child sacrifice was inhuman.

Some scholars believe sacrificial children were slain and tossed into a blazing fire. Others hold they were sacrificed alive in the outstretched arms of a super-heated bronze statue of Molech, and, as they slowly died, drums were played to drown out their screaming.

We cringe at such atrocities done in the name of religion. But are there even the remotest parallels between this ghastly crime and our present treatment of children?

Indeed, modern society has numerous sure but subtler ways of sacrificing children. The ancients brazenly killed their little ones swiftly and publicly. Our ways of child sacrifice are slower and hidden but just as lethal. We don't dedicate their deaths to idols, hoping to win their favor and assistance in life by appeasing their sadistic pleasure. Yet we gratify Molech's murderous inspirer, Satan, the "god of this world" (2 Cor. 4:4), by offering him our young through various sins of commission and omission.

For example abortion is feticide, the cruel sacrifice of the unborn to the callous will of the living. Sowing atheistic ideas in our children's minds feeds unbelief, preventing salvation by faith. Parental neglect—failing to show affection, give attention, and share conversation and activities with our kids—puts our offspring into Molech's destructive grip, since he attracts and corrupts every child we abandon. Failing to provide children's basic needs (food, shelter, clothing) through indolence or wastefulness is murderous. Indulging destructive addictions (drugs, alcohol, smoking) in their sight invites their self-destructive imitation. Physical or sexual abuse ignites enduring hatred and shame that consume their happiness. Settling our disputes with violence rather than reason silently instructs them to follow suit to their injury or death. And there's more.

Consistently modeling bad behaviors, such as promiscuousness, adultery, slothfulness, and financial irresponsibility, influences children to sow them—and reap sexually transmitted diseases, poverty, divorce, and other self-opposing consequences. Successive divorce and remarriage fueled by burning lusts leave families aflame and children's hopes in ashes. Condescending, condemning words—"Son, you've failed again! Can't you do anything right?"—consume children's confidence, crippling their ability to persevere in adversities and achieve in life. Planting and cultivating prejudices in children's minds consumes their love and sense of justice and creates twisted illusions of their racial, socioeconomic, religious, political, ethnic, or national superiority, and of the inferiority of everyone different.

These sins aren't limited to unbelieving parents. Like the Jews, born-again Christians also harm their young. We put our children in Molech's cruel arms by:

- Not loving them (not cultivating mercy for them and resolving to help them through life)
- Not disciplining them, when needed
- Ignoring God (not walking closely with our Father, the source of unfailing parental love)
- Lack of vigilance (not watching over their friends, activities, circumstances)
- Lack of daily intercession for them
- Failure to teach them God's Word, ways, worship (Deut. 6:6–7)
- Idolizing worldly values (money, possessions, popular trends) above eternal ones

I remember, years ago, our county fair having brazen vendors calling loudly to passersby: "Step up, sir, hit the target and win a prize for your lovely lady!" Or, "Come on, ma'am, toss the ball into the ring and win your little girl a stuffed animal!" What if some crazed religious leader were to openly advocate child sacrifice this way? "Child sacrifice, anyone? Step right up, parents, sacrifice your children, appease the gods, and win prosperity and success in life!" The public outcry would be deafening. Yet we do this very thing another way.

Quietly, privately, gradually, as described above, we yield our young to the god of this world. While his sadistic desire is being satisfied, the "drums" of our noisy, hyperactive, self-centered, non-contemplative lives rumble on. And no one protests the slaughter. But there's hope.

Scripture still promises, "He shall save the children of the needy" (Ps. 72:4). And God will, if we'll ponder Israel's tragic Molech worship and abandon child sacrifice, our way.

Chapter 73

HOPE FOR CRIPPLES—AND CARRIERS!

*L*UKE DESCRIBES A cripple who was "carried" and "laid daily" at the temple's "Beautiful gate" to "ask alms" (Acts 3:1–11). Those who carried this man set a remarkable example of unselfish love. Laying aside their desires, they gave their time, expended their energy, and surely lost some income, all to help this lame man live. They didn't do it for show; no one noticed them. Nor did they do it for money; the cripple didn't pay them. Nor just once or twice; they carried him "daily." Besides being a thankless task, theirs was hopeless.

The cripple had never walked, or even stood, since his birth over forty years earlier. Besides his paralysis, atrophy rendered his restoration to normal living impossible. Reason's verdict was in: he would never be healed, nor they relieved of carrying him, till he passed. Thus all optimistic options were incredible. Yet through Peter, Jesus did the incredible! When Peter ordered him to rise, "Immediately his feet and ankle bones received strength, and he, leaping up, stood and walked" (vv. 7–8). When he was set free, so were his carriers. Who were they?

Today we'd call them caregivers. They attended faithfully to his practical, protective, prayerful, and personal needs every day. Practically, they provided his bodily needs of food, clothing, hygienic care, nursing, lodging, and transportation. Protectively, they watched over him to prevent thieves from abusing and robbing him. Prayerfully, they interceded for his spiritual and worldly needs, uplifting his soul along with his body. Personally, they visited with him to cheer him with good conversation, biblical exhortation, and prayers and praises to Jehovah. This combined care "carried" him— literally, spiritually, and empathetically—through the longest, most hopeless season in his life. When after years of oppression he suddenly walked, leaped, and praised God, they did too!

Today carriers are those who provide practical, protective, prayerful, or personal assistance daily to "cripples"—anyone infirm, elderly, troubled, or needy. When they're liberated by Christ, so are their carriers!

Think: How many people are relieved when Jesus heals one cancer patient? Makes a weak heart strong again? Reinvigorates a paralyzed limb to full use? Delivers someone from demons, drugs, alcohol? Restores a psychotic mind to reality? Releases a troubled soul from depression? Parents, grandparents, spouses, children, friends, neighbors, pastors, intercessors, fellow church members, doctors, nurses, counselors—all these "carriers" sense the sweet relief of a lifted burden and joyous victory. Why? Wondrously Jesus touched the one they were carrying: "He laid his hands on every one…and healed them" (Luke 4:40). Not only this end but also the means glorify God.

Wearying as it is, "carrying" serves His higher purposes to:

- Give us a chance to be like Christ, who carries the whole church and its needs daily
- Help us pause and consider others' sufferings, and grow in compassion
- Prompt us to forsake self-centered thinking and living and enter the realm of true ministry, where Jesus lived, "not to be ministered unto, but to minister and to give" (Matt. 20:28)

Thus caregiving conforms our characters to Christ's. This is the chief reason God places cripples in our lives, but not the only one.

God especially blesses those who care for the needy. In Psalm 41 He promises to give committed care to committed caregivers: "Blessed is he that considereth the poor [or needy, in their time of trouble]" (v. 1). Specifically He promises to give them preservation, protection, earthly blessings, strength, pardon, nursing, healing, upholding, justice, and most importantly, the enduring, pure joy of His reviving presence daily: "You…set me in your presence forever" (v. 12, NIV). Thus He becomes a compassionate Caregiver to every compassionate caregiver.

Eager to prove this, He decided the Christian era's first-recorded miracle would benefit a cripple and his carriers in the temple courts. This merciful wonder involved a heavenly release from a hopeless burden at a "beautiful gate." It can be a beautiful door of hope to you.

Today Jesus still has yearning compassion and miracle-working power. If you're a physical, emotional, psychological, social, or financial cripple, ask and believe God for your healing. If you're a weary but faithful carrier, remember God's higher purposes in your service, believe Psalm 41's blessings are yours, persevere in caregiving, and expect to see your cripple "walking, and leaping, and praising God." And get ready to do some joyful jumping, yourself, because...

"God is not unrighteous to forget your work and labor of love, which ye have shown toward his name, in that ye have ministered to the saints, and do minister" (Heb. 6:10). That's cause aplenty for hope for cripples—and carriers!

Chapter 74

FROM WALKING TO WORRYING TO WORSHIPPING

*I*MMERSED IN IMPOSSIBILITIES, Peter did the incredible. He walked calmly on chaotic waters—with a little wavering!

Specifically, he walked steadily on, and thus overcame, a terrifying Galilean storm (Matt. 14:22–33). Then, after initially walking by faith, he sank by worrying. Once Jesus corrected him, Peter rose again to worship Him in fully restored confidence. His path through this turbulent test—from walking by faith to worrying in fear to worshipping in peace—mirrors ours. Let's note the particulars of his problematic situation.

Jesus "sent the multitudes away" (v. 22), isolating not only the apostles for a "church" test but also Peter for a very personal one. Then Jesus "went up into a mountain…to pray," where He surely interceded for not only the twelve but also for Peter (v. 23). (See Luke 22:31–32.) Soon night fell. When "the evening was come" (v. 23), as darkness temporarily prevailed over light, Jesus tested and built the faith of His light bearers in training. Soon Peter's boat, or divinely appointed scene of testing, was "in the midst of the sea [lake]," far beyond the reach of human help (v. 24). There it and he were "tossed," or agitated, by the repeated blows of dangerous, devilish "waves," all because the invisible but formidable "powers of the air" were working against them. As Matthew puts it, "The wind was contrary" (v. 24). And Jesus, by not intervening, seemed indifferent to their struggle.

Late in the night He finally revealed His presence and care: "In the fourth watch of the night, Jesus went unto them" (v. 25). He unveiled His supernatural power by "walking on the sea" (v. 25). He spoke reassuringly, "Be of good cheer; It is I; be not afraid" (v. 27). Inspired by Jesus' presence and Word, Peter rose, stepped out of the boat in faith, and overcame the watery onslaught, his attention now riveted firmly on the Way: "He walked on the water, to go to Jesus" (v. 29). But he wasn't presumptuous. Peter didn't exit the boat until he had a confirmed, divine Word to stand on: "Come [to Me on the water]" (v. 29). Thus, temporarily, he walked above his problems, strong, stable, and sure.

Then he became unsure—and his stability and strength wavered! "Beginning to sink" (v. 30), Peter called, and Jesus quickly saved His sinking student: "Immediately Jesus stretched forth his hand, and caught him" (v.

31). Ever the Teacher, Jesus then offered Peter precise correction and counsel. Peter sank because "he was afraid" (v. 30). He was afraid because he worried. And he worried because he doubted. Jesus said, "Why didst thou doubt [become double-minded]?" (v. 31). Trusting his understanding more than God's wisdom, Peter unwisely rethought his choice to trust Jesus' clear, confirmed Word of guidance. This doubt arose from a change of focus. Peter shifted his visual and mental focal point from trusting Jesus' faithful promise to considering his fearful problems: "He [now] saw the wind [wind-whipped waves,] boisterous" (v. 30). Divinely corrected and wiser, Peter drew near "and worshipped him" (v. 33). Then, with ruffled pride but restored faith, he resumed his close companionship with Jesus.

Since Peter's restoration, millions of Christians have needlessly retraced his steps from walking to worrying to worshipping. Are you one?

Has the Lord separated you from the distracted, distracting multitudes to create in you a deep, sure, focused faith in Him? Has a baffling spiritual "night" fallen in your previously Son-lit, favor-filled, easy-to-understand life? Has the Father permitted a cruel storm of trouble to envelop you and waves of difficulties, distresses, and discouragements to batter and toss you? Has the absence of Jesus' powerful intervention left you wondering? Worried? Wobbly? You have two options.

You can refocus on the facts revealed in Peter's trial, obey them, and overcome. Or you can fret at your waves, waver with doubt, sink with fear, and fall from your usefulness to God. For committed disciples, falling isn't an option.

So refocus on these facts. Jesus hasn't forgotten you. He's gone "up into a mountain [heaven]...to pray" you through this storm. There He "ever liveth to make intercession" for you (Heb. 7:25). Nor has He abandoned you. He'll return to your stormy life with sudden deliverance, open answers to your private prayers, and many other blessings and favors. He'll do "exceedingly abundantly above" everything you've asked or thought (Eph. 3:20). So don't doubt Him! Even in the exhausting "fourth watch" of your dark, trying, spiritual nighttime, remember the good news of Matthew 14. Rest in it. Hold it tightly!

Then you'll walk calmly on your chaotic Galilees, finding your way through every stormy challenge. You'll walk and worship without worrying—and never again waver from walking to worrying to worshipping.

Chapter 75

HIS WORK WILL GO ON...

*R*ECOGNIZING GOD'S WORK passes from one generation to the next, Stephen said:

> David found favor with God and asked for the privilege of building a permanent Temple....But it was Solomon who actually built it.
> —ACTS 7:46–47, NLT

So he illustrated how one generation often designs God's work and another delivers it. We sometimes forget this.

Shortsighted, we assume God will plan, prepare, and perform His visions, promises, and prophecies within our few short years on earth. Sometimes He does, but not always. Biblical and church history often show one generation finishing a former generation's work, due either to the former's negligence or sin, or God's sovereign timing.

For example, Joshua's generation executed the Canaan conquest Moses' generation envisioned. King David finished the subjection of Philistia Saul started. Elisha seized Elijah's mantle and continued his messages and miracles for another generation. The apostles continued Jesus' teachings and works in the church's early years. The church fathers extended the apostles' leadership. Other bishops then arose to feed and lead God's sheep. Wycliffe, Hus, and others prepared for the Reformation, and Luther, Zwingli, and Tyndale later rose to sustain it. When they passed, another generation, including Calvin and Knox, stepped up to lead Christianity's restoration.

Today this pattern persists. God uses one pastor to start a church, another to grow it, and yet another to establish it. He calls one missionary to plant an urban or foreign mission, another to enlarge it, and a new one to guide its outreaches to its city or nation. He raises certain donors to fund a church or ministry and, when they pass, others to continue it. He uses one dynamic leader to found a denomination and another to grow and lead its family of churches into the next stage of His plan.

This passing of the divine torch will reappear in the Tribulation. After the Church Age's final revival runs its course and Christ catches up His bride church, 144,000 Jewish believers will take up the church's mantle of Spirit-empowered ministry, use it to part the troubled waters of the Tribulation, and continue converting sinners and training disciples for Christ (Rev. 7).

This divine method purges pride and selfishness, creates humility and unity, and gives hope and joy. How?

Our pride and selfishness evaporate as we remember we're not creating a church or ministry on our own. We're just continuing the work of those who've gone before and growing it for those who follow. We'll pursue our work as far as God permits and, in God's time, selflessly lay it down and let others take over, without striving to control it further.

This heavenly humility and broadmindedness will grow as we agree that our work is God's, not ours. Like the ark of the covenant, we must carry it forward but never touch it—serving as God calls and gifts us yet never grasping it as if it were ours. The labor is ours, but all rights, fruits, and honors are His. This meek viewpoint grows as we realize we can do nothing without other believers' help. Paul couldn't disciple the Corinthians without Apollos: "I have planted, Apollos watered... [then] God gave the increase" (1 Cor. 3:6). Our unity in humility expands as we see and speak of our ministry, church, or mission as not an "I" but a "we" thing. Paul wrote, "*We* are laborers together with God" (v. 9).

Hope rises when we realize just as we need others to fulfill our calling, so they need us. Since our assistance is needed, we may confidently prepare ourselves and wait for Christ to send us to "enter into" others' labors. Jesus taught, "I sent you to reap that on which ye bestowed no labor; other men labored, and ye are entered into their labors" (John 4:38). Our joy will overflow in these last days as we join others and rejoice together in the rich, enduring, end-time harvesting work of converting sinners and training disciples: "He that reapeth... gathereth fruit unto life eternal, that both he that soweth and he that reapeth may rejoice together" (v. 36). So pause and remember.

Your work is God's, not yours. He gave the vision and plan for your "temple" and chose its pathway, provision, and builders. You need helpers to complete your task, but others also need your help. You haven't independently established anything. You're just continuing the work of your teachers, pastors, and mentors. Nor will you conclude anything. When you finish your race, you'll pass your baton to the next generation, if Jesus tarries.

And when He appears, we'll all go up, rejoicing together—and His work will go on...

Chapter 76

FIRM UP YOUR FOUNDATION

ODAY THE "FOUNDATIONS" are shaking—the natural and spiritual underpinnings of our human security. What are they?

Spiritually our souls are girded by our beliefs. If Christians, we're confident in God's unfailing faithfulness as revealed in Jesus Christ. If of another faith, we're relying on false deities, prophets, or doctrines. If atheistic, we're trusting in the goodness, wisdom, and power of humanity. Firm or feeble, these are the spiritual foundations upon which our houses of character rest.

Naturally, underneath our worldly lives are international, national, and personal props. Internationally our security lies in peace among nations. Wars, rumors of wars, and terrorism are shaking this foundation. Nationally we rest in our nation's president, government, economic stability, military strength, morality, justice, and unity. As I write, these too are quaking. Personally we rely on marriage, family, friends, a good name, jobs, and homes. These supports are also quivering and falling. There are two causes of these tremors.

First, as promised, God is shaking every false security so unbelievers will see He's the only foundation that "cannot be moved" (Heb. 12:28) and trust Him alone. Second, Satan is retaliating, using his agents to shake Christians, hoping we'll flee or turn from God to false but more familiar or popular securities.

In Psalm 11 David tells us how to keep our spiritual foundation firm when our natural foundations quake.

Our tremors begin when Satan's agents, "the wicked," cause troubles that disturb our international, national, or personal foundations: "The wicked bend their bow [and]...secretly shoot at the upright" (v. 2). Hoping to turn us, Satan starts giving us adverse advice—suggestions that, if obeyed, cause us to oppose ourselves: "If the foundations be destroyed, what can the righteous do?" (v. 3). Or paraphrasing, "You see the world shaking, the nation self-destructing, or your personal life unraveling. There's nothing you can do except 'flee' to your old 'mountains' of security—trusting human or self-help."

David would have none of it: "How say ye to my soul, Flee as a bird to your [former] mountain [refuge]?" (v. 1). Ancient facts held him firm in his current adversities. Let's review David's sacred stabilizers.

198

He knew there's something deeper than all our natural foundations—God Himself! Though everything else may change, He never changes. He's always holy: "The Lord is in his holy temple" (v. 4). He's always sovereign, in supreme authority over all creation: "The Lord's throne [of sovereign authority] is [still] in heaven" (v. 4). He always delights in His people, closely watching and controlling every detail of our lives: "His eyes behold...the righteous" (vv. 4–5). The shakings that visit us are examinations, not ends. God's testing our faith, not terminating it: "His eyelids test...the LORD testeth the righteous" (vv. 4–5). He always loves truth and fairness, never lies, injustice, or oppression: "The LORD is righteous [fair], he loves justice" (v. 7, NIV). One day His justice will stop those who won't stop hindering or harming us (vv. 2, 5–7). Then His favor will shine brightly on us: "His countenance [favor] beholds [shines on] the upright" (v. 7, NKJV). We'll also see His character-reflecting face more clearly: "The virtuous will see his face" (v. 7, NLT).

David steadied his soul with these facts at Ziklag. When all his personal foundations—marriage, family, home, possessions, friends, hope of divine service—were suddenly swept away by Satan's Amalekite agents, David first wisely reaffirmed his faith: "David encouraged himself [his faith, soul] in the LORD" (1 Sam. 30:6). Then, with his spiritual foundation restored, he readdressed his problems and, with God's help, "recovered all" (v. 18). Wisely follow his example.

When the enemy shakes or sweeps away one or more of your natural foundations, don't accept his adverse advice. Never flee to your old sources of help outside Christ! Your season of shaking is a passing, not a permanent change. It's an examination, not an end. With David, place full trust—utter dependence, complete reliance, total confidence—afresh in God's loving faithfulness, almighty power, and unfailing promises: "In the LORD put I my trust!" (Ps. 11:1). Then reaffirm your faith.

Feed your God-confidence by meditatively reading His Word, especially Psalms, and timely devotional and instructional writings. Patiently review passages and promises the Spirit emphasizes. Draw near and worship God with songs of praise and thoughtful adoration. Pray, talking, listening, and thanking Him for past answers. For further "building up," pray "in the Holy Spirit" (Jude 20). These simple disciplines will never fail to reaffirm your faith and restore your soul. Are your foundations shaking? Bending? Cracking? Collapsing? Take David's advice.

It's time to firm up your foundations.

Chapter 77

BLESSED AT JESUS' FEET

NE DAY JESUS "went up into a mountain" east of Lake Galilee and "sat down there" in full view of all passers-by (Matt. 15:29). Soon great multitudes came to Him.

Not from Israel proper but from the heavily Gentile Decapolis region they came, bringing many sick and severely handicapped people—"lame, blind, dumb, maimed"—whom they "put...down at Jesus' feet" (v. 30). There a fountain of marvelous miraculous mercies flowed freely, bringing healing, sight, speech, and wholeness.

These amazing blessings flowed not only because of Jesus' power but also the people's position. Jesus sat above them on the mountainside, exalted, while they assumed a place beneath Him, demonstrating humble submission to His authority. During Jesus' ministry others also received great blessings at His feet.

When the Syrophoenician "fell at his feet," worshipping and praying, Jesus delivered her daughter (Mark 7:25). After Jairus "fell at his feet," praying, Jesus resurrected his daughter (Mark 5:22). When a penitent prostitute "stood at his feet," kissing and washing them with tears, Jesus forgave her sins (Luke 7:37–38). When Mary of Bethany "sat at Jesus' feet," pondering His teaching, she received life-changing insights (Luke 10:39). "Sitting at the feet of Jesus," a demoniac received deliverance and psychological healing (Luke 8:35). When a healed Samaritan "fell down at his feet, giving him thanks," Christ gave him a comforting commendation (17:15–16). When after Jesus' resurrection two women "came and held him by the feet," He spoke, reassuring and guiding them (Matt. 28:9). While the apostle John "fell at his feet as dead," Jesus gave him a divine vision and prophetic revelation (Rev. 1:17). Will we receive these blessings?

Today Jesus isn't seated on a hillside by Lake Galilee. He's enthroned on a much higher "mountain"—the kingdom of heaven. But the same fountain of miraculous mercies flows freely, if only we'll position ourselves figuratively at His feet.

We do so as we:

200

- SURRENDER TO JESUS' LORDSHIP. Realizing Jesus is Lord of heaven, earth, and the church, we should humbly submit to His rule. Abandoning our right to have our way, we should always do as Jesus' Word says and Spirit guides in every area of our lives, day by day, decision by decision.

- HUMBLY STUDY AND OBEY HIS TEACHING. First-century Jewish and Greek disciples sat at the feet of their respective teachers and philosophers in intellectual submission, eagerness to learn, and willingness to obey. As we prayerfully study and diligently obey God's Word in the same teachable spirit, like Mary, we sit at the feet of the greatest Teacher-Philosopher.

- FAITHFULLY PRAY HIS MERCIES UPON OTHERS. The Syrophoenician interceded successfully for her daughter's deliverance "at Jesus' feet." Abigail and the Shunammite begged mercies at the feet of David and Elijah, who foreshadowed Christ. Will we intercede "at Jesus' feet" for the sick and sinful with the same meek but determined mercy they displayed?

- LABOR HUMBLY AND HEARTILY IN HIS SERVICE. In the ancient East servants attended the humble duty of washing the feet of their masters' guests. Will we meekly do "whatever" tasks, including the humblest, "heartily, as to the Lord"? (Col 3:23).

- COMMIT OUR RESOURCES TO HIM IN TRUST. Early Christians laid their financial gifts "at the apostles' feet" (Acts 4:35), fully entrusting them to the agents of Christ's will. We should submit our gifts to our churches in the same spirit— as His resources for His servant-leaders to use as He wills.

- WORSHIP IN SPIRIT AND TRUTH. We worship at Jesus' feet by complying with His request for worship "in spirit and in truth" (John 4:23–24). We worship with our spirit, inspired and instructed by His Spirit, and in truth, loving and living His Word-truth and confessing our sins truthfully.

Many Christians, however, are positioned not properly but problematically.

Some are trying to put Jesus at their feet. They pridefully and persistently exalt their desires, methods, and plans over His, seeing Him as their helper, not their Head. Others are positioning themselves at men's feet. Unconsciously idolatrous, they adore and praise people—politicians, preachers, entertainers, achievers, athletes, celebrities, business moguls—excessively, as if they were gods. These inappropriate positions offend Christ and hinder His mercies. Are you positioned problematically?

If so, reposition yourself at Jesus' feet. Then through your prayers, charities, and ministries, a fountain of miraculous mercies will open and flow out, with deliverances, insights, reassurances, guidance, and visions. The wonders of Jesus' Decapolis ministry will reappear. The "blind" will see His greatness. The "lame" will rise to walk with Him. The "dumb" will speak, testifying of Him. And He'll restore "maimed" friendships, marriages, families, and churches to wholeness—all blessed at Jesus' feet.

Chapter 78

PHILIP WENT DOWN—WILL YOU?

IVINELY LED, PHILIP obediently "went down" to share Christ with the Samaritans, whom the Jews despised as half-breeds and heretics (Acts 8:5). The phrase "went down" is significant. Literally, Philip went "down" in elevation from Jerusalem. Figuratively he went "down" in several ways:

- SOCIALLY, in the view of prejudiced Jewish Christians who still despised Samaritans

- RELIGIOUSLY, in the opinion of the proud Jewish religious leaders, who "had no dealings" with Samaritans (John 4:9)

- PSYCHOLOGICALLY, in his self-esteem—by accepting God's call to a despised people and place

Yet as he discharged this lowly duty faithfully, Philip's "pride of life" (1 John 2:16) shrank and his Christian humility grew. So by going down, Philip went up!

His divine approval increased, as God greatly blessed his efforts in Samaria (Acts 8:5–8). Philip's heart was also transformed—he now loved those he formerly loathed. Philip's ministry was transformed—this mundane deacon became a mighty deliverer, like his Master (vv. 6–7, 13). God made him a spiritual role model—other leaders went down to minister to the Samaritans, as he had (vv. 14–17, 25). God honored him—He dedicated almost an entire chapter of Acts to memorialize Philip's exemplary obedience, in Samaria (vv. 5–24) and on the Gaza road (vv. 26–40). Though wonderful, Philip's obedience wasn't unique. Many others have gone down to obey God in humble places of testing, labor, ministry, or suffering.

As a youth, Jesus "went down" from conferring with respected rabbis in the temple courts to obeying His parents in Nazareth for eighteen years (Luke 2:51). He later came down from His exalted Sermon on the Mount to minister to a despised leper (Matt. 8:1–2). Paul came down from his high ministerial hopes in Jerusalem to a decade of hidden preparation in his hometown (Acts 9:30). David came down from the honor of serving in King Saul's court to the humility of keeping Jesse's "few" sheep (1 Sam. 17:14–15,

28). Daniel came down from years of advising King Nebuchadnezzar to years of humble endurance on a "shelf" of disuse—until suddenly recalled to high service (Dan. 5:11–13). Jeremiah willingly went down into a pit of suffering for declaring the truth that Jerusalem's siege was God's judgment and calling Judah to repent (Jer. 38:6). While the other apostles received a miraculous deliverance from prison (Acts 5:17–20), Paul escaped persecution in Damascus by being "let down" in a humble laundry basket (9:23–25).

Like Philip, these who willingly went down when God called also went up spiritually—in closeness to God, knowledge of His ways, hearing of His voice, discernment of His hand, strength of character, spiritual power, fruitfulness in God's service, and transformation into Jesus' likeness. Why? They were following Jesus.

Jesus was the first to "come down" in this Christian era—to become one of us, reveal the Father, minister to us, teach us, redeem us, and set us an example. He said, "I am the living bread that *came down* from heaven" (John 6:51; see vv. 33, 38, 41–42, 50, 58). Christians who willingly go down to places of testing, preparation, service, or suffering are gradually transformed into His image. As in Jesus' life, God's Word is thoroughly "worked out" in them, and they're positioned for promotion in God's time and way (Phil. 2:5–11, 12–16). Along the way they learn to avoid "going down" wrongly.

They don't go down from:

- A properly separated life to one unequally yoked with sinners, as Jehoshaphat did (2 Chron. 18:2)
- Fully trusting God's help to foolishly trusting man's, as Judah did (Isa. 31:1–2)
- Faithfully pursuing God's call to faithlessly fleeing from it, as Jonah did (Jon. 1:5)

Thus they're ready, in God's time, to go up.

Everyone wants to go up to a more respected, comfortable, prosperous, or useful place, but God is looking for believers who are willing to first go down when He calls. When divinely led to do so, will you humbly submit to human authorities, prepare for ministry, accept a small job, occupy faithfully on the shelf, serve despised people, minister to Christians of other cultures, or endure a pit of rejection for speaking the truth, until God releases you? If you sow Philip's humility, you'll reap his honors.

God will visit your humble "Samaria" and greatly bless your labors.

You'll work out Christ's nature until you love those you formerly loathed. God will use you to joyfully deliver and heal the oppressed. Then He'll raise your influence to help His people, build His kingdom, and honor Him. Others will note and follow your example. And Philip's. And Jesus'. So I have only one question.

Philip went down—will you?

Chapter 79

THE NEW WINE IS BETTER

W HEN JESUS POURED out the Spirit at Pentecost, some by-standers mocked, "These men are full of new wine" (Acts 2:13). This was true, but not as they thought.

To them "new wine" was either freshly pressed grape juice or recently fermented wine. The first was nonalcoholic and available only seasonally. The second was a sweet, light alcoholic wine bottled before its fermentation was complete. Thus it wasn't "old," or aged wine, but "new." Peter affirmed no one was drunk, since devout Jews fasted before the 9:00 a.m. prayer hour during festivals. He added that Jesus, now exalted in heaven, had poured out the Spirit as prophesied (Acts 2:15–18, 32–33). His conclusion? The 120 were drunk with Christian "new wine," or *Holy Spirit freshly given.*

So at Pentecost Christ gave His engaged bride, the church, her first "drink" of new wine.[1] It was a delicious foretaste of her future earthly spiritual outpourings and heavenly marriage supper (Rev. 19:7–9).

Today Jesus gives us new wine whenever:

- We're born again (John 20:22)
- We're baptized with the Spirit (Acts 19:6)
- We read God's Spirit-filled Word believingly (2 Tim. 3:16)
- We pray, with understanding or "in the Spirit" (Eph. 6:18)
- We praise or worship God
- Jesus spontaneously refills us (Acts 4:8, 31)

The benefits of our new wine parallel the characteristics of ancient Jewish new wine.

Still fermenting, ancient new wine was stored in new wineskins, which had enough elasticity to expand as the wine released gases. Christian new wine is only fit for "new wineskins," or regenerated (reborn) souls (Luke 5:37–38), not those still rigidly bound by sins or works-based plans of salvation.

Ancient wine imparted gladness: "Wine that maketh glad the heart of man" (Ps. 104:15). Our wine makes believers glad—to be saved from sin, to have a new purpose to live, to have a growing closeness to God, to have hope for a joyous eternity.

Ancient wine loosed tongues to speak freely, without social inhibitions. Our wine removes hindering fears, enabling us to speak freely about our faith, salvation, Savior, and His Word, power, appearing, judgments, and kingdom.

Ancient wine stirred warriors' emotions to fight battles and shout victories, "like a mighty man who shouteth by reason of wine" (Ps. 78:65). Our wine inspires our hearts to fight spiritually and confess victories by faith—like the Israelites at Jericho and David before Goliath!

Ancient wine was an anesthetic, relieving sufferers of their pain. Our wine, the "Comforter," relieves us during spiritual "operations"—amputations of wrong relationships and habits and surgeries removing cancers of unforgiveness, envy, covetousness, or false doctrine.

Ancient wine was addictive: "I will seek it [wine] yet again" (Prov. 23:35). Our wine is also habit forming. Once we taste it, we keep coming back for more "drinks" night and day!

Ancient wine inspired songs: "They shall not [any more] drink wine with a song" (Isa. 24:9). Every outpouring of new wine in church history has produced new hymnists, songwriters, and singers who "sing unto the Lord a new song" (Ps. 149:1).

Antiquity's disinfectant, ancient wine cleansed wounds (Luke 10:34). Our wine convicts us of sin and, when we repent, cleanses our sin-wounds, leaving us forgiven, restored, and thankful. But ancient wine had its downside!

It intoxicated! This was especially true when drunk undiluted[2] or to excess. Intoxication alters one's consciousness of reality, leaving one confused and deceived (Prov. 23:33, NIV). Today the wine of false Christianity intoxicates millions. It substitutes impressive rituals, music, architecture, and vestments for God's real presence, truth and working, leaving worshippers deceived with false devotional fervor, or "drunk with the wine of her fornication [unfaithfulness to God]" (Rev. 17:2).

Ancient wine also caused excesses of bad behavior, resulting in hangovers, depression, and weakened characters (Eph. 5:18). (See Proverbs 23:29–35.) Here we find a contrast. Our wine creates the opposite: righteous living, joy, and strong characters that overcome adversities! So it's superior. Truly, the new wine is better! And the best is yet to come!

Jesus always saves the best for last (John 2:10). In these last days He'll pour out His best wine on us, a long, powerful, reviving drink of *Holy Spirit freshly given* to finish what He began at Pentecost. To release this wine, He needs human "grapes" that have been chosen, crushed, and bled.

Will you be one? By obeying Jesus daily, will you let Him crush your stubborn sin and willfulness so the precious new wine in you may flow out to bless others with Christlike love, truth, hope, charity, intercession, service, and other ministries? Why's this important?

The Baptizer wants the whole world to know the new wine is better.

Chapter 80

INVERTED CHRISTIANS

*W*HEN CALLED TO speak to the Jewish councilors, Stephen responded with a powerful, Spirit-led Bible lesson (Acts 7:1–50). It was just what God wanted to say—and they didn't want to hear.

Nevertheless Stephen's talk was inspired, timely, and focused, a direct message from heaven to their hearts. He closed by boldly applying the message to his hearers, hoping to prompt repentance (vv. 51–53). But instead they rebelled—while he faithfully and graciously described his vision of Jesus' glory! "Behold, I see the heavens opened, and the Son of man standing on the right hand of God" (v. 56).

A body of professing believers in the only true God, the Sanhedrin here represents a church. But not a good one! It models not an inspired but an inverted church. Everything was turned upside down. Let's review its reversals.

After hearing Stephen's inspired message, call to repentance, and heavenly vision, this congregation should have cried out with conviction and brokenness of spirit. Instead "they cried out" (v. 57) in protest against God's spokesman. Rather than praise God loudly, they denounced His messenger and message "with a loud voice" (v. 57). Thus when God tried to bless them, they battled Him.

Having heard God's truth rightly divided, they should have opened their ears to receive more truth. Instead they "stopped their ears" (v. 57) to ensure they'd hear Stephen's sound doctrine no more. So God honored their wishes, using their persecution to send His messengers elsewhere: "At that time...they [Christians] were all scattered abroad...preaching the word" (Acts 8:1, 4).

After being discerned so accurately, they should have realized Stephen's counsel was from God and run to him for more. Instead they "ran upon him" (Acts 7:57) angrily to harm the minister they should have heeded.

Stephen's spontaneous vision of Jesus enthroned in heaven should have powerfully convinced them to unite to publicize the good news, as Christ prayed (John 17:21, 23). Instead they were of "one accord" (Acts 7:57) to stop the Word God wanted to spread. Thus they united in obstinacy, not obedience.

SWEETER THAN Honey

After hearing Messiah's anointed messenger, the Council church should have invited him to speak to them again. And again. And again! Instead they "cast him out of the city" (v. 58) to ensure its temple courts and synagogues would never again hear his gracious, wise, and life-giving words. Ever!

After Stephen offered them the gift of saving grace, they should have offered him gifts of gracious gratitude—words of appreciation, fellowship meals, or material or monetary love-offerings. But instead of rewards, they offered rocks! "They stoned Stephen" (v. 59) until, wounded, broken, and bleeding, he stopped preaching. And praying. And breathing.

The Sanhedrin's follies mirror those of inverted Christians. Sometimes they form a murmuring minority in otherwise great congregations. In others, sadly, they comprise the majority. Let's examine them.

When pastors preach very challenging messages, inverted Christians "cry out" in anger, not appreciation. When elders offer convicting counsel, they "stop their ears," not their sin. When traveling teachers deliver timely, corrective Bible messages, inverted churches "cast them out" spiritually by blocking their return. Strangely, the harder some Stephenesque pastors work to offer Spirit-led talks and Spirit-filled worship, the more indifferent and unresponsive—or adversarial—their people become. The more watchful undershepherds run to correct sin-sick or wounded sheep, the more they run from, not to, their guidance. The more effectively ministers pray God's blessings and benefits down upon inverted ones, the more they toss hard looks and words their way—until they're ministerially "stoned," rendered ineffective by their churches' stony rejection or voted from their pulpits. So, like the ancient Jewish council, these congregations battle those sent to bless them. How does God respond?

Sometimes He passes over them. The Cornerstone and His "stoned" ministers move on to churches that want real ministry and steady spiritual growth. At other times He providentially roots out inverted ones. Indignant, they leave seeking "better" ministers and churches. If we respond to this as Stephen did, interceding for our inverted ones, God will ultimately awaken many of them.

Acts implies that Stephen's prayers helped convert one very inverted rabbi, Saul of Tarsus (Acts 7:58–60; 9:1–9). Once right side up, this man, who had been the church's worst foe, became its best friend and the apostle Paul! Are you an embattled Stephen?

If you're troubled, vexed, baffled, or opposed by inverted Christians or congregations, learn from Stephen. When they rebel, remain faithful. Keep sharing timely biblical messages. Keep describing Jesus' glory. Continue examining and counseling your sheep. Maintain your intercession. Then, though others are upside down, you'll remain right side up, possibly win a "Paul," and surely convert many inverted Christians.

Chapter 81

MUST WE TITHE?

*N*OWHERE DOES THE New Testament order Christians to tithe. Neither Jesus, the apostles, nor the epistles require it. Since tithing was part of Moses' law, some Christians reject it as legalistic bondage. Others, unsure, ask, "Must we, may we, should we tithe?" The first mention of tithing is illuminating.

After defeating Chedorlaomer's army to liberate Lot and the Sodomites, Abraham gave "tithes of all" the spoil to Melchizedek (Gen. 14:20), who, as king of Salem (Jerusalem) and priest of the most high God, foreshadowed Christ, our King and Priest. This act—the father of faith giving tithes to Melchizedek—foreshadows the people of faith, Abraham's spiritual children, giving "tithes of all" to Christ. Three facts about this pre-Mosaic tithing stand out.

First, it was voluntary, not compulsory. Second, it signified gratitude for God's redeeming grace, Abraham's material "thank you" for God saving Lot without merit from just judgment. Third, the second and third patriarchs of faith also tithed. Jacob pledged and paid God the tenth (Gen. 28:20–22). And when Abraham tithed to Melchizedek, Isaac (like Levi) was present "in [the seed of] Abraham," tithing with him (Heb. 7:9). So all three pioneers of the faith life tithed voluntarily and to thank God for redeeming grace. Again, this occurred before Moses' law.

Under the law God ordered tithing for symbolic and practical reasons. The Jews' tithes expressed gratitude for God's saving grace and the awareness that all their possessions and earnings belonged to God. Tithing was also God's way to support Israel's temple and its priests and Levites. Special tithes collected every three years supported Israel's unsupported ones: orphans, widows, and foreigners (Deut. 14:28–29). To encourage faithful tithing, God promised to "pour out" blessings on everyone giving tithes and offerings (Mal. 3:10) and did so (2 Chron. 31:4–10). Though Jesus criticized the scribes' and Pharisees' many sins and omissions, He commended their tithing (Matt. 23:23). Christian tithing reaches back before this legal tithing to the example set originally by Abraham and the other pioneers of faith.

Though Christ hasn't ordered tithing, He has ordained that we support our ministers and churches (1 Cor. 9:14). We must "not muzzle" the ministerial oxen who tread out the grain of the Word to feed our souls (vv. 9–11). Also, by using the example of the tithes-and-offerings-supported Jewish temple and priesthood to urge Christian giving, 1 Corinthians 9:13 subtly links Old Testament tithing with New Testament ministerial support. As the Jews' tithes supported their priests and temples, we should support our ministers and churches "in the same way" (v. 14, NLT). Furthermore, since we're heirs of Abraham's promises by faith (Gal. 3:6–9, 14), Malachi 3:10 promises us as well as the Jews that God will faithfully bless all who give tithes and offerings. If we'd obey this challenge, church fund-raisers would cease. Instead of piles of unpaid bills, we'd have "heaps" of excess funds, ready for use as needed (2 Chron. 31:6–10)! The alternatives—giving less than 10 percent or nothing at all—undermine our Christian testimony.

When giving less than tithers, can we truly claim to be fully devoted? Do we really appreciate our ministers if we give them nothing while they "give themselves continually" for us (Acts 6:4)? How can our righteousness "exceed" that of the scribes and Pharisees, who tithed zealously, if their giving exceeds ours (Matt. 5:20)? When other Christians joyfully give to Christ even in need, can we honestly claim our love for Him is equally sacrificial? Non-tithing also often betrays other sinful attitudes: greed, unbelief, unthankfulness, and pride (denying God's ownership of our wealth).

Summarizing, since Jesus didn't command tithing, churches can't require it. But they may request it. And we should give it, faithfully giving a tenth of our income. This isn't just advisable, it's advantageous.

Voluntary Christian tithing:

- Demonstrates gratitude for God's redeeming grace
- Shows we're faith children of Abraham, Isaac, and Jacob
- Acknowledges God owns everything we have and earn
- Honors God with our substance (Prov. 3:9–10)
- Faithfully supports our faithful ministers and churches
- Shows and grows faith in Jesus' principle of giving (Luke 6:38)
- Releases God's hand to provide for us and bless us (2 Cor. 9:6, 9–10; Mal. 3:10)
- Confirms our Christian testimony
- Makes our giving as righteous as the scribes' and Pharisees'

- Is better than giving nothing, or less than a tenth

So when pondering whether to tithe or not to tithe, let's remember: Must we tithe? No. May we tithe? Yes. Should we tithe? Yes. That's the best. And giving tithes and offerings is even better!

Then we'll never again wonder or ask, "Must we tithe?"

Chapter 82

ABOUT OVERCOMING CHRISTIANS AND CHURCHES

*P*HILIP'S MINISTRY TO Samaritans and an Ethiopian official in Acts 8 models overcoming Christians and churches. Let's examine his character and actions.

Philip endured adversity well. When the "great persecution" broke (v. 1), he didn't break—break fellowship with Christ or break off ministry—but instead persevered in painful times. He was humble. Philip willingly went "down" to minister to the lowly, despised Samaritans when others wouldn't (v. 5). He was without prejudice. By ministering salvation freely to Samaritans and Ethiopians (vv. 26–39), he manifested God's redeeming love for all people, without racial, ethnic, cultural, or denominational bias. His message was Christ-centered: "Philip...preached Christ unto them" (v. 5; see also v. 35), without focusing on politics, worldly issues, or personal interests. He had no envy. Rather than compare and compete with the apostles Peter and John, Philip received and cooperated with their leadership and their baptismal (vv. 15–17), corrective (vv. 18–24), and teaching ministries (v. 25). He was Spirit led. He fully trusted the Spirit's unerring wisdom, obeying His confirmed directives without requiring explanations, proofs, or human agreement (vv. 26–27).

Additionally, Philip wasn't greedy. Out to gain souls, not silver, he ministered for Christ's sake freely, without soliciting special gifts from the Samaritans or the Ethiopian official, whose occupation (royal treasurer) and possessions (chariot, Isaiah scroll) show he was wealthy (vv. 27–28). He obeyed God promptly. When God spoke clearly, Philip "arose and went" quickly (v. 27), without contention or complaint; later he "ran" with confidence God was working all things for good (v. 30). He was uncompromisingly true to core Christian doctrines. He baptized the Ethiopian only after he confessed not passive but passionate faith (v. 37). True to the Master's "must" (John 3:7), Philip preached real rebirth, not mere religious rites. He taught timely biblical insights. A man of the Book, Philip fed on and fed others biblical "meat in due season" (Ps. 104:27), preaching and counseling the right scripture to the right soul at the right time (Acts 8:30–31). These were Philip's ways and works. What followed is equally notable.

When Philip finished his work, God removed him. After evangelizing Samaria, Philip was called away to the desert (v. 26). Again, after evangelizing the Ethiopian, he was "caught away," or seized bodily by the Spirit and transported to Azotus (vv. 39–40). Philip's personal "rapture" concludes Acts 8's description of the church's initial evangelization of non-Jews. The next chapter refocuses on saving Jews (Paul, Acts 9:1–9). Philip also left behind disciples. In the desert and Samaria, after Philip's departure his converts continued walking joyfully with Jesus and learning His ways and works (Acts 8:8–17, 39). Moreover, Philip ministered again. After being "caught away," he resumed preaching in other cities (v. 40). Finally, he gained a new home. Philip settled in Caesarea, where he received and fellowshipped with believers, apostles, and prophets (Acts 8:40; 21:8–14).

Philip illustrates overcoming Christians and their assemblies perfectly! Let's compare key points.

Like Philip, overcoming Christians and churches accept seasons of persecution as part of their calling (Phil. 1:29). Humble, they embrace whatever duties God assigns, including the lowest. They harbor no prejudice, nurturing goodwill for everyone made in God's image. Their thoughts, conversations, and teachings focus on Christ's person, plan, and people, not political obsessions or media frenzies. Cleansed of envy, they seek to please God, not outshine others. They follow the Spirit's leadings confidently, not anxiously. They minister freely to royal treasurers and common Samaritans alike without requiring excessive fees or expensive gifts. They obey God swiftly, not slowly. Uncompromising, they won't abandon or modify biblical truth to agree with popular opinions or false doctrines. Discerning conditions accurately, they consistently minister God's Word "in due season."

When these overcomers finish their work in this world's "desert," like Philip, they'll be "caught away"—not to any city but to heaven! (1 Thess. 4:13–18). This sudden, supernatural, departure will end this present "chapter" of God's salvation of non-Jews, the Church Age. God will immediately begin the next Jewish "chapter," the Tribulation, by converting and commissioning 144,000 Jewish evangelists as suddenly and powerfully as He did Paul (Rev. 7). Christian overcomers will leave disciples behind, as the 144,000 and their Jewish and Gentile converts will feed on and follow their teachings in the Tribulation. Overcomers will also minister again. After returning with Christ at Armageddon, they'll help administrate His earthly kingdom for a thousand years. Finally they'll receive a new home—New

Jerusalem—where they'll fellowship forever with the Lord and His prophets, saints, and apostles. Including Philip!

So overcome! Relive Philip's character and actions in the "desert" of this world, and pray your church does also. Don't delay! The church's "chapter" will soon end and Israel's begin. It's time we become, like Philip, overcoming Christians and churches.

Chapter 83

HE KNOWS WHERE TO FIND YOU

*I*F YOU'RE A faithful Christian, yet long-delayed prayers have you worried that God has forgotten you, here's good news: He knows where to find you! Acts 9 showcases this.

After his conversion Paul was in deep seclusion for three days in a Damascus safe house praying for Jesus to show him what he should do. In response Jesus appeared to Ananias, ordering him to find Paul and minister to him. Note how specific His directions were: "Go into the street which is called Straight, and inquire in the house of Judas for one called Saul of Tarsus; for, behold, he prayeth" (v. 11). As if guided by a heavenly GPS,[1] Jesus' instructions led Ananias straight to Paul—on "Straight Street" (NLT)! Matthew Henry wrote, "Christ very well knows where to find out those that are his in their distresses. They have a friend in heaven, that knows in what street, in what house...in what frame [room] they are."[2] Thus God and Ananias found Paul.

This discovery, despite Paul's hidden condition, confirms Jesus' teaching that our heavenly Father "seeth" us whenever we pray, fast, give alms, or obey "in secret," and will "reward thee openly" (Matt. 6:6, 4, 18). The moment He's ready to give us an open answer or divine appointment, He'll do so. Provided, of course, we live as Paul did, on "Straight Street"—righteously, without crookedness, falsehood, or unfaithfulness.

Scripture repeatedly shows God finding faithful ones to:

- GIVE BIBLICAL INSIGHT. Jesus sent Philip to find an Ethiopian proselyte—traveling on a highway!—to explain God's Word to him (Acts 8:26–35).

- SAVE THEM. When Cornelius "prayed to God always" for salvation, two findings followed (Acts 10:2). First, Jesus sent an angel to find Cornelius (v. 3). Second, the angel told Cornelius where to find Peter—precisely! "Send men to Joppa, and call for one Simon.... He lodgeth with one Simon, a tanner, whose house is by the seaside" (vv. 5–6). Thus Cornelius and his household were saved.

- REASSIGN THEM. Having faithfully "fulfilled" their teaching ministry in Antioch, Paul and Barnabas sought their next ministry assignment (Acts 12:25). Finding them in a leader's prayer meeting, the Spirit reassigned them: "Separate me Barnabas and Saul for the work unto which I have called them" (Acts 13:2).

- RELEASE THEM FROM INJUSTICE. Though at peace while unjustly incarcerated for righteousness' sake, Joseph still prayed for justice. After two years, through a friend's belated favor, God found and released him (Gen. 40:14–15; 41:9–14).

- PROMOTE THEM. When David's musical gift was needed, someone recommended him glowingly to King Saul. Saul found David faithfully keeping his father's "few" sheep and appointed him court musician (1 Sam. 16:17–19; 17:28).

- REVIVE VISIONS. When Moses' youthful vision of delivering God's people seemed hopelessly dead, God found him in the remotest location—"the backside of the desert" (Exod. 3:1)—and revived the long-delayed vision.

- RECALL TO SERVICE. After Daniel had been on a dusty shelf of disuse for many years, God found him through the queen mother's recollections and recalled him to fruitful government service (Dan. 5:12–13; 5:30–6:3).

- PROVIDE MATERIAL SUPPORT. When a poor Phoenician widow and her son were starving, God sent a foreign prophet, Elijah, to their land and city to find and feed them (1 Kings 17:8–16).

All these faithful ones looked and felt forgotten by God. But they weren't. He saw them and heard their prayers all along and responded in His time.

Like them, you may be praying in secret for employment, sales or work orders, increasing income to meet increasing expenses, a buyer for property you must sell, favor in a legal dispute, wisdom in a perplexing situation, or release from an injustice that's oppressed you for years. Or you may be praying for spiritual needs.

You may be seeking closer intimacy with Christ, deeper understanding of God's Word, opportunities to use your spiritual gifts, your next missionary assignment, recall to teaching or pastoral ministry after a season on the "shelf," or the fulfillment of a long-hindered vision.

If so, however remote your location—a Syrian safe house, deserted highway, the backside of a desert, one of your heavenly Father's small church "flocks," prison, a foreign land—God knows where and how to find you. Provided, of course, you're living on "Straight Street."

So live righteously. Abandon besetting sins and selfishness. Obey God's Word and guidance joyfully. Be faithful and content with your duties, vocation, or ministry. Pray persistently in secret, presenting your needs to your loving, watchful, heavenly Father with faith and thanksgiving, and expect His open response. Why?

You know He knows where to find you.

Chapter 84

REFOCUSING ON THE FAMILY OF GOD

OUR CULTURE'S DISINTEGRATING marriages and families have understandably caused many Christians to refocus on family values and responsibilities. Critical as this is, we should also refocus on our new, eternal household, the family of God.

Paul welcomes all believers into God's family of the redeemed: "Ye are no more strangers...but...of the household [family] of God" (Eph. 2:19). This brotherhood of former sinners related by Jesus' blood has both earthly and heavenly members: "Of whom the whole family ['his whole family,' NIV] in heaven and earth is named" (Eph. 3:15).

By repeatedly calling Christians "brother" or "sister," the New Testament confirms we're already in God's family unit:

Brother Saul...

—ACTS 9:17

Phoebe, our sister...

—ROMANS 16:1

I, John...your brother...

—REVELATION 1:9

As in earthly families, God's family members share many things in common.

Believers in Christ share a common Father: "Our Father, which art in heaven" (Matt. 6:9). Whether our earthly fathers were good, bad, or indifferent, we now have a perfect Father. We have a common "mother," the comforting, abiding, truthful but tender Holy Spirit: "The Father...shall give unto you another Comforter...the Spirit of truth" (John 14:16–17). So whether our natural life-givers were caring or callous, we all have a loving mother now. We share the same eldest Brother, Jesus, whose first post-resurrection message was decidedly family oriented: "Go tell my brethren...go into Galilee" (Matt. 28:10). Whether our natural older brothers were helpful or hateful, we now have a wondrously attentive, instructive, and inspiring Sibling to look up to—and, as Lord, worship!

As we enter natural families by physical birth, we enter God's family by spiritual rebirth. The Firstborn insisted, "Ye must be born again...born of the Spirit" (John 3:7–8). Believers share a unique kind of life. While everyone has immortal life, or unending existence, we alone enjoy eternal life,[1] or everlasting personal fellowship with God: "This is life eternal, that they might know thee, the only true God, and Jesus Christ" (John 17:3). We share the same faith, interpreting all matters in light of our core, childlike trust in God's infallible Word. We share a common passion, an abiding love for learning and living biblical truth: "My mother and my brethren [my family] are these who hear the word of God, and do it" (Luke 8:21). We share a favorite pastime, praising and worshipping God. All day, every day, in every circumstance, we thank God and sing to Him with "psalms and hymns and spiritual songs" (Eph. 5:19–20). Why? It blesses Father! Our "Father seeketh such to worship him" (John 4:23). And there's more.

We share a common ambition, to increasingly know God and fully do His will in life. Our Brother said, "My meat is to do the will of him that sent me, and to finish his work" (John 4:34, KJV). We share a general predestination to be "conformed to the image" of our Father's firstborn, Jesus (Rom. 8:29). We share common character traits. As families share similar values and virtues, we exhibit the Christlikeness of the "fruit of the Spirit" as we grow in grace (Gal. 5:22–23). Like some families, we share a large business— building our Father's kingdom by faithfully exercising our gifts and pursuing our ministries and vocations. Again, our Brother said, "I must be about my Father's business" (Luke 2:49). We share a common heritage. All our spiritual ancestors feared God or stood in awe of His awesome power and believed both His promises and warnings: "Thou hast given me the heritage of those who fear thy name" (Ps. 61:5). We share a common motto: "Known by Our Love!" Our Brother ordered us to "love one another; as I have loved you," adding, "by this shall all men know that ye are my disciples [family learners]" (John 13:34–35). We share common enemies, the prince and "rulers of the darkness of this world" (Eph. 6:12), whom we defeat by obeying and spreading the light of God's Word and praying persistently in the Spirit. That's not all!

Soon we'll share a family reunion like no other! When Christ appears, He'll suddenly catch away all faithful believers, living and dead, to be reunited with each other and Him forever (1 Thess. 4:13–18). Ultimately we'll share a common home. Pilgrims with "no continuing city" (Heb. 13:14) in this secular world, our family's sweet home place is our "Father's house"

(John 14:2), New Jerusalem, the "better country" our Father and Brother have prepared for us. This new family and home will forever eclipse our old ones.

So while praying, working, loving, and learning to build or restore our natural families, let's also refocus on the family of God.

Chapter 85

AMAZING GRACE INCARNATE

HEN ANANIAS OBEDIENTLY "went his way" through Damascus' streets to find and pray for the repentant Christian killer, Saul of Tarsus (Paul), he was amazing grace incarnate (Acts 9:17).

Not only the heavenly Father and Son but now their earthly servant showed stunning unmerited favor to a man who, only hours ago, was the most angry, active, injurious, feared, and notorious enemy of Christians alive! But Jesus' Damascus Road visit had thoroughly broken this seemingly unbreakable enemy of the Way, leaving him thoroughly cleansed, open-hearted, and ready for God to fill and use. So Ananias, Spirit-led and Spirit-filled, spoke kindly: "*Brother* Saul" (Acts 9:17). It was as if he was saying, "Saul, you're my spiritual brother now, one of us in God's family of the redeemed." This must have deeply comforted Saul, who was completely surrounded by adamant rejection, despised by Jews as a traitor and distrusted by Christians as a deceiver (v. 26)!

Ponder the past sins of this self-described "chief" of sinners (1 Tim. 1:15). Saul gladly assisted Stephen's executioners, dragged women as well as men from their homes, prosecuted and whipped them in synagogues for heresy, blasphemed Jesus as a demonic false messiah, forced Christians to renounce Him, and imprisoned or executed others all over Israel. Not content to limit his Christian hunting to Israel, he journeyed abroad to Syria to apprehend, accuse, and abuse them. The key fact we must grasp is that Ananias knew all this: "Lord, I have heard by many…how much evil he hath done to thy saints" (Acts 9:13).

It was this same vicious enemy whom, after his repentance, Ananias called "brother." Thus Ananias:

- Blessed a brother who had cursed his brothers
- Received into God's family one who had split Christian families (v. 17)
- Prayed for the healing of one who had injured many Christians (vv. 17–18)

- Restored sight to one who blinded many to the Light (v. 18)
- Ministered the Spirit to one who had resisted the Spirit (v. 17)
- Baptized in Jesus' name one who had blasphemed Jesus' name (v. 18)
- Fed one who had starved many Christians in prison (v. 19)
- Restored to strength one whose harassment had weakened many Christians (v. 19)

Ananias' embrace of his former enemy showed Christlike compassion, the very amazing grace of God incarnate!

It's like a creationist helping a newly converted evolutionist. Or like an Israeli Christian ministering to a former Palestinian terrorist. It's like a North Korean or Chinese Christian receiving a former Communist government informant. Or like a Northern Irish Protestant receiving a former Catholic adversary. It's like African Christians receiving converted African Muslims, who previously slaughtered members of their tribe. Get the picture yet? Let's zoom in closer.

It's like having a chance to lead to Christ a spouse who abandoned you years ago. Or like a neighbor who previously hated, slandered, and sued you now seeking reconciliation. Or like a relative who has long mocked your faith coming, now bankrupt, to ask for financial help. It's like a bitterly atheistic supervisor, who tried repeatedly to have you fired, getting saved and asking you to disciple her. How about now? Is Ananias' amazing grace coming into focus?

Ananias also manifested other gracious Christlike attitudes and behavior.

What kindness! He didn't speak a single word to Saul about his past sins. What faith! He trusted the Holy Spirit totally, believing if Saul's conversion wasn't genuine, the Spirit, who knows everything, would alert him (Prov. 3:5–6; John 14:2). What courage! He risked his life to help restore another. What submission! Though Christ's command was most unpleasant, after a brief, prudent inquiry Ananias yielded and obeyed without the slightest resistance. What humility! Ananias surely sensed some Christians would misjudge and criticize him as helping an enemy, but he obeyed anyway, knowing Jesus would be pleased and would defend him. Will He be pleased with us?

Jesus wants to do in us what He did in Ananias—so fill us with His gracious love that we too are amazing grace incarnate! But as with Ananias, we must cooperate with the Spirit's quiet, private, convicting work within our hearts for this to occur. Whom is the Spirit urging you to show mercy to today? If you yield and obey, more of Jesus' compassion will be seen in your life—and His other graces, such as kindness, courage, faith, submission, humility, and so forth. If you don't yield, this won't happen. You'll remain amazingly ungracious. Which way will you go?

Go your way on your mission of mercy today, through the streets of your Damascus, to find and minister to your Saul. Like Ananias, be amazing grace incarnate.

Chapter 86

OUR ORIGINAL DENOMINATIONS

$\mathcal{W}$HEN WE MEET other Christians, our first question is often, "What's your denomination?"

As if anticipating this, the New Testament states various "denominations," or names and designators that identify Christ's devotees. Since they're biblical and predate all post-Reformation Protestant groups, they're our original denominations—inspired names that most initially, authoritatively, and accurately describe followers of Christ.

Each is a message from Christ, revealing a key truth for meditation—and molding, or helping conform us to the image of the name. Let's consider them.

- CHRISTIAN (Acts 11:26). "Christian" is taken from the Latin *Christianus*, whose suffixes (-ianus; plural, -iani) refer to one's allegiance or loyalty. The Pompiani were loyal to Pompey, Caesariani to Caesar, and Herodians (Gk. *Herodianoi*) to Herod.[1] Christians, therefore, pledge their loyalty to Christ and His loyalties—the Father's will, Word, people, plan, and call.

- BELIEVER (Acts 5:14). This designation reveals the core of what we are and do. While others deny or doubt the Creator, we believe everything He is and says. "Believer" means I fully trust in and confidently rely on the integrity of God, His Son, and His Word.

- DISCIPLE (Acts 9:1). "Disciples" were deeply serious student-followers of Jewish rabbis or Greek philosophers, who disciplined themselves to be and teach like them. Jesus said His disciples "continue" in His word (John 8:31). So "disciple" means I discipline myself to continue learning, living, and spreading Jesus' Word and ways.

- BRETHREN (Acts 9:30). As "neighbor" speaks of community, "brethren" speaks of family. Whether our earthly family is delightful or dysfunctional, "brother" or "sister" means we now have a wonderful new family, the eternal "household of God" (Eph. 2:19).

- FRIENDS (John 15:15). Jesus said, "Ye are my friends," and then added, "if ye do whatever I command you" (v. 14). By consistently obeying Jesus, we qualify for friendship benefits: special biblical insights, warnings, secrets, manifestations of Christ (John 14:21–23), and "sweet, satisfying companionship" with Him (Ps. 25:14, AMP). "Friends" are Christ's obedient, intimate companions.

- OVERCOMER (Rev. 2:7). An "overcomer" is "one who subdues,"[2] a conqueror of adversaries and adversities. Basic Christian overcomers conquer this world's unbelief (1 John 5:4–5). Master overcomers also rise above every challenge to their Christian walk, whether from their sin, self-will, or failures, or adversaries.

- SAINTS (Rom. 1:7). "Saints" are "holy ones,"[3] believers who are sanctified and set apart unto God by saving faith in Christ. Jesus prayed we'd be further sanctified by keeping His Word (John 17:17). Paul calls believers "saints" (Rom. 1:7) and shows us how to sanctify ourselves so God can "wholly" set us apart for His fellowship and use (1 Thess. 5:23, 12–23).

- ELECT (Rom. 8:33). Foreknowing we'd freely choose Jesus, the Father "elected," or chose, us before this world was, to be saved and play a part in His redemptive plan. Just as God chose the Jews, Christians are also now His "elect."

- SECT OF THE NAZARENES (Acts 24:5). This derisive name mocked Christ's followers as a cult of dangerously deceived heretics who ignorantly believed in a Galilean instead of a Judean Messiah. Accepting it, or its modern equivalents, means we're willing not only to be "magnified" (Acts 5:13) but also maligned. Paul was (Acts 24:14). So were the Huguenots, Puritans, Separatists, Methodists, Baptists, and others scornfully named.

- PEOPLE OF THE WAY (Acts 9:2). The "way" is Christ, the only way to God and eternal salvation: "I am the way...no man cometh unto the Father, but by me" (John 14:6). We assert

He's the way, we live in His ways, and we're on the way—not residents but pilgrims in this world bound for God's kingdom.

- PEOPLE WHO CALL ON THIS NAME (Acts 9:21). In every problem or perplexity we call on "this name," seeking help first not from human wisdom or strength but from our heavenly Father, whose name (character) alone we fully trust. "In everything by prayer" (Phil. 4:6) is our motto and modus operandi.

By recommending these original denominations, I'm not suggesting that joining modern denominations is sinful or divisive. Not at all.

But I advocate we change our self-perception. We shouldn't think or speak of ourselves first or solely in denominational terms but rather simply as *Christians* who attend various denominational or nondenominational churches. Idealistic? Yes. Irrelevant? No. This will help foster unity in our denominationally splintered postmodern church world. Inspired, biblical, and meaningful, these original denominations are pure, authentic, nonsectarian, and truly ecumenical in spirit.

Consider them well. Conform to their message. Confess them. When asked, "What's your denomination?" why not respond simply, "Christian"? That's one way to remember and revive our original denominations.

Chapter 87

JUST A MUSTARD SEED

ESUS' PARABLE OF the mustard seed depicts God's very small works becoming very large (Mark 4:30–32). Let's consider two applications.

Primarily, the phenomenal growth of Jesus' proverbial mustard seed—from a Palestinian garden's smallest seed to its largest plant (10-foot to 15-foot tree!) in one season—represents the dynamic growth of the present spiritual, hidden form of God's kingdom, the church, as recorded in Acts. After the Holy Spirit filled Jesus' few surviving followers in the Upper Room, within hours their 120 became 3,000. Within days thousands more were added. Within weeks their faith infiltrated all Jerusalem and Judea. After a few decades this "mustard seed" church was a thriving network of Christian assemblies throughout the Mediterranean world—despite relentless opposition from venomous, violent enemies!

Secondarily, the mustard seed pattern describes any kingdom-building work God creates and fosters to bless His people. These mustard-seed works may be spiritual movements (reformations, revivals), churches, ministries, or individual believers. All these works of the Spirit begin small yet contain biblical truth and "faith as a grain of mustard seed" (Matt. 17:20). To grow from obscurity to significance, these minuscule but mighty seeds must undergo death experiences (John 12:24), in which they appear hopelessly defeated or destroyed for a season. Then, in God's time, the Spirit blesses their growth, raising them from small beginnings to distinctly larger ends: "Though thy beginning was small, yet thy latter end should greatly increase" (Job 8:7). Note Jesus' key words.

"Less than all" emphasizes the mustard seed's smallness—like a petunia seed or flake of ground pepper (Mark 4:31). One commentator says Jesus' surprising point is, "That the mighty kingdom everyone expected could issue from apparently obscure beginnings—like Jesus and the disciples."[1] How true!

Everything about Jesus and His disciples was, from His culture's viewpoint, small as a mustard seed. His occupation was minute. Jesus was a carpenter, not a priest, scribe, or Pharisee. His public profile was insignificant.

230

He was a quiet man, not a protesting, prominent revolutionary. His education was modest. Though biblically literate and rhetorically gifted, He lacked the extensive oral theological training rabbis typically received in the schools of Shammai or Hillel. His social image was small. He hailed from Galilee, a region noted for common fishermen, laborers, and Gentiles, not from Judea, which boasted uncommon priests, prophets, and aristocrats. His wealth was infinitesimal. Besides His clothes, Jesus owned nothing, not even a bed! What an unlikely choice this small man was to become the larger-than-life Messiah sent to save Israel!

His disciples were equally insignificant: several "unlearned and ignorant" fishermen (Acts 4:13), a despised publican, a zealous nationalist, a converted harlot, a brooding traitor, a handful of women, and some former followers of an ascetic, beheaded prophet named John!

Furthermore, they were numerically "less than all" other religiopolitical sects sown in Israel's religious garden. Jesus' post-crucifixion followers tallied a mere 120. Meanwhile the popular Pharisee party numbered 6,000, and the Sadducee, Herodian, Essene, and Zealot parties, though smaller, were still far more numerous than Jesus' followers. By every measure, then, Jesus' "way" was a mustard seed. Their chance of survival, much less significant fruitfulness, was very small. But their God was very big! After "sowing" them in a death experience—Jesus' ministry-shattering betrayal and crucifixion—God left them ministerially "underground," hidden for fifty days in the Upper Room. Two waterings followed: a sprinkling "breath" of His Spirit on the night of the resurrection (John 20:22) and a heavy watering at Pentecost. Spiritual germination ensued and, growing, they were soon "greater" than the other religious trees (Mark 4:32). Their mustard tree gradually produced "great branches," or ministers, ministries, and missions, that provided refuge and rest in Jesus for all who came under its influence, or "shadow" (v. 32).

God has worked similarly throughout church history. Oswald Chambers said:

> In the history of God's work you will nearly always find that it
> has started from the obscure, the unknown, the ignored, but the
> steadfastly true to Jesus Christ.[2]

Truly, God can take any faithful, humble Christian individual or group, however small, and, by sowing, growing, and releasing His powerful Spirit and favor, make them a huge blessing to the church and world.

Is your Christian influence so small you feel you're "just a mustard seed"? Has God "sown" your life, ministry, church, or movement in a baffling death experience? Though hidden "underground," are you still growing and maturing spiritually? Pray persistently for the Spirit's "watering," and wait expectantly until God raises you from obscurity to significance, from your small beginnings to distinctly larger ends—to bless His people and build His kingdom!

And praise Him you're just a mustard seed.

Chapter 88

ANANIAS' EXTRAORDINARY CHARACTER

*T*HERE WAS A certain disciple at Damascus, named Ananias; and to him said the Lord in a vision, Ananias…Arise, and go" (Acts 9:10–11). With these words Scripture introduces us to Ananias of Damascus.

He is mentioned only in this and one other biblical reference (Acts 22:12–16). Some traditions suggest Ananias rose to prominence, that he was one of the seventy, later became bishop of Damascus, and was ultimately martyred for the faith. But in Scripture he remains one of God's unsung heroes, like Micaiah, Huldah, Epaphras, Onesiphorus, and others, who, while honorably mentioned, are not central players in the biblical drama.

But whatever Ananias lacked in fame, he made up for in faithfulness. The record reveals a man of outstanding Christian character.

No less than the apostle Paul testified Ananias was "devout" (Acts 22:12), or God-fearing and devoted to a life of seeking God daily in private devotions. Apparently Ananias' secret pleasure was the "secret place" of prayer, Bible meditation, and worship (Ps. 91:1). He was "of good report" among the Jewish believers in Damascus (Acts 22:12). Those who knew him best knew he was one of the best, a man of integrity without chronic character flaws. He was beautifully obedient. Once sure God wanted a course of action, he swiftly complied, without delaying or murmuring. This made him one of Christ's friends: "Ye are my friends, if ye do whatever I command you" (John 15:14). He knew God's voice well. When God spoke, Ananias expressed no surprise that He spoke, only about what He said (Acts 9:10). His calm response, "Behold, I am here, Lord," hints he heard from his Friend regularly, with clarity and understanding. Let's learn more.

Ananias was a man of reason. His request that Jesus clarify His strange orders (to aid a notorious persecutor!) showed not rebelliousness but thoughtfulness and wisdom. He prudently faced facts and likely consequences before, not after, acting. Yet he was first a man of faith, trusting his Redeemer's wisdom above his own and always following His confirmed guidance with childlike abandon (Prov. 3:5–6). He was a man of love, willing to forgive even his worst enemy (Saul), if repentant, and was quick to speak kindly to comfort Saul's broken, desolate heart now rejected by Jews and doubted by Christians. Ananias' courage was exceptional. He must have realized Saul might betray and harm him or the Damascus Christians misjudge and reproach him, yet Ananias went steadily forward on his mission to please Jesus. He prayed with power. When Ananias laid hands on Saul, so did Jesus. The results were powerful and manifest: "Immediately there fell from his eyes as it had been scales; and he received sight" (Acts 9:18; see James 5:16). Tradition aside, we know these things to be true of Ananias.

These attitudes and actions reveal the stuff of spiritual greatness. Though hidden, Ananias was holy. Though ordinary, he was an overcomer. Though obscure, he was seen, known, and used by God—mightily!

Warren Wiersbe noted:

> God can use even the most obscure saint. Were it not for the conversion of Saul, we would never have heard of Ananias; and yet Ananias had an important part to play in the ongoing work of the church...Saul of Tarsus became Paul the apostle, and his life and ministry have influenced people and nations ever since.
>
> Behind many well-known servants of God are lesser-known believers who have influenced them...On April 21, 1855, Edward Kimball led one of his Sunday school boys to faith in Christ. Little did he realize that Dwight L. Moody would one day become the world's leading evangelist....
>
> God keeps the books and will see to it that each servant will get a just reward. The important thing is not fame but faithfulness (1 Cor. 4:1–5).[1]

Indeed, without Ananias' faithful hidden ministry there would be no famous apostle Paul—no model missions to the Gentiles, no revelation of the mysteries of the emerging church, no clear description of the Rapture, and no inspiring example of Jesus' grace, power, and sufferings in Paul's life and ministry. The whole subsequent history of the church, in Acts (Acts 13–28) and beyond, hinged upon this unknown layman's remarkably courageous, humble, and faithful obedience. There's another reason God introduced us to Ananias.

He wants his character integrated into ours. Will we learn and live Ananias' ways in Christ? If we'll have his character, we'll hear His call: "Arise and go!" So let's aim to be not famous but faithful. Not special but steadfast. Not religious but real. While many fret over their reputations let's focus on our characters—and build one like Ananias' extraordinary character.

Chapter 89

GO WITH A STRAIGHT COURSE!

WHEN CALLED TO Macedonia by a heavenly vision, the apostle Paul obeyed "immediately" (Acts 16:10). To him procrastination was not an option.

From the busy port of Troas he selected the shortest, straightest way to obey God: a ship bound for the Macedonian port of Neapolis. Seeing Paul's promptness, God responded promptly, giving favorable winds. Luke wrote: "We came with a straight course" (v. 11), or "sailed with the wind at our backs." These east-west winds enabled their ship to maintain a straight Northwest course, without having to tack.[1] Consequently Paul's ministry team crossed the Aegean in two days instead of the five it would have required if sailing against the wind (Acts 20:6).

Key here was Paul's expeditiousness, or swiftness in accomplishing a task. He didn't rush or act hastily, yet he expedited God's work by prayerfully discerning the things that might hinder his mission and avoiding them. For instance, an overland route through Thrace would have taken more time and money, so he ruled that out. The sea route from Troas to Neapolis was quick, oft-used, and less expensive, so he took it. God's favorable response wasn't unique. The Old Testament shows God's "wind"—His Spirit's powerful help and favor—at the backs of others who obeyed Him quickly.

Abraham's servant searched for Isaac's bride expeditiously. He prayed for "good speed" (Gen. 24:12), refused to feast before discussing his proposal (v. 33), and, once it was accepted, returned to Abraham immediately, without lingering at Laban's estate (vv. 55–56). Responding, God's Spirit blew favorable responses his way. The servant found Rebekah immediately, she fulfilled the sign he requested, and she was willing to leave right away—and Laban was agreeable to it all!

When King Hezekiah moved decisively to restore Judah's dilapidated temple, he found himself assisted by divine wind. God prospered the Levites' work by enabling them to cleanse and restore the temple and its courts in only sixteen days, thus clearing the way for the resumption of national worship (2 Chron. 29:12–19).

Lifted by Haggai's inspiring prophecies, the post-Exile Jews set a straight course to finish rebuilding God's temple. Seeing their initiative, God intervened, giving them favor with King Darius. When he ordered their Samaritan enemies to help them, they complied "speedily"—and the Jews responded by finishing the temple with equal swiftness (Ezra 6:13–14).

When the Spirit stirred Nehemiah's heart over Jerusalem's desolate condition, Nehemiah responded swiftly by offering to help rebuild Jerusalem's walls. Soon he found God's favorable winds at his back. With Artaxerxes' royal support and the assistance of the small but faithful Jewish remnant, Nehemiah rebuilt Jerusalem's walls in only fifty-two days! (Neh. 6:15–16). The New Testament also recommends expeditious obedience.

Having a divine appointment with a cross, Jesus "steadfastly set his face" to go to Jerusalem without delay while traveling through Samaria (Luke 9:51). When returning to Jerusalem, Paul sailed by Ephesus, stopping briefly at nearby Miletus to exhort the Ephesian elders, because he hoped to deliver the Gentile churches' donations to the Jerusalem church at Pentecost. Paul also repeatedly recommended the single life as a way to serve God expeditiously, or "without distraction" (1 Cor. 7:35). Now let's consider the alternative.

When we obey God's guidance slowly or not at all, our procrastination creates the opposite scenario: the wind of the Spirit blows *against* us—and it's a long, hard, five-day sail to "Macedonia"! Why? The same God who "gives grace" to the humble, "opposes the proud" (James 4:6, NIV). Jonah's experience confirms this. His stormy story should convince us to obey God with a straight course. Whenever God calls, will we identify and eliminate the distractions that hinder our obedience?

Some common distractions are:

- Preoccupations with money-making, entertainment, sports, politics
- Excessive social interests, activities, relationships
- Bad attitudes—self-pity, judgmentalism, prejudice, envy, anger, fear, unbelief, and so forth
- Giving excessive attention to communication technologies such as television, Internet, cell phones, iPads, and other fascinating devices
- Anything else that, while perfectly legitimate, may interfere with our obedience to God's call or guidance

These are just some of the things that entangle us and render our obedience slow, lethargic, or nonexistent. We mustn't let them keep us from running "the race" set before us with God's wind at our backs (Heb. 12:1). The next time God calls, respond like Paul.

Choose the most direct way to obey. Prayerfully consider what you can change, minimize, or remove to expedite your obedience. Deal with it promptly, "forgetting" what's behind, "reaching forth" to what's before, and "pressing" on toward the "mark" (Phil. 3:13–14). Then expect God's "wind"— the Spirit's strength and favor—to help you go with a straight course!

Chapter 90

KEY TIME

CRIPTURE DECLARES, "THERE is…a time to every purpose under the heaven" (Eccles. 3:1), including "key time"—the time to lock or unlock things. Let's consider the purpose and use of keys.

Keys turn bolts that open locked doors or lids, behind which are closed chambers and otherwise inaccessible secret things. These chambers may be as small as a jewelry box or as large as a kingdom. The secret things are typically valuable property, such as treasures or important documents. Or they may be valuable people—Eliakim's keys opened a door of access to Judah's King Hezekiah (Isa. 22:22).

Giving someone our keys implies we share a close, trusting relationship and therefore grant them authority and privileges not granted others—for instance, the authority to act in our name and the privilege of accessing us or our property. Carrying someone else's keys signifies we accept responsibility to use them properly or according to the owner's will. When Jesus told Peter, "I will give unto thee the keys of the kingdom of heaven" (Matt. 16:19), He put him, and us, on notice: key time is coming!

Historically the keys Jesus gave Peter, though intangible, were very real. They were evangelistic authority to open the door to God's kingdom to Jews and Gentiles in salvation. Peter used them first at Pentecost (Acts 2) and later at Cornelius' house (Acts 10). On both occasions, as Peter spoke Jesus' gospel he unlocked the door to the kingdom of heaven to the world's two major people groups, giving them access to its King and the treasures of His Word and Spirit. But Peter wasn't the only key holder.

Other apostles unlocked God's kingdom, King, and treasures to races, nations, and continents. Thomas used his keys in India, Andrew in Russia, and Paul in Asia Minor, Macedonia, and Achaia.

Non-apostles also used kingdom keys. Philip turned his gospel key and released Christ to the Samaritans. He used it again to unlock the King's Word to a traveling African government official and through him, tradition says, his nation. Aquila and Priscilla's teaching key opened Christ's Way "more perfectly" to the devout Alexandrian scholar, Apollos (Acts 18:26). These examples prove Peter's kingdom keys were not given to apostles only but rather to every Christian having a personal relationship of trust with their Owner. So today every abiding, born-again Christian has the same authority Peter had to open kingdom doors and secrets to bless others. To do this effectively, we must cooperate with the Holy Spirit.

This collaboration begins when we learn to recognize when it's "key time." Key time occurs whenever God opens "door(s) of utterance," or divinely timed opportunities for us to speak to others (Col. 4:3). When the Spirit grants these precious openings, we must boldly use them to unlock the King and His kingdom treasures and Word to those with whom we speak. This may involve evangelizing a lost soul or edifying a fellow Christian with a timely word of encouragement, warning, correction, or instruction.

Thus, as Peter and other key holders before us, we:

- Open the door to the kingdom to the unsaved
- Open a door "of knowledge" (Luke 11:52) to Christians eager to learn
- Unlock the meaning of biblical passages to puzzled Christians
- Unlock God's end-time plan to untaught or confused believers
- Open truths that free spiritual captives from fear, oppression, or errors
- Open doors to vital spiritual experiences, such as the baptism with the Holy Spirit
- Open the door of faith that heals the sick and makes them whole
- Open the door of increased access to the King—a deeper, closer, sweeter walk with Jesus

Two important facts remain. First, if we refuse to speak in key times, we repeat the sin of the Jewish religious leaders, whom Jesus rebuked for not using their key of knowledge to open salvation or edification to others (Luke 11:52). Second, we must recognize when not to use our keys. When people are not ready or willing to hear, keep your keys inactive and mouth closed. Even Jesus couldn't use His keys when people stubbornly held to their sins or adamantly rejected Him. When the Jewish leaders conspired to "trap Jesus into saying something for which he could be arrested" (Matt. 22:15, NLT), His words were discreet and few. When Herod Antipas questioned Him, He said "nothing" (Luke 23:9). Why? It wasn't key time.

Used wisely, keys change lives. One turn of a key and a spiritual prisoner walks out a free man in a captive world. Stay close to the Owner of your kingdom keys, ready to use them whenever it's key time.

Chapter 91

THE WALLS WILL COME DOWN!

$\mathcal{W}$ HEN CORNELIUS' GENTILE messengers visited Peter in Joppa, Peter, a Jewish Christian, "called them in, and lodged them" (Acts 10:23). Since devout Jews didn't associate with Gentiles, this shows "the walls were coming down"[1]—specifically the wall separating Jewish and Gentile Christians.

God does the same in our day. Whenever His Spirit visits and revives us, God tears down all man-made walls in the body of Christ. One by one the needless partitions tumble.

Race no longer separates the redeemed. Suddenly we're color blind! Nationality no longer keeps us apart. Love of country abides, but national pride is eclipsed as we praise the greatness of Christ's coming kingdom. Political partisanship fades. Unbiased, we fellowship with Christians of differing parties, policies, and views. Sectarianism no longer matters. We freely worship and serve with born-again believers of every denomination. Education no longer parts us. Unscholarly and scholarly Christians study Scripture together and marvel at the wisdom that inspired and indwells it. Rich and poor no longer draw back from each other. Their respective disdain and envy fade as they unite to seek eternal, spiritual riches, or "gold tried in the fire" (Rev. 3:18). Styles of worship and music no longer bar fellowship. "Where the Spirit of the Lord is, there is liberty" (2 Cor. 3:17)— and we let others praise and adore God the way their conscience approves, whether we prefer it or not.

We no longer separate over forms of church government. Whether bishops, superintendents, pastors, boards, or congregations make final decisions, we all decide to fellowship. Congregational size no longer matters. Small, medium, and large churches serve, study, and sing together, oblivious to how their numbers compare. Meeting places also mean nothing. Believers congregating in stone cathedrals receive those who cluster in steepled sanctuaries, storefronts, homes, and huts. Clergy-only ministry restrictions fade. The Spirit raises laymen to minister beside clergy, speaking from their hearts and studies with simplicity and scholarship. We become gender blind. Men and women minister to congregations hungry for biblical

241

messages given and witnessed by the Spirit, whether delivered by Pauls or Priscillas.

These and other troublesome spiritual walls are washed away whenever the mighty river of God pours down from heaven and surges into the church. But not automatically!

To remove them, we must cooperate with the Spirit's unifying work, even during extraordinarily powerful revivals. This requires a humble willingness to change wherever God desires it and a courageous determination to please Him rather than Christians who stubbornly cling to their old divisive walls. Are we willing to be bold spiritual pioneers who, when God confirms His intention to change our flawed practices, forge trails of spiritual progress for others to follow? Peter was one.

When Cornelius requested ministry, Peter laid down his old Jewish prejudices and adopted new kingdom values, boldly stepping out to receive believers of another group—and be criticized for it! (See Acts 11:1–3.) The apostle Paul was another wall breaker.

Paul emphatically denounced our historic divisions and announced our kingdom unity:

> For ye are all the sons of God by faith in Christ Jesus.... There is neither Jew nor Greek, there is neither bond nor free, there is neither male nor female; for ye are all one in Christ Jesus.
>
> —GALATIANS 3:26–28

We should follow his brave example, abandoning man-made biases and adopting scriptural attitudes, confident "God shows no favoritism" (Acts 10:34, NLT). When Christians unwilling to do so judge us—and they will!—rather than retreat into their darkness, we should pray them into our light. Then *all* the walls will come down. With the Spirit's help we'll build the wondrous unity Christ prayed for (John 17:21, 23) and the psalmist praised: "Behold, how good and how pleasant it is for brethren to dwell together in unity!" (Ps. 133:1). But some walls will continue standing.

Scripture erects key spiritual and moral barriers to preserve God's holiness and blessing in our lives and churches. Though committed to love, we mustn't pretend fellowship with professing Christians who condone sinful practices, accept false religions, reject Scriptural authority, or adopt this world's ungodly values to avoid its rejection. Biblically broad-minded, we won't join these. We can't. Not with a clear conscience. But we will pray for them. Such barriers must stand—or we'll fall from God's favor!

But all other walls between us will fall. They must. They won't exist in heaven, so we mustn't allow them on earth. They fell in the first century and subsequent revivals. They'll fall again. When the Spirit revisits us, He'll give us wall-breaking love and courage. Let's get ready now, knowing, when He moves, the walls will come down!

Chapter 92

MEMORIAL DAY IS COMING!

*S*OMETIMES IT SEEMS God has forgotten our devotion. We've obeyed, given, and prayed for years with little visible results. But Cornelius' experience assures us God hasn't forgotten us. Our "memorial day" is coming!

For years Cornelius, a God-fearing Roman military officer, poured out his heart in daily prayers to God and charitable contributions to God's people. We don't know how many open answers to prayer the Lord had sent Cornelius, but it's certain none were as dramatic as the one he received when an angel suddenly appeared during his afternoon prayer time.

Cornelius' celestial guest informed him, "Thy prayers and thine alms are come up for a memorial before God" (Acts 10:4). "Come up for a memorial before God" meant Cornelius' years of prayer, obedience, and giving had now come afresh to God's memory, prompting Him to send an immediate and full reward. For Cornelius, life was about to change—in a big way!

Since Cornelius greatly honored God, God greatly honored him with seven distinctions:

1. God favored Cornelius with a visit from an angelic messenger.

2. God sent His most respected minister, Peter, to evangelize Cornelius.

3. God honored Cornelius' home as the site of "Pentecost II," a powerful outpouring of the Spirit on Gentiles like that given Jews in the Upper Room.

4. God adopted Cornelius as His child. Once born again, he entered God's family, heaven's citizenship, and a personal relationship with Jesus.

5. God filled Cornelius with the Holy Spirit, making his body God's living temple.

6. God selected Cornelius' "household" (Acts 10:2, NAS)—relatives, friends, and servants—to be the first Gentile church.

244

7. God honored Cornelius' name and character in the church's
first history book, Acts, for all future Christians to ponder
and emulate.

No accident, God sent these honors to fulfill His key promises, "Them
who honor me I will honor" (1 Sam. 2:30), and "Whatsoever a man soweth,
that shall he also reap" (Gal. 6:7). They created a sweet memorial day—a
monument of blessings commemorating all Cornelius' seemingly forgotten
good works. God rejoiced when these long-delayed answers to prayer suddenly broke through to shower blessings on His humble, patient servant.
Others also experienced memorial days.

After five long years[1] of negligence, King Xerxes finally remembered
Mordecai saved his life by reporting an assassination plot. By God's inspiration he then commemorated Mordecai's honorable deed in a citywide
parade proclaiming him, "The man whom the king delighteth to honor"
(Esther 6:7, 9, 11). Mordecai knew, then, that God had heard his prayers and
seen his obedience all along.

After approximately twenty long, lonely years on the "shelf" of professional disuse, Daniel may have wondered if God had forgotten all his daily
devotions, prayers, gifts, and years of excellent service. If so, such doubts
vanished when King Belshazzar suddenly summoned him to interpret the
enigmatic handwriting on his palace wall. Daniel's subsequent successful
interpretation and rapid promotions to service in Belshazzar's and Darius'
administrations settled it: God had *not* forgotten his lifelong devotion and
service (Dan. 5:10–6:3).

After thirteen disappointing years of slavery and prison, Joseph may
have been tempted to think that, for whatever reason, God no longer wished
to fulfill his dream. Then God intervened. Pharaoh's butler remembered
Joseph, Pharaoh sent for him, and, suddenly, Joseph was raised to the high
service he had envisioned years earlier. Why? Nationally Egypt's great famine was at hand. But personally it was Joseph's memorial day. God remembered his past devotion, obedience, charity, and prayers and prompted His
immediate, full reward. There are also more recent examples.

For instance, in 1722 a small group of Moravians settled in Herrnhut,
Saxony,[2] determined to build a godly community. For years they served
God faithfully without significant breakthroughs in prayer or ministry.
Then in August 1727, God answered, raining a mighty outpouring of His
Spirit on their city of faith—from which sprang a hundred-year nonstop

prayer vigil and church-and-world-changing missionaries! Are you devoted yet discouraged?

Worrying, as we often do, that God has forgotten your labors, gifts, and prayers? The experience of Cornelius, whose name means "the beam of the sun,"[3] can be a bright ray of hope in your long, dark valley of unrewarded service—if you believe its lesson. The author of Hebrews believed it: "God is not unrighteous to forget your work and labor of love, which ye have shown toward his name, in that ye have ministered to the saints, and do minister" (Heb. 6:10). Why not share his faith? Believe God has seen your devotion and granted your prayers.

Look up! Your life is about to change—in a big way! Memorial day is coming!

Chapter 93

REESTABLISHING THE HEAD

*S*IX TIMES! THAT'S how often the New Testament asserts the headship of Jesus over the church and every Christian.[1] This inspired repetitiveness should make us pause and ponder what God is saying.

"The Father of glory...gave him [Jesus] to be the head over all things to the church, which is his body" (Eph. 1:17, 22–23). In this and similar biblical references God through Paul uses the human body as a model of His church. Let's explore this.

Physically, all our thoughts, words, actions, reactions, and bodily functions, conscious and unconscious, are commanded by our heads (brains) via impulses transmitted through our nerves. Spiritually, Christian individuals, churches, and ministries should function just like this. We should be commanded and controlled by our spiritual Head, Jesus! By identifying Him as our Head, Scripture delegitimizes and forbids any other. Nowhere does the Word authorize any person, office, or council to assume Jesus' headship. Every reference to the church as Christ's body quietly but persistently reaffirms He, and He alone, is its Head. Unless God created the church a headless body!

Acts 10 reveals Christ's headship in action. At Cornelius' house we see Jesus in full, uncontested command of everything that happened and everyone who participated.

The preacher, Peter, was selected by Jesus' express order conveyed by an angel (v. 5). Cornelius obeyed the Head by summoning Peter (v. 7). So did his messengers by traveling from Caesarea to Joppa to find Peter (v. 8). Meanwhile the Head prepared Peter for his mission by giving him a special vision informing him he should now accept Gentile believers (vv. 9–17). Then, by His Spirit, He ordered Peter to return to Caesarea with Cornelius' messengers, "doubting nothing" (vv. 19–20). Peter complied immediately— the Head had spoken! The next day Peter, six witnesses, and Cornelius' messengers departed promptly, as the Head had ordered (v. 23). Meanwhile, Cornelius waited in Caesarea and invited guests implicitly approved by the Head through prayer (vv. 24, 27). Upon Peter's arrival, Peter and Cornelius disclosed the instructions each had received from the Head (vv. 27–33) and then joined their guests, who were eager to hear the message the Head had given Peter—and obey it (vv. 33–48).

The Head's response? He suddenly and powerfully saved and Spirit-baptized everyone present, launching a dynamic church. How beautiful!

And hopeful! We can have similar rewarding experiences, if we'll live under Jesus' peaceful, rewarding command and control. As He did at Cornelius' house, the Spirit will bless what we do and say "exceedingly abundantly above" anything we ask or imagine (Eph. 3:20). Scripture implies Cornelius had been asking God how to be "saved" and if Jesus, as reported, was indeed the Messiah (Acts 10:4, 14, 37). God not only spoke but also demonstrated His answer with angels, visions, miracles, salvation, signs, and great joy! Thus His wise and benevolent plan—to redeem Gentiles equally with Jews—marched forward. Why? The body obeyed the Head.

In his last written message A. W. Tozer lamented that this too often is *not* the case in the church. Comparing Jesus to a constitutional monarch, he wrote: "Nominally he is the head over all, but in every crisis someone else makes the decisions."[2] If Christ is not making the decisions in our personal lives, families, and churches, who is? Who are the false heads commanding and controlling us?

The pope? Yes, but he controls only devout Roman Catholics, not others, and certainly not Protestants, Orthodox, or independents. So who are our false heads? Superintendents? False apostles? Hyper-influential pastors? General councils? Possibly.

But here are some more likely unauthorized controllers:

- Our heads, or intellects—human reasonings not submitted to God's Word or Spirit
- Willful wealthy or powerful people
- Materialism
- Lustful impulses for sinful pleasures or excessive leisure
- Religious tradition
- Blind denominational loyalty
- Worldly trends
- Prejudices
- Wanting people's approval

- Any person, thing, or interest that influences us more than Christ's Word or guidance in a given issue

These are the illegitimate heads most likely to captivate and steer us, usurping Christ's headship and causing us unnecessary trouble, spiritual failure, and grief. And note this. The real "brain," or core controlling force, pulsating within all these false heads is self-will: all impulses to disobey Christ spring from a root desire to please ourselves. Thus self-will is the secret sovereign rivaling Jesus' headship in our lives.

Let's end his manipulation by rededicating our lives, churches, and ministries to Jesus' control. As we seek the Head's will by prayer and Bible meditation, and steadily obey it, He'll bless us as surely as He did Cornelius' house. So, "whatsoever he saith unto you, do it" (John 2:5). That will reestablish the Head.

Chapter 94

ALL THAT CALL ON THY NAME

ONE OF THE unofficial names given Christ's followers in the New Testament was "all that call on thy name" (Acts 9:14).[1] What does this unofficial but inspired label say about us?

It reveals Jesus' followers are a praying people. Some folks worry, reason, or imitate their way through problems. Others steal, cheat, or bribe their way to what they want. Still others lie, fight, or manipulate their way through life. Unlike these self-sufficient individuals, Christ's born-again people pray their way through life! Our biblical watchword is, "In everything by prayer" (Phil. 4:6). What makes us this way?

We have an advantage—an all-sufficient, ever-present, super-attentive, marvelously loving heavenly Father! Whether we were well or poorly parented, as God's own adopted children we may now call on our wondrously faithful Father for every need, worldly or spiritual. As we learn to lean on Him for everything, we begin thriving. Soon we're overcoming problems, perplexities, and persecutors the same way Jesus did—by praying early, often, simply, patiently, expectantly, and with praise. Let's review this prayerful lifestyle.

We pray in private, "When thou hast shut thy door, pray to thy Father, who is in secret" (Matt. 6:6), and in public, "They continued steadfastly...in prayers...in the temple" (Acts 2:42, 46). We pray at set times, "Peter and John went up...at the hour of prayer" (Acts 3:1), and at all times, "Praying always" (Eph. 6:18). We pray with purpose, "If we ask any thing according to his will" (1 John 5:14), and with persistence, "Pray without ceasing" (1 Thess. 5:17). We petition with faith, "When ye pray, believe that ye receive" (Mark 11:24), and with thankful praise, "In everything by prayer...with thanksgiving" (Phil. 4:6). We pray with obedience, "Whatever we ask, we receive...because we...do those things that are pleasing in his sight" (1 John 3:22), and without presumption, sure that "God heareth not sinners" (John 9:31). There's more.

We appeal in the city, "Prayer was made...[in] the house of Mary [in Jerusalem]" (Acts 12:5, 12), and in the countryside, "We went out of the city by a riverside, where prayer was [offered]" (Acts 16:13). We plead for kings, "I exhort…supplications, prayers, intercessions…be made…for kings" (1 Tim. 2:1–2), and for criminals, "If he [Onesimus] hath wronged thee…put that on mine account" (Philem. 18). We call on God in palaces, "The chief man of the island…received us and lodged us…to whom Paul entered in, and prayed" (Acts 28:7–8), and in prisons, "They cast them into prison.…And at midnight Paul and Silas prayed" (Acts 16:23–25). We pray for our ministers, "Ye also helping together by prayer for us" (2 Cor. 1:11), and they pray for us, "We will give ourselves continually to prayer" (Acts 6:4). We intercede in our native tongue, "And I will pray with the understanding" (1 Cor. 14:15), and in other tongues, "I will pray with the spirit" (v. 15). That's not all.

We offer petitions for friends, "The Lord give mercy unto the house of Onesiphorus, for he often refreshed me" (2 Tim. 1:16), and for enemies, "Lord, lay not this sin to their charge" (Acts 7:60). We pray for messages, "[Praying always] for me, that utterance may be given unto me" (Eph. 6:19), and for missions, "When they had fasted and prayed…they sent them away" (Acts 13:3). We request open doors, "That God would open unto us a door of utterance" (Col. 4:3), and closed doors, "For there are many…deceivers…whose mouths must be stopped" (Titus 1:10–11). We appeal for boldness, "Behold their threatenings; and grant unto thy servants, that with all boldness they may speak thy word" (Acts 4:29), and for wisdom, "If any of you lack wisdom, let him ask of God" (James 1:5). We cry out for the Spirit's fullness, "I bow my knees unto the Father…that ye might be filled with all the fullness of God" (Eph. 3:14, 19), and to have our worldly needs fully supplied, "Pray to thy Father…Seek ye first the kingdom of God…and all these things shall be added unto you" (Matt. 6:6, 33). Thus, "in everything by prayer" we prevail—thanks to Father!

Born-again one, have you forgotten to lean on your fabulously faithful Father lately? Are you worrying, reasoning, or arguing your way through problems? Fighting, manipulating, or imitating your way to what you want? Stressed out, exhausted, miserable? Remember your New Testament name: "All that call on Thy name." Live out this label and be a light to this hopeless, prayerless, Fatherless world. Awesome answers await.

"By awesome things in righteousness wilt thou answer us, O God" (Ps. 65:5), and all that call on Thy name.

Chapter 95

WILL YOU SEE JUDGE JESUS?

To MOST CHRISTIANS Jesus looms large—as Savior, Lord, Messiah, Redeemer, Son of God, Son of man, prophet, preacher, teacher, counselor, baptizer, healer, deliverer, intercessor, head of the church, general of heaven's armies, and coming King. But this image isn't large enough.

Besides these facets of His glorious character, Jesus is also a judge. And not just any justice, but the most active, righteous, powerful, and enduring! To understand Jesus' role and work as judge, let's review those of ideal human judges.

Excellent judges aren't just legal authorities decreeing orders, fines, incarcerations, and executions. Ideally they dispense justice in an unjust world, empowering the truthful and exposing false accusers. They end controversies, stopping villains and rescuing victims. They uphold the rule of law, backing lawmakers, punishing law breakers, and rewarding law keepers. They deter crime, ensuring peace, order, and prosperity. Their decisions release good influences and shut down harmful ones. In these ways they produce and preserve a healthy, secure society. No nation or kingdom can long survive without wise, just, and compassionate judges. They also foreshadow "Judge Jesus."

Peter testified Jesus ordered the apostles to preach not only His saviorship and lordship but also His judgeship: "He commanded us to preach…and to testify that it is he who was ordained by God to be the Judge of living and dead" (Acts 10:42). So the Great Commission includes the message of Judge Jesus, "the Judge of living and dead." Without it our gospel is inaccurate and commission unfulfilled.

Jesus also said the Father committed not part but all divine sentencing to Him: "The Father judges no one, but has entrusted all judgment to the Son" (John 5:22, NIV). Paul added that Jesus' judgments occur at divinely appointed times: "He [the Father] hath appointed a day, in which he will judge the world in righteousness by that man whom he hath ordained [Jesus]" (Acts 17:31). But when? How?

Here are ten times and ways Jesus issues or executes decisions:

1. Presently He's judging everyone (the "living") daily, not directly but providentially. He guides human authorities' and judges' decisions concerning us (Prov. 21:1). Seeing our sowing, He determines which blessings or adversities we'll reap. Justly yet mercifully, He orders these decisions according to biblical principles (Gal. 6:7)—and chastens human judges who misjudge us (Ps. 18:25–27).

2. Before the Rapture He'll judge His bride, the church, examining and purifying her. God's end-time judgment, or assessment and reordering of all things according to His righteousness, must begin at His "house" (1 Pet. 4:17–19). Through godly leaders' corrective decisions, Christ will steadily restore divine order—biblical truth, ministries, methods, and goals—among us. This restoration will remove sin, separate the lukewarm from the committed, and spark revival.

3. The Rapture itself will be a judgment. Our being taken or left depends upon whether we're ready, watching, and worthy in Christ's view (Matt. 25:10, 13; Luke 21:36).

4. After the Rapture Jesus will judge us again in heaven. There He'll evaluate our life-works, not to determine our salvation but to decide what rewards and responsibilities we'll have in His kingdom (2 Cor. 5:10).

5. At the close of the Tribulation He'll judge the Antichrist, his armies, and the false prophet, permanently condemning and punishing them (Rev. 19:17–21).

6. After returning to earth, He'll judge the Tribulation survivors, separating and searching them for saving faith reflected in their treatment of the believing Jewish remnant (Matt. 25:31–46).

7. Before the Millennium begins, He'll judge Israel's dead, resurrecting, reviewing, and rewarding righteous Jews (Dan. 12:2).

8. During the Millennium He'll judge and rule all nations, deciding all controversies through His judiciary of apostles and overcomers (Matt. 19:27–28; Rev. 2:26–27).

9. As the Millennium ends, He'll judge Satan and the rebels he incites, executing them in a fiery judgment (Rev. 20:7–10).

10. After the Millennium He'll judge the wicked "dead" of all ages, resurrecting, reviewing, and assigning them degrees of eternal punishment according to their works (Rev. 20:11–15).

These are Judge Jesus' known judgments. Does our vision of Him include them? Are we ready for Judge Jesus?

The first-century Jews saw their coming Messiah only as a conquering King. This limited view left them unprepared for His coming as a sacrificial Lamb. If we see Jesus only as we prefer and not as Scriptures proclaim, we're repeating their error—and totally unprepared for Jesus to be "revealed from heaven…taking vengeance" on His enemies (2 Thess. 1:7–8). And the time is short: "Behold, the judge standeth before the door" (James 5:9).

Will you believe the whole revelation? Fulfill the whole commission? Preach the whole gospel? Will you see, and expect, Judge Jesus?

Chapter 96

CALLING CONSUMMATE CONGREGANTS

*A*T CORNELIUS' HOUSE Peter found some extraordinary believers (Acts 10:23–48). Though technically still Jewish proselytes, they perfectly represent "consummate congregants"—Christians gathered in a state of maximum receptivity toward God.

Self-examined and spiritually hungry, Cornelius and friends were a well-laid fire awaiting a spark named Peter. All Peter did was speak and the Spirit did the rest: "While Peter yet spoke these words, the Holy Spirit fell on all them who heard the word" (v. 44). Like these believers, consummate congregants are quiet, undistracted, and concentrated come meeting time—or in biblical terms, "in the Spirit on the Lord's day" (Rev. 1:10). They come together not for tradition, ritual, entertainment, or thrills, but to hear from God through their ministers. They're ready to receive all things He says, truths that are new or familiar, comforting or challenging, complimentary or critical: "We are all here…to hear all things…commanded thee of God" (Acts 10:33).

Submissive to truth, they don't argue with Bible facts, but rather accept, ponder, and practice them. They come looking for something to believe, something to work out, something to build their lives on. They're open to counsel and willing to change, realizing every truth they applaud must be applied—to themselves, not others.

They come prepared, sure God is always ready for all who are ready for Him. Knowing Jesus promised, "Behold, I stand at the door, and knock [ready to bless whoever opens it]" (Rev. 3:20), they believe He's always ready to:

- Speak to anyone ready to hear
- Work for anyone who's ready to work with Him
- Revive any church that's ready to pay the price of spiritual progress

Human unpreparedness negates this divine readiness. No matter how ready the Lord is, nothing happens if we're unprepared. All God could do remains undone. All we could know remains unknown. All we could be we never become. All the fruit we could bear we never bear.

Yet how powerfully God moves when He finds spiritual readiness! Peter was only a few sentences into his sermon when God interrupted, releasing an explosive flood of blessings: "As I began to speak, the Holy Spirit fell on them" (Acts 11:15). The energy with which God burst in among these congregants shows we're not waiting for God nearly as much as He's waiting for us. How eagerly He's searching for Christians who want eternal truth instead of ecclesiastical tranquilizers and who will do whatever He asks to have more of His life. Wherever He finds such hearts, He bursts in to release, renew, correct, direct, and mature them. These Christians realize their attitudes, dispositions, and moods are very important.

They know wisdom commands us, "Keep thy heart [soul, including one's mind, will, and emotions] with all diligence, for out of it are the issues of life" (Prov. 4:23). When our internal state is wrong, we can't receive from God, no matter how clearly or powerfully He speaks. Almighty God spoke to mighty Moses, and he in turn preached mightily to the Israelites, but "the word preached did not profit them" (Heb. 4:2). Why? Unbelief undermined the Word. Unbiblical attitudes toward people and situations, complaining or judgmental dispositions, angry or fearful moods, all these prevent us from receiving the Word, even from a minister as mighty as Moses!

So each of us must accept our responsibility to be ready. We can't compel others to be ready when we come together, but we can be consummate congregants ourselves. We can determine to prepare for every gathering of our church by examining our thoughts, judging our actions, confessing our sins, forgiving our offenders, adopting biblical attitudes, correcting our moods, and listening expectantly for God's voice.

If by these disciplines we consistently prepare ourselves, we'll be amazed how consistently God responds. He meets ready souls readily: "Unto them that look for him shall he appear" (Heb. 9:28). In not some but every meeting, we'll experience a personal, internal Cornelius-like rebaptism of the Spirit as our "Peters" speak God's Word. The Spirit will give new insight into Bible verses, characters, and incidents. He'll personalize timely truths, making us sense, "This is for me!" We'll find refreshing "living water" and sweet "honey from the rock" in every meeting and always emerge stronger and more fit for life. So Cornelius' congregants challenge us to examine ourselves.

When we gather, are we casual hearers or worthy listeners? Lukewarm churchgoers or fervent Christian disciples? In or out of the Spirit? Cornelius' church also summons us to become like them—spiritually prepared, hungry souls who consistently gather in a state of maximum receptivity toward God. They're not alone. Listen...

Christ is also calling consummate congregants.

Chapter 97

ECCLESIASTICAL EXCELLENCE

*U*PON ENTERING CORNELIUS' home, Peter found a gathering of people who would soon become an outstanding church (Acts 10:25, 23–48). Their condition and actions, and those of their leaders, model ecclesiastical excellence—a church in the highest state of spiritual life and readiness.

Let's look more closely at this church's outstanding spiritual condition and actions.

Everyone present in Cornelius' home was called of God. While Peter was approaching from Joppa, Cornelius, acting as God's agent, busily "called together his kinsmen and near friends" (v. 24). They waited on God. While Peter, his six witnesses, and Cornelius' three messengers traveled toward them, "Cornelius [and his church] waited for them," patiently expecting God to bless them through His servant Peter (v. 24). They were spiritually minded. Believing they were "present before God" (v. 33), they trusted God had personally ordered Peter's message and so prepared to hear what was "commanded thee of [by] God" (v. 33). That's not all.

They were focused on vital issues. Undistracted by trivia, religious fads, or mere biblical curiosity, they were focused on God's Word, which alone establishes, develops, and matures right relationship with God: "Words, by which thou...shall be saved" (Acts 11:14; ct. 2 Tim. 3:6–7). They were willing to hear everything God said through His messenger. Eagerly they listened to Peter explain "all things...commanded thee of God," without preferring or excluding any subjects (Acts 10:33; ct. 2 Tim. 4:3–4). They had godly leaders. Cornelius and Peter, symbolizing resident pastors and visiting teachers respectively, sought God's will regularly by prayer and fasting (Acts 10:2, 9, 30–31), obeyed divine guidance (v. 29), and willingly taught not what people demanded but what God commanded—and shared their pulpits with other ministers so committed. The Acts' description goes on.

They humbly received God's grace. Once told the gospel, they readily received God's forgiveness not by their works but by Christ's cross alone (vv. 39–43). They were spiritually hungry, open to not only God's Word but also His Spirit's fullness and gifts. In this unprejudiced condition, the Spirit "fell on all them" who received Peter's message (v. 44). They readily obeyed biblical ordinances and teaching. When so taught by Peter, the record implies they quickly submitted to water baptism (v. 48). They wanted more of God in their lives. Though well-fed by Peter's sermon, they urged him to "tarry certain days," so they could receive more truth, power, and growth (v. 48). They lived prepared for revival. The Spirit's sudden outpouring confirms that, as best they could, they had gotten their lives in order before Christ visited them through Peter (v. 27). They were spiritually unified. Their leaders, Cornelius and Peter, worked together harmoniously, and the people demonstrated the same depth of spiritual oneness as their leaders. Their story continues.

They feared God. Cornelius' message states, and Peter's remarks imply, that they stood in awe of God's awesome immensity, authority, and power: "He that feareth God [as you do]...is accepted with him" (v. 35). They were Spirit-baptized. That Peter and others "heard them speak with tongues and magnify God" implies they subsequently continued praying and praising God in His Spirit and truth (v. 46). Churches like theirs exist and enjoy God's favor in every nation. Their Gentile status and Peter's inspired comments reveal this: "God is no respecter of persons; but in every nation he that feareth him, and worketh righteousness, is accepted with him [as you are]" (vv. 34–35). There are many such churches worldwide. That Peter found "many" (v. 27), or "a large gathering of people" (NIV), at Cornelius' house suggests ever so subtly that there are "many" similar groups of believers in the Gentile world—though, like Israel's God-fearing remnant in Elijah's day, they're relatively unknown. And they live on.

All spiritually excellent churches today are distant reflections of Cornelius' exceptional *ekklēsia*.[1] They're God-fearers called apart from the world who humbly receive God's gracious salvation and His Spirit's fullness. They're spiritually minded, unified, and focused on God's Word. They willingly hear whatever God says, readily obey it, and live ever hungry for more of God. Led by godly leaders, they pray "in the Spirit" (Eph. 6:18), worship "in spirit and in truth" (John 4:23), and wait expectantly for His blessings. By living in divine order daily, they're always ready for revival—or the Rapture! Though comparatively few are celebrated, many of these excellent assemblies exist, and they're in not some but every nation. Every time they gather "present before God," God presents Himself before them anew!

Study the ways of Cornelius' church. Follow them till you reach the highest spiritual life and readiness. Master them until your Master responds: "The Holy Spirit fell on all them" (Acts 10:44). Why will He respond?

He loves ecclesiastical excellence.

Chapter 98

RE-CROWN HIM LORD OF ALL

*I*N CAESAREA PETER boldly proclaimed Jesus "Lord of all" (Acts 10:36). Thus he asserted, as we do, that Christ is the sovereign ruler of everything and everyone worldwide. But are we who proclaim Christ's lordship publicly, honoring it privately?

Christian history reveals repeatedly that honoring Jesus' lordship brings peace with God, the Spirit's power, and spiritual and church growth. But if we deny Christ's lordship by letting sin or selfishness rule parts of our lives, we forfeit His peace in our souls, power in our ministries, and growth in our lives and churches. Are we in any way denying, and thus dishonoring, Christ's lordship?

Many assert, "If Jesus isn't Lord of all, He's not lord at all." Theoretically they're right. Jesus isn't ruling us if we consistently *overrule* Him in even one issue in our lives. Yet this assessment isn't entirely true to life. Many Christians sincerely yield their hearts to Christ yet lack the will to surrender everything to Him. Like James and John they worship Jesus, yet sometimes desire "a certain thing" more than pleasing Him (Matt. 20:20). Thus they surrender to Christ yet retain, as Oswald Chambers said, their "right to themselves" when their selfish desires are very strong.[1] These profess Christ "Lord of all," but He's not. Yet it's equally untrue to say He's "not Lord at all." More accurately, He's "Lord of most." Scripture illustrates this incomplete submission.

In Midian Moses obeyed all God's commands except one: he failed to circumcise his second son. Jehoshaphat and Josiah lived and worshiped as Jehovah ordered yet didn't initially destroy all of Judah's idolatrous "high places." David's heart overflowed with love for God, yet on one occasion he ignored God's biblical commands about transporting the ark of the covenant. Eli ministered acceptably, even training young Samuel, yet failed to discipline his evil sons. Though positionally "just" and "righteous" (2 Pet. 2:7–8), Lot sought wealth and power in Sodom more than favor and influence with God. After initially rebelling against God's call, Jonah repented and preached to Nineveh—yet didn't change his impudent attitude and speech. Even Peter, who declared Jesus "Lord of all," let his former Gentile prejudices resurface briefly in Antioch (Gal. 2:11–14).

All these believers were generally subject to God, yet they resisted or refused His control in specific issues where their contrary desires were excessively strong. God's lordship over them cannot be denied, yet neither can their insubordination in selected areas. Like them we may be only letting Jesus be Lord of most.

For instance, we may submit our minds generally to Him yet hold specific imaginations, desires, or motives contrary to His teaching. We may not use money as He wishes, spending lavishly for personal desires yet being remiss in tithing, giving, or paying debts. We may condone immorality, thinking lightly of off-color jokes, risqué dress, or soft pornography. Our eating habits may be insubordinate, leaving us indulgent and controlled by our appetite. We may not use time wisely, preferring to waste the time God wants us to spend praying or studying His Word. Our devotional life may be irregular when it should be a fixed daily appointment with Jesus. We may leave a church Christ called us to join to attend a lukewarm assembly with less challenging teaching and no corrective counsel.

We may spend too much time, energy, or money on entertainment. We may not control our tongue, often speaking in a manner displeasing to Christ. We may be "unequally yoked" in close friendships with sinners or carnal Christians. We may obey God's Word in our family and church yet not at work. We may be "entangled" in hobbies or other interests that, while acceptable, hinder our discipleship (2 Tim. 2:4). We may love God with part but not "all thy strength" (Mark 12:30), serving Him when we feel well but not when we're tired or sick. We may freely praise and worship God at church yet forget to do so at home. We may "give thanks" in some but not "all circumstances" (1 Thess. 5:18, NIV). By consistently disobeying Christ's will in one of these areas, we deny Him His rightful lordship over all our lives—dethroning and dishonoring Him. He's calling for self-examination.

"Why call ye me Lord, Lord, and do not [all] the things which I say?" (Luke 6:46). Inspect your life thoroughly. Are you in any issue still asserting your right to yourself? Letting idolatrous "high places" remain? Overruling your Ruler? Reducing Him to Lord of most? Act now, not later.

New peace, more power, and exciting growth await, if by completing your obedience you re-crown Him Lord of all.

Chapter 99

REMINDED BY THE SPIRIT

PETER TESTIFIED THAT at Cornelius' house the Spirit spontaneously reminded him of Jesus' Words: "There came into my mind the words of our Lord, when he said, 'John indeed baptised with water, but you will be baptised with the Holy Spirit'" (Acts 11:16, PHILLIPS). These weren't just random sayings of Jesus.

They were divinely aimed Word-arrows. They perfectly fit and satisfactorily explained Peter's immediate situation—at that very moment Jesus was baptizing Cornelius' household with the Holy Spirit! Grasping this explanation, Peter accepted the surprising events he may otherwise have resisted. We may consider this spontaneous recall of Scripture extraordinary.

But it's not. Jesus promised the Spirit would remind us of His Word as we need it: "The Holy Spirit...will remind you of everything I have said to you" (John 14:26, NIV). These spontaneous recalls of Scripture come for:

- CORRECTION, after we've thought, said, or done something wrong
- GUIDANCE, when we're pondering what to do or say, or which way to turn
- WARNING, when the Spirit sees spiritual, moral, or physical danger looming
- PREPARATION, just before a difficult test arises
- EXPLANATION, giving "understanding [insight]" (Prov. 2:11) to help us interpret what we're experiencing, witnessing, or hearing of (Acts 11:15–16)
- CONFIRMATION, corroborating teachings or counsels
- COMFORT, relieving anxiety, despair, shock, or grief
- REASSURANCE, reviving our faith when contradictory events have shaken it (Mark 5:35–36)

No coincidences, these perfectly timed Bible reminders are God's present voice to us. His Spirit, who inspired these Words originally, is re-inspiring and re-speaking these ancient texts to meet our current needs.

These reminders come when the "still, small voice" of the Spirit speaks in our hearts or consciences (1 Kings 19:12), our dreams (Acts 16:9), or our daily activities (Acts 11:16). They may come as we awake in the morning or through a Bible teaching, sermon, book, or e-mail. They may speak through a friend's exhortation, a minister's counsel, or any other way we're reminded of a biblical truth just when we need it. Can our spiritual ears hear God's voice?

Jesus' letters to the churches of Asia Minor show that, sadly, not every Christian develops their ability to hear the Spirit: "He that hath an ear, let him hear what the Spirit saith unto the churches" (Rev. 2:7). Our spiritual ears may be clogged with sin, hyperactivity, doctrines asserting God no longer speaks to men, or other blockages. If so, we should "wash" our ears by obeying the applicable "water" of "the Word" (Eph. 5:26). Then when the Spirit speaks, we'll hear Him.

When Jesus promised His disciples the Spirit would remind them of His sayings, He implied they already knew them. Today the Spirit's reminders are typically Bible portions we've already heard, read, or studied. Stored in our cerebral computers, they're awaiting recall when needed. But the Spirit sometimes exceeds this grace. In rare instances He recalls Scriptures we've never even learned! Though we mustn't presume He'll do this, if He does, He's calling us to learn these texts now...and live them! All these loving reminders are prompts—inspired words given to spur inspired action.

Will they successfully prompt you, as they did Peter? To ensure this, do the following whenever the Spirit brings God's Word to mind.

Wonder at the Word, standing in awe of your heavenly Father—the Most High God!—for taking time to speak to you. Worship Him for the Word, thanking and praising Him for speaking and causing you to detect His voice. Inscribe His Word, noting in your diary or notes when the Spirit spoke, what He said, and what it concerned. Meditate on His Word, prayerfully pondering its meaning and reading its biblical setting and parallel references to discover everything God wants to say to you in your situation. Obey the Word, faithfully complying with God's communication. If it's guidance, follow it. If it's a correction, change. If it's a warning, heed it. If it's an explanation, accept it. If it's a confirmation, trust it and doubt no more. If it's a reassurance, believe it and keep hope alive. If it's comforting, receive it and rest in God. If it comes to prepare you, take steps to get ready.

Finally, share the Word, telling another spiritually minded Christian what and how the Spirit spoke to you. This will bless and educate them in the Spirit's ways and make you more like Peter, who told others when, how, and why the Spirit reminded him of Jesus' words at Cornelius' house.

With Peter's example and these instructions, you're ready to recognize it and respond wisely whenever you're reminded by the Spirit.

Chapter 100

NEED A FRIEND?

*D*ISTRUSTED ON EVERY side, newly converted Saul of Tarsus (Paul) needed help being accepted by the churches of Damascus, Jerusalem, and Antioch. And everyone knew why.

Every Christian had heard how Paul had "made havoc of," or shamefully injured and destroyed, the church in Jerusalem, "entering into every house and, haling [dragging] men and women, committed them to prison" (Acts 8:3). And not a few, but many. He later testified, "I caused many believers there to be sent to prison [and] . . . condemned to death" (Acts 26:10, NLT). Obsessed, Paul did so not apathetically but zealously. Every time he jailed, flogged, or stoned another Nazarene, he rejoiced: "I punished them often in every synagogue, and compelled them to blaspheme; and being exceedingly mad against them, I persecuted them even unto foreign cities" (v. 11).

Due to this campaign of terror, the name "Saul of Tarsus," like more recently "Gestapo" or "jihadist," rang like a death knell in every Christian home from Sinai to Syria. Many graciously forgave Paul but couldn't forget the merciless monster who had so joyfully wounded or executed their loved ones. Then God's lightning struck this son of blitzkrieg.

The Light of the world personally appeared and suddenly terminated Paul's terrorism near Damascus. Now converted and equally zealous for Christ, Paul stood before an Everest of a problem: How could he convince Christians that he, their chief enemy, was now a chosen minister? Only God could move this mountain of mistrust! He did so by sending Paul two friends.

Like everyone in Damascus, Ananias knew Paul's infamy. He protested to Jesus, "Lord, I have heard by many of this man, how much evil he hath done to thy saints" (Acts 9:13). But Ananias humbly received Jesus' correction and quickly befriended his former adversary: "Ananias went his way, and . . . said, Brother Saul" (v. 17). After Ananias relayed Jesus' message to the Damascus Christians, that Paul was genuinely converted and chosen for special service, "then was Saul . . . [accepted for fellowship] with the disciples who were at Damascus" (v. 19).

Like Ananias, Barnabas was good-hearted (Acts 11:24). When Paul told Barnabas of his special conversion and call to help Gentiles, and the Spirit

266

confirmed this, Barnabas quickly accepted Paul. But when Paul visited the Jerusalem church, to his dismay "the disciples...were all afraid...and believed not that he was a disciple" (Acts 9:26). So Barnabas spoke up for Paul: "Barnabas took him, and brought him to the apostles, and declared...how he had seen the Lord in the way, and that he had spoken to him" (v. 27). Once convinced Paul wasn't a wolf in sheep's clothing, the church's shepherds accepted him. Soon the sheep followed their lead, and Paul "was with them coming in and going out" (v. 28).

A few years later God launched a key new church among the Greeks at Antioch. Sensing the time for Paul's Gentile ministry had come, Barnabas journeyed to Tarsus to find Paul and bring him to Antioch. There again he recommended Paul, this time to the leaders of Antioch's fast-growing assembly. Once accepted, Paul assumed a leadership post with the other trusted "prophets and teachers" (Acts 13:1).

So at three crucial junctures—in Damascus, Jerusalem, and Antioch—when Paul needed favor, God provided it through key friends. Before their intervention Paul was encircled by a frustrating wall of impossibility. Afterward he was surrounded by a protecting shield of favor. Got a "Saul of Tarsus" problem?

Has adversity or persecution caused you to be distrusted, demonized, or deserted? Instead of favor, do you find frustration in your church, ministry, or mission field—though God expressly led you there? Are opportunities denied you due to your past reputation, though now, like Paul, your character is thoroughly changed? Though the Good Shepherd personally blesses and helps you daily, do some of His sheep still fear you're a wolf and doubt your conversion or ministry? Or are you being rejected in your workplace, neighborhood, or city for other reasons: your faith, race, gender, nationality, education, poverty, religious background, political convictions, divorce, or just because you're a newcomer? Don't be dismayed by the wall of disadvantages encircling you.

Instead, remember Paul! Faithfully abide in Christ, pursue your work, and pray for Christ's help, as Paul did in Damascus. God hasn't changed. He's still able to replace your wall of frustration with a shield of favor: "For surely, O LORD, you bless the righteous; you surround them with your favor as with a shield" (Ps. 5:12, NIV). In faith thank Him for your "Ananias" and "Barnabas"—and that Paul's situation was far worse than yours! And look up.

Things aren't nearly as bad as you think. You just need a friend.

Chapter 101

PRAYING UNTIL...

S UDDENLY KING HEROD Agrippa executed the apostle James! A
few days later he arrested Peter and held him for execution! To
the Christians in Jerusalem, things looked grim—Satan was at-
tacking and Jesus sleeping (Acts 12:1–4).

But just as suddenly the believers rose to the challenge, fighting back
with their most powerful weapon: persistent prayer! "But prayer was made
without ceasing by the church unto God for him" (v. 5). No average prayer
meeting, this was a prayer mission! These Christians committed themselves
to *pray until*... That is, they didn't know when, where, or how God would
respond, but they knew He would. So they resolved to keep praying, with
faith and thanksgiving, until He did so. Why were they so confident?

They knew their God and His will in the matter. Their teaching and
experiences convinced them that "God is faithful" (1 Cor. 10:13), or utterly
reliable, and always ultimately does whatever He prophesies, promises, or
threatens. They were also confident that He never denies petitions aligned
with His will. John wrote, "This is the confidence that we have in him, that,
if we ask anything according to his will, he heareth us; and if we know that
he heareth us, whatever we ask, we know that we have the petitions that we
desired of him" (1 John 5:14–15).

More specifically, they knew Peter's release was not just theirs but also
God's will. God's calling, prophecy, and correction convinced them.

Jesus had called Peter to "feed my sheep" (John 21:15–17), so it wasn't
His will to remove Peter from shepherding. Jesus also prophesied Peter
would "stretch forth his hands" as a martyr when he was "old": "When
thou shalt be old, thou shalt stretch forth thy hands, and another shall gird
thee, and carry thee whither thou wouldest not" (v. 18). Since Peter was still
young, it couldn't be his time to die. Finally, after the church committed itself to prayer, the Spirit didn't check them. If He didn't want Peter released,
He would have spoken "a word" of correction, as Isaiah taught: "Thine ears
shall hear a word behind thee, saying, This is the way, walk ye in it, when ye
turn [away from God's will] to the right hand, and...to the left" (Isa. 30:21).

Therefore they prayed "without ceasing" or doubting—and God answered without delay (Acts 12:7–12).

Bible and church history reveal the extraordinary power of unwavering believing prayer.

The Bible says the Shunammite kept seeking Elisha's help until it was well with her son. The Syrophoenician woman kept asking Jesus' help until He delivered her daughter. Elijah prayed for rain until a great rain fell in Israel. Jesus prayed for a blind man from Bethsaida until his vision became perfectly clear. Daniel prayed for a revelation of God's end-time plan for Israel until he received it. The 120 in the Upper Room prayed in unity until Jesus, as promised, poured out the Spirit. Cornelius "prayed to God alway[s]," and apparently also asked Him if Jesus was the Savior, until God sent Peter with the answer (Acts 10:2).

Church history adds that in the Third Great Awakening (1857–1859) laymen all over America, especially in larger northeastern cities, began meeting for prayer and testimony daily—and didn't stop praying until the Spirit visited the nation, saving an estimated one million souls.[1] In England George Mueller prayed daily for his orphanages' and ministries' many needs—and never stopped until help arrived, sometimes at the last possible moment.

All these prayed persistently because, like the Jerusalem church, they knew God and His will in the issues before them.

Do we know how utterly faithful God is to His promises? Do we know His will in our current problems? Then it's our duty to pray unwaveringly until Jesus:

- Helps our troubled child
- Releases our neighbor from addiction
- Saves our relative or coworker
- Visits and grows our church
- Empowers and increases our ministry
- Establishes our mission
- Heals a sick friend
- Awakens a backslider
- Softens and convicts a hardened enemy
- Provides employment or housing
- Guides us through a perplexing dilemma

- Gives our ministers timely messages and counsels

To some Christians this "I will not be denied" praying seems simplistic, foolhardy, or even presumptuous. But wise ones will ponder and practice this secret of spiritual victory. However long, painful, discouraging, or exhausting their tests, they'll keep praying in faith—until their "Peters" are free!

More "acts" always follow. Angels intervene, miracles happen, breakthroughs occur, divine fear falls, rejoicing erupts, and, chiefly, God is honored! Are you "praying always...in the Spirit...with all perseverance...for all saints" (Eph. 6:18)? Why not?

Today start praying until...

Chapter 102

BE CHRISTIAN OR DIE!

E CHRISTIAN OR die!" was Norwegian King Olaf's hasty demand as he began forcing Norway's pagan tribes to turn from Thor to Christ.[1] An experienced warrior, physically imposing, and zealous, Olaf and his Viking "gospel" were hard to resist. Few did and lived to tell it.

Olaf's sincere but misguided way of spreading the faith was typical of the Medieval Age's coercive kings—Christian monarchs who felt it their duty to enlarge Christendom by conquering pagans and forcing their conversions to Christianity. Olaf's successor continued this practice, as did other European rulers before and after, including Frankish King Charlemagne and Vladimir of Kiev. Even the medieval church used coercion.

The church's infamous Inquisition tortured thousands of alleged heretics to wrest confessions (and possessions) from them, reclaim their souls, and prevent their errors from spreading. The church also launched its ill-conceived Crusades to reclaim the Holy Land from the unholy Muslims, all in the name of the Prince of Peace, who told His first militant follower *not* to wage holy war—"Put up thy sword into the sheath" (John 18:11)—and touchingly healed the man he had just injured. Perhaps many reasoned the Muslims deserved it. A few centuries earlier Muhammad's successors (caliphs) led Muslims on a series of military campaigns stretching from Palestine through North Africa to Spain, by their actions crying, "Be Muslim or die!" Sadly, Christ's people followed the caliphs' practices, forgetting that Christ insisted one "must" be "born again" by not sword but Spirit (John 3:3–8). The Crusaders' coerced conversions were superficial, not saving, and proved they didn't know the Prince they professed. Or did they?

There's a rich spiritual truth hidden deep in Olaf's shallow watchword. Ever since Christ died for our sins, His Spirit has been crying, "Be Christian or die!" Let me explain.

To truly "be Christian" is to be spiritually reborn by faith in Christ's sacrificial death and His Spirit's regenerating touch. Such genuine converts will never perish but live forever with Christ (John 3:16). But let's go deeper.

The word *Christian* means literally "Christ's loyalists," or "Christ's

271

men"[2]; or, followers of Christ. This implies that after conversion believers should follow Christ's teachings and ways with loving loyalty. Biblically, "or die" implies:

1. Physical expiration (a lifeless body)

2. Spiritual death (a lifeless soul)

3. Second death (eternal separation from God)

These definitions illuminate Olaf's dark dictum.

All the unsaved will one day expire. If they don't receive Jesus in life, they'll subsequently die a "second death"—eternal separation from God in a hellish place called "the lake of fire" (Rev. 20:15). Jesus asserted He was the only way to escape this and enjoy eternal life with the Father: "I am the way, the truth, and the life: no man cometh unto the Father, but by me" (John 14:6). His apostle John insisted no one who rejects Jesus' Saviorship will receive the Father's salvation: "Whosoever denieth the Son, the same hath not the Father" (1 John 2:23). The apostle Peter also proclaimed Jesus' exclusive Saviorship: "Neither is there salvation in any other; for there is no other name under heaven given among men, whereby we must be saved" (Acts 4:12). Clearly Christ and His apostles believed everyone will be Christian or die—the second death. But there's more.

Born-again Christians also live by this rugged mantra. In every issue or decision that tests us daily, we'll either be "Christians"—Christ's loyalists, obedient to His Word, correction, guidance, and call—or "die." That is, if disloyal, we'll bring spiritual death upon ourselves. Disobedience immediately weakens or deadens the Holy Spirit's influence in our hearts. His anointings cease, grace diminishes, and His voice becomes quieter. Prayer becomes empty. Bible study grows dull. Praise and worship are lifeless. Church meetings become meaningless. Christ's sweet touches diminish. Our strength and peace wane. Our fellowship with Christian friends no longer edifies. Our love for others cools and ministry to them slows—then stops. Our faith falters and outlook grows hopeless and cynical. Why is this?

Like a body deprived of nourishment, our soul-branch is cut off from the Christ-Vine. We're drying, failing, dying. Our relationship with Christ remains, but our fellowship connection—wondrous, loving, invigorating communion and communication with Him—is expiring. If we don't revive it by confessing our sins and repenting, we'll become like the Sardis

Christians, who, though saved, had grown "dead" to their Savior (Rev. 3:1). So we too die if we're not loyal to Jesus. Prepare to be shocked.

Wrong as he was, Olaf got it right. His crude Norse ultimatum is still true. We all, pagans and believers, will, "Be Christian or die!"

Chapter 103

HE GIVES LIGHT IN PRISONS

*W*E KNOW WELL the gospel of Acts 12—how Herod jailed Peter but the church prayed and God miraculously released him. But something else very significant occurred. "A light shined in the prison" (v. 7, KJV). Note this divine illumination occurred not after but "in" Peter's prison experience. At the time prisons had little or no light. So when Herod's dark prison suddenly filled with light, it was most extraordinary—but not unique. God does the same for us.

No matter what kind of "prison" we're in, God's "light" will find its way there if we'll humble ourselves, trust and obey God, and pray for light.

Ours may be a literal prison. With or without cause we may be incarcerated in a federal, state, or local detention center. Or ours may be a figurative prison, such as:

- Lengthy, seemingly endless tests of faith and patience
- Hard employments with oppressively unfair or indifferent superiors
- Long unemployment with few or no job prospects
- Oppressive nations whose laws severely limit our rights and activities
- Difficult marriages yoking us to troubled or hateful spouses
- Chronic illnesses or disabilities limiting our mobility and quality of life
- Wearying duties in which love or loyalty binds us to help sick or troubled ones
- Rough neighborhoods riddled with drugs, gangs, and violence
- Financial constraints caused by reduced income or increased expenses
- Judicial restraints, awards, or other unfair and oppressive rulings

In these dark life-prisons, like Peter, we need light. Figuratively, *light* means many things.

Light is truth, or the true knowledge of God that dispels the darkness of ignorance of or misinformation about Him. The apostle Paul ministered light in Athens: "Whom...ye ignorantly worship, him declare I unto you" (Acts 17:23). Light is the correct interpretation and application of the Bible, dispelling the darkness of erroneous biblical teaching or misapplication of biblical principles: "The entrance of thy words [rightly interpreted and applied] giveth light" (Ps. 119:130). Light is faith, confidence in the Bible's Author and assertions, dispelling the darkness of doubt and unbelief. Light is insight, dispelling the darkness of perplexing circumstances or issues. Light is divine guidance, dispelling the darkness of not knowing the right way. Light is divine prophecy, dispelling the darkness of fearful uncertainty of the future. Light is hope, or bright new prospects, dispelling the oppressive darkness of despair. Need light?

Biblical promises assure us God will give us light in our dark prisons: "Unto the upright there ariseth light in the darkness" (Ps. 112:4). And biblical history shows Him doing so.

For example, the Lord gave Paul the light of prophecy while he was detained in Jerusalem's jail (Acts 23:11). He gave him the light of hope when he was detained for "many days" on board a ship helplessly adrift in a fierce hurricane (Acts 27:23–24). He gave him the light of guidance when he was forced to wait for God's directions at Troas (Acts 16:6–10). He gave Elijah the light of guidance as he sat, unhelped yet obedient, in the dark confinement of uncertainty by the brook Cherith. He gave the apostle John the brightest prophetic light—the Book of Revelation—as he endured his darkest prison, Patmos, while still in fellowship with the Light.

Centuries later God gave Martin Luther the light of insight for translating the New Testament into German during his nine-month confinement in Wartburg Castle.[1] He gave William Tyndale similar intellectual light to translate the Bible into English while living secretly in Antwerp, Belgium. These are only a few high-profile recipients of the divine light God has given to countless others. Want to be among them?

What's your discouraging, dark prison? A lengthy test, hard workplace, or prolonged unemployment? An oppressive nation, difficult marriage, or chronic illness or disability? An exhausting duty, financial constraints, or judicial restraints? A rough neighborhood, incarceration, or other limiting, hindering, or oppressive circumstances?

Whatever your prison, Jesus will give you light—true knowledge of Him, sound biblical interpretation, insight, faith, guidance, prophecy, or a timely message of hope. Not later but now. Not outside but in your prison. Not after but before He makes your chains fall off, opens your impassable iron gate, guides you by His angel, and releases you! (See Acts 12:3–10.) What moved God to send Peter light?

Earnest, expectant prayer! So ask the Lord for light. Seek it earnestly in meditative Bible study, teachings and sermons, and godly counsel. Then expect what you've asked—what Peter got and God promises: "Christ shall give thee light" (Eph. 5:14). And don't forget to praise and worship Him!

Aren't you glad He gives light in prisons?

Chapter 104

OBEY YOUR ANGEL!

*A*s THE CHURCH prayed steadily, God acted suddenly, sending an angel to deliver Peter from Herod Agrippa's prison and certain execution (Acts 12:5–12). But the angel didn't act alone.

Peter's full cooperation was required. When the angel ordered Peter in rapid succession to "Gird thyself," "bind on thy sandals," "cast thy garment about thee," and "follow me," Peter immediately complied without question, contention, or delay (v. 8). Luke writes, "So he did...and he went out, and followed him" (vv. 8–9). As Peter obeyed the angel, he went free, in this case by supernatural means. God's mystical power caused Peter's chains to fall off, his two personal guards to remain asleep, two other guards posted outside to not see him, and an impassable iron gate to open—without being touched! Is "Herod" after you?

Thoroughly evil, Herod symbolizes Satan, who ruled his spirit and influenced his actions. If we let sin or selfishness rule our lives, we give Satan the right to harass and oppress us with excessive adversity. If instead we consistently trust and obey God, Satan will try to disrupt our godly walk and work by prompting people to reject, oppose, or persecute us, as Herod did Peter. If in either case we ask God's help, He'll send angels to free us from Satan's harmful control or frustrating hindrance. But liberation won't be automatic. Like Peter, we must obey our angels.

Angels are "ministering spirits" divinely sent to minister to our needs (Heb. 1:14). While they minister in many ways—protecting, teaching, guiding, strengthening—their chief ministry is delivering messages. Angels carry our prayer requests to God and His answers to us (John 1:51). Thus "angel" is taken from the Greek *angelos*, which means "messenger."[1]

These heavenly angels are specially created to be God's personal representatives and couriers. Hebrews says some believers have "entertained angels unawares" (Heb. 13:2), or encountered heavenly angels temporarily assuming human form and mistaken them for ordinary people. We're in danger of a similar misidentification.

There are also figurative "angels"—humans whom God uses to represent or speak for Him. Jesus repeatedly addressed Asia Minor's pastors as "angels" (Rev. 2:1).[2] Since we usually assume all angels have wings and halos and suddenly appear and disappear, we easily overlook the human kind—pastors, teachers, and elders. We may interact with our human angels without realizing that, though neither supernatural nor faultless, they're still God's personally appointed messengers to us. If we recognize God is speaking through them to strengthen, train, purge, and mature us, we'll be inclined to obey them "as to the Lord" (Col. 3:23). If we don't, we may dismiss their heaven-sent counsels casually—as mere human opinions or preferences—or even catastrophically. If Peter had disobeyed his angel, he would have died prematurely!

To save us from sins, selfishness, and early death, God sends us human angels. Moses was Joshua's angel. Mordecai was Esther's angel. The apostle Paul was Timothy's angel. Through his writings Wycliffe was Hus' angel. Calvin was Knox's angel. Not just Joshua but all these "left nothing undone" that their angels taught them (Josh. 11:15). Every mature Christian has wise human angels representing and speaking for Christ in their lives, especially during their early years in Christ. But these Elijahs don't walk with us, their Elishas, forever. When our training is complete, like Peter's angel, they "depart" (Acts 12:10).[3]

Because our angels are divinely selected and sent to us, "ministers...the Lord gave to every man" (1 Cor. 3:5), our attitude and response to them is crucial. If we disobey their biblical counsel, we'll never grow up and escape "Herod's prison"—Satan's oppressive influence in our lives through our sin or selfishness, or his hindering wiles and opposition. If we obey them, we'll go free, and grow freer, until we're "free indeed" (John 8:36). Recognize your angels?

They're the pastors, teachers, elders, and mentors God has placed in your life to teach you His Word and model His ways of living. Will you acknowledge that their messages are bringing His "light," His opportunely expounded and applied Word, into the "prison" of your sin-, self-, or persecution-hindered life?

Like Peter's angel, they're telling you to:

- "Gird thyself [your soul]" with biblical and other studies, and prayer
- "Bind on thy sandals," preparing to walk in good works and personal evangelism (Eph. 2:10; 6:15)

- "Cast thy garment about thee," clothing yourself, as Christ's bride, with "righteous acts" of devotion, obedience, charity, faithfulness, and ministry (Rev. 19:8, NIV)

- "Follow me" in God's ways (spiritual daily life habits), the Spirit's unerring leadings and warnings, and character transformation

Want Peter's freedom? Follow his example. Obey your angel!

Chapter 105

SLEEPING THE SLEEP OF FOLLY?

*I*N SCRIPTURE, SLEEP refers to not only desirable nightly physical restoration but also an undesirable spiritual condition—the "sleep" of folly.[1]

The sleep of folly occurs whenever Christians are in a wrong spiritual or moral condition. Something about us isn't in God's wise and loving order. It may be:

- UNCONFESSED SIN—unacknowledged and unforsaken wrong attitudes, acts, or words

- FOOLISHNESS—unwise decisions or behavior

- NEGLIGENCE—not responding to biblical teaching or correction, or God's prompts or calls

- LACK OF VIGILANCE—failure to watch for our adversary's wiles, works, and temptations

- HOPELESSNESS—discouraging disbelief in God's promises, especially Jesus' return

Jesus prophesied the sleep of folly, in one form or another, would hinder all Christians in these last days: "While the bridegroom tarried, they all [wise and foolish virgins] slumbered and slept" (Matt. 25:5). To understand this figurative sleep, let's consider natural sleep.

When physically asleep, we're temporarily insensible and inactive. Our sensory systems aren't as responsive, our internal activities are slower, and our external activities stop.

More specifically, we're unconscious of reality, or out of touch with actual conditions. We're moved by imaginations, as dreams of unreal events stir real emotional reactions of fear or joy. We're unaware of dangers, as fires or floods may rage around us without our noticing. We're unaware of enemies, as thieves may steal everything but the bed we're sleeping in. We're unaware of our friends, who may be praying for or betraying us without our knowledge. We're unaware of blessings, as food, gifts, or money may be given us without our appreciation or appropriation. We're unaware of time passing, unsure if we're sleeping six or eight hours. We don't notice changes occurring around us, as births, deaths, or significant events may occur, changing our lives. We're silent, not conversing with, witnessing to, or exhorting others.

Additionally, our bodily systems are less active when we're asleep. Our metabolism, heart rate, and respiration slow down and our body temperature cools. And our physical activity virtually ceases. Besides occasionally shifting positions, we're motionless—not walking, working, reading, ministering, or giving.

All these conditions of soul and body that attend natural sleep reappear in a corresponding form when we fall into the sleep of folly.

When spiritually asleep, we stop facing reality, preferring to take a rosy view of the past, present, or future rather than face things as they are. We let imaginations move us, as doubt-filled reasonings, anxious thoughts of tomorrow, and offensive memories stir bitter or paralyzing emotions. We're unaware of spiritual dangers and enemies, as the "thief" (Satan) steals God's Word and peace from us, the "roaring lion" devours our spiritual growth, and the "rulers of darkness" hinder our prayers. We lose sight of our blessings and friends and fail to appreciate or thank God for them. We lose track of the brevity of time and overlook detrimental changes in our habits and spiritual condition. We fail to notice missed opportunities, the urgency of preparing for Jesus' appearing, and wrong trends in our churches. And we become silent, no longer sharing the gospel, teaching God's Word, exhorting others, or praising and worshipping God regularly.

Additionally, our souls' healthful internal activities decrease. Our spiritual metabolisms slow, as we convert our spiritual food—God's Word—into the action of energetic obedience less often. Our heart rates decrease, as God's compassion pulses in us for others less frequently. Our respiration decreases, as we breathe in God's Spirit in prayer, praise, and worship and release the toxins of sin through confession less often. Our temperatures drop, as our core spirit of devotion decreases from fervent to lukewarm to cold. We stop walking, no longer staying close to Jesus through each day as Enoch did when he "walked with God" long ago (Gen. 5:22, 24). We stop working well, no longer lifting up Christ and His teaching by doing "whatever" we do "heartily, as to the Lord" (Col. 3:23). We stop reading wisely, no longer studying biblical passages, teachings, and related subjects regularly to be "approved unto God" (2 Tim. 2:15). We stop ministering kindly, no longer forgiving, assisting, fellowshipping, or interceding. We stop giving generously, forgetting Jesus said it's "more blessed to give than to receive" (Acts 20:35). Spiritual sleep always produces these conditions. We can't afford them!

It's late, Jesus is coming, and God's calling us to "awake" to full spiritual diligence, vigilance, and sensitivity to Him. Not later but now! "Now it is high time to awake out of sleep" (Rom. 13:11). "Awake thou that sleepest" (Eph. 5:14). Are you sleeping the sleep of folly?

Chapter 106

ON THE SIDELINES?

MPRISONED IN CAESAREA, Paul found himself set aside from his beloved missionary travels "two years" (Acts 24:27). How strange that God's most valuable minister should be left on the ecclesiastical sidelines.

In American football, first teamers never want to be on the sidelines during a game. They want to be on the field, rushing, passing, receiving, scoring, blocking, tackling, and making plays! But injuries, sickness, fatigue, ejections, or breaking team rules force them onto the sidelines. There they eagerly watch and wait for a chance to reenter the contest.

While Paul was sidelined in Caesarea, many ministers were carrying the gospel football by evangelizing and teaching God's Word. Some were passing it to new disciples, who then ran with the good news. Others were scoring kingdom touchdowns by planting churches all over the Mediterranean world! But not Paul. He could only watch and wait. How disappointing.

And confounding! Jesus had appeared in Jerusalem to personally promise Paul he was going to Rome (Acts 23:11), yet Paul remained in Caesarea, pending the arrival of his defense witness, Lysias (Acts 24:22). The governor, Felix, knew Paul was innocent but wasn't about to displease his Jewish constituents by releasing him. As the weeks became months, and then years, Paul realized this—and surely wondered why Jesus permitted the lengthy, unfair, and contradictory delay. It made no sense. When Paul should be sailing to Rome, he was sidelined instead in Caesarea. Felix repeatedly summoned Paul to talk, but only hoping for a bribe, never to hear his case or release him (vv. 25–26). Why did God permit a corrupt official to delay His best minister's itinerary two years?

We don't know. But we know it wasn't because Paul was injured, sick, or had broken God's rules. So we're left to guess.

Perhaps these exercises in waiting for God and resisting temptation (to bribery) were meant to refine Paul's patience and character. That would make the wine of his ministry even sweeter. Maybe his imprisonment was a sabbatical. Paul certainly needed an extended rest after years of fruitful but wearying ministry. Maybe Jesus used this quiet period to draw near Paul with new revelations of Himself and His purposes for the church (2 Cor. 12:1). That would certainly be worthwhile. Perhaps He was letting His unjustly detained servant show us how to be cross-bearing overcomers. Doesn't his example inspire us to carry our crosses, as Paul did, with honor and hope? Whatever God's reasons, Paul recognized His loving control and wise timing and acquiesced. He also received the ministry of memory.

He surely recalled how God kept him waiting years to minister in Asia Minor, detouring him through Macedonia and Achaia until His time came (Acts 16–18). When it finally arrived, Paul enjoyed his best season of ministry: three years of prolific evangelism, teaching, and miracles that powerfully impacted the whole region (Acts 19:26–27)! Paul understood God had made him wait only to be more gracious to him and the people of Asia Minor (Isa. 30:18). These memories likely helped him wait, again, for God's time for Rome—and occupy himself well in Caesarea.

There he sought Jesus daily in prayer and study of the Scriptures. Knowing Paul's character, past experience, and teaching, we may assume he offered thanksgiving "in" his unpleasant circumstance (1 Thess. 5:18), praised and worshipped God (Acts 16:25), and submissively chose to be "content," though "abased" (Phil. 4:11–12). He probably stayed busy writing epistles and fellowshipping with local ministers, church leaders, and other Christians he met during his travels.[1] We know he practiced his personal evangelism and debate skills in his many conversations with Felix, thus sharpening his speaking gifts. We may assume he also made a few tents! Thus Paul wisely made the best of a bad situation. Is your situation similar?

Are you an aspiring first teamer in your trade, craft, business, industry, profession, or ministry, yet find yourself sidelined while others in your field are running, passing, and scoring touchdowns? Are you a:

- Caring pastor between churches?
- Skilled but unemployed worker?
- Committed missionary without a sponsoring church?
- Fervent evangelist without any scheduled meetings?
- Gifted teacher without a position?

Paul understands your frustration. So does God. Ask Him why you're sidelined. If you've broken His team rules, repent, patiently obey Him, and prepare to labor another day. If you haven't, accept His sovereign delay and occupy well, remembering He's delaying only to be more gracious to you and others. And have hope: In God's time Paul arrived and thrived in Rome!

You'll arrive and thrive too in God's time. So don't rebel on the sidelines. Excel on the sidelines!

Chapter 107

SEEK CONFIRMATION

HREE YEARS AFTER his conversion Paul visited the Jerusalem church (Acts 9:26–31). But after only fifteen days his visit ended abruptly. Why?

The church's leaders unanimously decided he should leave Jerusalem for Tarsus. This pivotal decision was prompted by two factors: the church's reasoning and its Redeemer.

The apostles and elders noticed Paul was following in Stephen's footsteps, out-debating the Greek-speaking Jews in their synagogues and already evoking assassination plots: "They [the Jews] went about to slay him" (Acts 9:29).[1] If Paul was martyred, it might spark another dreadful "great persecution" like that prompted by Stephen's execution (Acts 8:1). So they reasoned it was best for everyone—Paul and the church—for Paul to depart. But reason alone didn't move Paul.

Sometime during this crisis the Redeemer personally appeared to Paul to inform him that, since the Jews had adamantly rejected his ministry, he should leave Jerusalem. Not eventually but immediately: "Make haste, and get thee quickly out of Jerusalem" (Acts 22:18). Jesus encouragingly revealed Paul would continue ministering, but primarily to Gentiles rather than Jews: "I will send thee far from here unto the Gentiles" (v. 21). Paul relayed Jesus' message to the church leaders. Thus doubly advised by reason and Redeemer, they promptly "sent him forth to Tarsus" (Acts 9:30). Note what followed.

"Then [after Paul's departure] had the churches rest throughout all Judaea...and were edified; and walking in the fear of the Lord, and in the comfort of the Holy Spirit, were multiplied" (v. 31). This verse reveals God showed His approval of their decision by giving them:

1. REST. "Then had the churches rest..." Stress vanished and tranquility visited. They "rested" from the present agitation— threats of more assassinations and persecution—and received and enjoyed renewed peace.

2. EDIFICATION. "And were edified..." Sitting under steady Spirit-inspired Bible teaching, they were "edified"—built up

and recharged in faith, hope, and love. This enhanced their devotion, reenergized their ministries, sweetened their fellowship, and strengthened their unity.

3. INCREASED AWE. "Walking in the fear of the Lord…" They walked forward, or made progress, in the holy, healthy fear of God, growing more aware of God's awesomeness—His unique majesty, immensity, power, and sure promises and threats. This drew them into closer fellowship with Jesus, increasing their experiential knowledge of Him and His wisdom (Prov. 9:10). Closer and wiser, they knew God and respected Him more deeply.

4. SOUL COMFORT. "In the comfort of the Holy Spirit…" The Spirit gave them numerous new, sweet consolations: biblical insights, timely remembrances of God's Word, touches of Christ's presence, spontaneous refillings of the Spirit, answers to prayer, hope-inspiring dreams and prophecies, corrective warnings, and guidance. These reassurances comforted their souls.

5. GROWTH. "…were multiplied." This speaks of increase, or new growth, numerical and spiritual. Numerically they received an influx of new disciples. Spiritually they increased in knowledge of God, enduring faith, spiritual discernment, Christlikeness of character, and awareness of God's purposes. This rich, new "fruit" proved the Jerusalem "branch" was still vitally connected to its "Vine" and "Vinedresser" (John 15:1–8).

These five blessings confirmed that it pleased Christ to send Paul away and that He had indeed so ordered Paul. If He had been displeased, the opposite would likely have happened.

The Lord would have withheld their peace, leaving them with a gnawing sense of unrest (2 Chron. 15:5–6). They would have become unedified—weaker in faith, devotion, ministry, and love, and less unified. Their fear of God would have decreased and they would have begun straying from Christ, His ways, and His righteousness, and thinking lightly about sin and judgment. The "comforts of the Holy Spirit" would have dried up, leaving them without the sweet daily touches, words, insights, refillings, answers to prayer, and other blessings that make a close walk with Jesus so special. And they would have decreased in disciples, churches, knowledge of God, insight into His plan, and Christlikeness of character. Though negative, these unwanted changes in their condition would still have been a confirmation.

They would have proven that the "branches" were disconnected from their "Vine." Somewhere they had departed from His will and needed to examine themselves to discover where, when, and why, and repent. Let's learn from them.

Whenever you make key decisions or changes, God wants to confirm—verify and firmly establish—your decision. If after such changes you experience more soul rest, edification, awareness of God's awesomeness, comforts of the Spirit, and numerical or spiritual increase, be confident you've pleased God, and thank Him for the confirmation! If the opposite occurs, quickly acknowledge you've turned aside—and turn back!

Made changes lately? Was the Redeemer, or just your reasoning, leading? Seek confirmation.

Chapter 108

RAPID RIGHTEOUS REVERSALS

*H*OWEVER DIFFICULT, DRAWN OUT, or discouraging your tests, never lose hope. At any moment God can execute a rapid righteous reversal—quickly and justly turning the tables on your troubles.

Acts 12 illustrates this. By chapter's end the Jerusalem church's situation was the exact opposite of what it was at its beginning. At its beginning the church looked ruined—fallen, silent, and buried in a spiritual death experience symbolized by James' literal death and Peter's scheduled execution. But by chapter's end it was resurrected—walking in newness of life, spreading God's Word, and growing in influence. Note these facts.

In the beginning the church's chief persecutor, Herod Agrippa, was healthy, powerful, and hotly pursuing Christians, "to vex [injure[1]] certain" of them, killing one key leader and imprisoning another (vv. 1–4). By the end Herod was weak, sick, and dying (v. 23), and the Christians were healthy, reenergized by Peter's miraculous deliverance, and growing: "The word of God continued to spread, and there were many new believers" (v. 24, NLT).

At the beginning Herod suddenly arrested Peter and bound him with painful chains for seven days intending to kill him on the eighth (vv. 4, 6). At the end an angel suddenly arrested Herod and bound him with a painful intestinal affliction for five days, after which he died (v. 23).[2]

At the beginning the Christians were hemmed in, praying for Peter's release, and, under threat of arrest, holed up in their quarters (v. 12). At the end they were free and ready to spread salvation throughout the Gentile world (vv. 24–25; cp. Acts 13–14).

At the beginning Herod "stretched forth his hands" (Acts 12:1) to persecute Christians. At the end God, by His angel, stretched forth His hand to judge Herod (v. 23).

At the beginning the Christians were praying steadily for God to rescue Peter and stop Herod (v. 5). At the end many Jews were no doubt praying for Peter's recapture and Herod's rescue.

At the beginning the Christians were stunned by Herod's execution of

289

James and arrest of Peter. At the end they were stunned by God's release of Peter (v. 16).

At the beginning the unbelieving Jews' hopes were high and the Christians' were dashed (vv. 3–4). At the end the Jews' expectations were dashed (v. 11) and the church's high.

At the beginning the church had lost two effective leaders, James and Peter (vv. 2–4). By the end it had gained two new effective leaders, Paul and Barnabas (Acts 12:25–13:2).

At the beginning the church was "vexed" (Acts 12:1) and its Jewish enemies were glad (v. 3). At the end the church was glad (v. 14) and their enemies were vexed.

At the beginning it appeared God had forsaken the church and was favoring Herod and the Jews. At the end it was apparent He had forsaken Herod and the Jews and was favoring the church.

At the beginning it looked like God was impotent and His church vulnerable. At the end God demonstrated He was irresistible and His church undefeatable.

Thus, at the beginning of Acts 12 it looked like the end for the church. But by chapter's end the church was experiencing yet another dynamic new beginning. Why?

The Redeemer executed a rapid righteous reversal. He completely reversed His people's fortunes—their tables were turned. He did so righteously—in perfect fairness, by the just principles and promises of His Word. And He did so rapidly—in just a few weeks at most. It wasn't the first time.

Consider these renowned reversals:

- MORDECAI. As arrogant as he was vengeful, Haman erected a 75-foot impaling pole[3] so everyone in the Persian capital of Susa could witness Mordecai's ghastly execution. But the next day Mordecai was honored in a citywide parade—led by Haman—and the day after, all Susa watched Haman, not Mordecai, die on that stake! (Esther 5:14–7:10).

- JESUS' DISCIPLES. When Jesus ascended, His 120 disciples were still secluded from their emboldened enemies and praying unitedly for "power from on high." Just ten days later, filled with that power, they emerged and boldly transformed Jerusalem (Acts 1:12–2:47).

- PAUL. One morning the church's worst enemy was nearing Damascus hasting to arrest and punish more Christians. By noon *he* was arrested by Christ, converted, and fellowshipping with those very Christians (Acts 9:1–22).

And we could go on.

So when the enemy, like Herod, stretches out his hands to shock, intimidate, hinder, or overwhelm you with trouble, hoping to end your faith, church, mission, or ministry, don't lose hope. Remember how Acts 12 began—and ended! Believe God can quickly turn your troubles, and patiently and confidently ask Him to do so.

Then watch for *your* rapid righteous reversal!

Chapter 109

LORD, OPEN MY EYES!

*W*HEN PAUL ARRIVED in Paphos, a power struggle quickly arose. But not a typical one.

Power struggles usually arise over the top positions. We strive to be president, not vice president; champion, not runner-up. But in Paphos the contest was not to be the top man but to be near him. Let's review the facts.

Before Paul's arrival, a Jewish false prophet and sorcerer named Elymas was "closely associated with" (AMP), or "an attendant of" (NIV), the Roman governor of Cyprus, Sergius Paulus (Acts 13:7). Elymas was likely Sergius' court sorcerer, employed to advise, predict the future, or use magical arts to try to thwart Sergius' adversaries—and his own rivals![1] With access to and influence over Cyprus' top man, Elymas had everything he wanted—an honorable position, financial security, and professional success. Then Paul and his gospel arrived.

Immediately Elymas feared the worst. If Sergius believed Jesus' teachings, his belief in Elymas' counsel would plummet, leaving Elymas without position, honor, and salary. To prevent fear from becoming fact, Elymas went on the offensive. When Sergius called Paul "to hear the word of God" (Acts 13:7), Elymas "withstood" Paul, "seeking to turn away the deputy from the faith" (v. 8).

Just as quickly God launched His counteroffensive, moving Paul to pronounce a stunningly miraculous judgment: "Thou shalt be blind, not seeing the sun for a season" (v. 11). It followed without delay: "Immediately there fell on him a mist and a darkness" (v. 11). Though severe, this intervention was necessary and just. God's punishment showed Sergius Christ's power was superior to Elymas'. He was suddenly and soundly converted: "The deputy [Sergius], when he saw what was done, believed" (v. 12). And Elymas reaped precisely what he sowed.

Elymas tried to keep the governor spiritually blind, unable to see the light of heaven's "Sun of righteousness" (Mal. 4:2). So God blinded Elymas to the light of earth's sun, though, mercifully, only "for a season" (Acts 13:11). Elymas tried to quench Paul's influence with the governor. So God ended his influence. He hoped to ruin Paul's ministry in Paphos. So God spoiled his dark, occult "ministry." Thus the proud magician whose satanic counsel had misled others now "went about" disoriented, humiliated, and blind, "seeking some" to lead him (v. 11). Scripture describes similar power struggles.

Miriam's reproach of Moses' Ethiopian wife probably arose in part from a fear that she would usurp Miriam's influence with Moses (Num. 12:1–3). The apostles' "dispute" over who would be "greatest" in the kingdom (Mark 9:34) was really a contest to be Jesus' greatest assistant. Similar struggles continue.

Christians often contend for power. Elders, deacons, worship leaders, and associate ministers compete for the senior pastor's ear. He in turn may contend with other pastors in his denomination for their bishop's praises. Children frequently contend for their parents' time, attention, and approval. Students race to outperform one another to become the teacher's pet. Employees vie to win the compliments and favors of their managers or business owners. All these undeclared competitions spring from the "Elymas" hidden in our sin nature—the rivalrous ambition of our pride. If we'll walk in Jesus' humility and love, they won't occur.

Rather than seek people's attention and praise, we'll seek God's presence and favor. Instead of trying to unseat others, we'll try to finish our courses. Rather than fight rivals, we'll love and pray for them—and fight the good fight of keeping the faith. Instead of enviously competing with one another, we'll "love one another" (John 13:34). In this kind humility we'll enjoy peaceful unity, fulfill our calling, and please the One who called us—and see Him. Unlike Elymas, we'll discern the "Sun of righteousness" shining daily.

We'll see insights He opens to us from His Word. We'll see His answers to our prayers. We'll see His hand giving us favor, opening doors, blessing our work, and subduing our adversaries. We'll see His guidance warning and directing us. We'll see His viewpoint toward our times, discern His plan, and perceive what He wants us to do. You can have this wonderful vision—or Elymas' woeful blindness.

To see the "Sun of righteousness" daily, remember:

- Elymas' blind, rivalrous ambition lives in our sin natures.
- It may rise at any moment, in us or others, to compete for attention, favor, position, or influence.
- Acts 13 reveals God's judgment is upon it.
- Like Paul, we should deal with it quickly.

So when "Elymas" rises in you, repent, confess, and return to an attitude of humble love. When it rises in others, counsel them and intercede for them to repent.

Meanwhile pray, "Lord, open my eyes!"

Chapter 110

WHOSE HEART ARE YOU AFTER?

GOD DESCRIBED DAVID as a man "after mine own heart," or one *seeking after and conformed to* Him (Acts 13:22).[1] David passionately and persistently pursued God's heart—to perceive, perform, please, produce, and proliferate it. Let's explore this.

Primarily, David was after perceiving God's heart—discovering and understanding His innermost being. David often got alone with God to pray, worship, and meditate in Scripture, all to investigate the core of the Creator. There, with unbroken fascination, he studied God's psyche, what and how He thinks. He researched God's values, what He loves and hates. He explored God's judgments, His decisions on various issues. He prayed to know God's purposes, His goals for His people. He studied God's methods, how God wanted His people to reach His goals. Perceiving these things fully and deeply was David's top priority, so he went after it. This was just the beginning.

David also performed God's heart—converting revealed knowledge into real action. God continues, "[David] Who shall fulfill all my will" (Acts 13:22). David realized knowledge wasn't an end in itself but a guide for action. Once perceived, God's heart must be performed, and fully! David remembered well God's grief over King Saul's incomplete obedience. Determined not to repeat Saul's error, he went after full obedience to God's Word and guidance: "Who shall fulfill *all* my will." Whenever he failed, he quickly confessed his sin, corrected his deficiency, and kept after his goal of performing all God's heart. His motivation?

David's inner driver was his deep desire to please God. God's testimony proves David succeeded. "A man after mine own heart" implies "a man I love" (Acts 13:22, WEY). When God saw David learning and living His heart, His heart went out to this humble soul who was so utterly committed to satisfying Him. Thus David's love stirred God's love and moved Him to go after David's heart—pleasing him with blessings, deliverances, victories, a dynasty, and other tokens of His love. So David reaped what he sowed: David pleased God and God pleased David. He went after God and God went after him. This was productive.

Going after God's heart produced a new heart in David. As David chased God's heart, God changed his heart. The Holy Spirit reproduced, grew, and shaped God's extraordinary heart in David's ordinary soul. Gradually David became transformed. Softened, cleansed, and remolded, his soul became a living earthly model of his heavenly Maker and Master's soul. He became "a man [remade] after [the pattern of] my own heart," or a man whose thoughts, loves, and ways were now like God's. Changed from inside out, David was "conformed to the image of his son" (Rom. 8:29) in being and behavior. Such transformed hearts can't remain barren.

They must proliferate, or reproduce their own kind in other souls. David's heart did this—and still does! To this day David's God-seeking is infectious. It spreads to other souls—by psalms and other biblical readings, testimonies, books, sermons, songs, and word of mouth—and enters and duplicates itself in them. Greatly! God is remaking many Christians today after His own heart because of David's example, and those of other God-pleasers, such as Moses, Samuel, and the apostle John, who was so eager to discover Christ's heart he leaned on His breast (John 13:25)! But some Christians aren't living after God's heart. Why?

They're after something else. Outwardly they practice their devotions, yet inwardly they deify, pursue, and serve their own hearts—self-serving desires and plans. Paul said their god is "their belly [human appetites or desires]" (Phil. 3:19). They're not the first to go after other things.

Long ago Eli's sons pursued their "heart" for illicit pleasures and excessive offerings. The scribes and Pharisees of Jesus' day pursued theirs for men's praises and seats of honor, "For they loved the praise of men more than the praise of God" (John 12:43). Balaam pursued his for the wages and honors of unrighteousness. Demas, Paul's assistant, pursued his for "this present world" (2 Tim. 4:10). Simon pursued his by using any means, even bribery, to try to gain and hold religious influence in Samaria.[2] Will you go after them or David?

David and others like him went after God's heart so passionately that they willingly paid a high price—working hard, suffering rejections, enduring hardships, waiting long—to know and be remade after God's heart. Will you pay a price to be a Christian "after God's own heart"?

If so, seek after God's heart persistently to perceive, perform, please, produce, and proliferate it. Today, whose heart are you after?

296

Chapter 111

PHILADELPHIA CHRISTIANS IN A LAODICEAN ERA

ORE THAN HISTORIC letters, Jesus' messages to the churches of Asia Minor foretell the path of church history and describe types of Christians present in every generation (Rev. 2–3).

Prophetically, Philadelphia's church represents Christianity in revival, covering roughly the period from the Great Awakenings to the early twentieth century (Rev. 3:7–13). The Laodicean church previews Christianity falling into lukewarmness and apostasy, from approximately the mid-twentieth century forward (vv. 14–22).

Symbolically, "Philadelphia" (revived) and "Laodicean" (lukewarm, apostate) Christians have existed throughout the Church Age. Today we're living in the Laodicean era, when spiritual and moral compromise and materialism typical of the ancient Laodiceans control many believers. But we don't have to be Laodicean. We can be Philadelphia Christians in this Laodicean period. Let's learn how.

Philadelphia means "brotherly love"[1] and refers to the exceptional brotherly loyalty the city's founder Attalus II showed for his brother Eumenes.[2] This suggests that Philadelphia's church was built on brotherly love—Christlike compassionate care for one another—in obedience to Christ's prime command (John 13:34–35). The "bond of perfectness," love matured and united them (Col. 3:14).

Jesus commended their obedience to His teaching: "Thou hast…kept my word" (Rev. 3:8). They were apparently humble, self-examining "doers of the Word," not self-righteous, spiritually negligent "hearers only" (James 1:22). In every trying circumstance, they diligently sought and obeyed Christ's appropriate teachings. And they "held" them "fast" by further studies, reflection, prayer, and vigilance (Rev. 3:11).

Loyal, they remained true to Christ's "name"—divine identity and character.[3] They steadfastly confessed Jesus alone is Lord and Savior and His character-reflecting teachings are absolute truth, while other churches swayed, changing their confessions with the winds of every new Caesar, philosopher, prophet, or heretic.

Notably they received no criticism from Jesus. Since all Christians then and now need correction, this implies they had already received Jesus' corrective counsels. No needed improvements were currently outstanding.

Pleased, Jesus gave them an "open door" (v. 8)—divinely arranged and blessed opportunities to grow His spiritual kingdom by sharing His inspired words and compassionate works. And these ministry calls and channels were secure: "No man can shut it."

Yet they faced strong opposition, gospel-rejecting Jewish persecutors whom Jesus called, "The synagogue of Satan" (v. 9). Wherever God's people are in revival, Satan's children are in resistance. The Philadelphians' Jewish adversaries apparently:

- Slandered them relentlessly, claiming God didn't "love" them and Jesus' Messiahship was a "lie" (v. 9)
- Tried to "shut" their open doors, though unsuccessfully (vv. 7–8)
- Continued stubbornly resisting the Christians (v. 10)

But as the Philadelphians overcame, Christ used this strong opposition to make them even stronger and more determined than their enemies!

They developed enduring faith. Jesus said, "Thou hast kept the word of my patience" (Rev. 3:10), or "my command to endure patiently" (NIV). When they apparently requested a quick deliverance from their fiery tests, Jesus ordered them instead to wait and endure. Humbly, they complied. Though trial-weary, with only "a little strength [remaining]" (v. 8), they nevertheless learned to renew their strength in God's presence and Word daily. As they endured in His unfailing power, they obtained "gold tried in the fire"—the priceless faith and knowledge of God purified in fiery tests that Jesus challenged the Laodiceans to buy (v. 18).

This assured victory and vindication. Jesus promised to convert their enemies and bring them, humbled, under their leadership: "I will make them to come and worship before thy feet [under your leadership]" (v. 9).

He also gave them tribulation security, vowing to keep them "from" the tribulation period: "I also will keep thee from the hour of temptation, which shall come upon all the world, to try them" (v. 10). Why? They had already had their tribulation and needed no further testing.

They were now master "overcomers" who trusted, obeyed, and endured so consistently that they rose above every challenge and challenger.

Jesus promised to make them pillars in His temple (v. 12), a figurative description of stable leaders in the church (Gal. 2:9).

Finally, they received the ultimate honor. Jesus promised to inscribe His, His Father's, and New Jerusalem's "name" (monogram) upon them. This signified the divine character, or the Trinity's family likeness, was fully integrated into their characters and New Jerusalem was indeed their proper eternal home. These were the Philadelphians. Now that you know them, follow them!

Walk in brotherly love. Obey God's Word. Loyally hold Jesus' lordship and teachings. Receive His correction. Patiently endure your present tribulation, buy God's "gold," and overcome. As you follow the Philadelphians, expect their blessings—open doors, victory, vindication, tribulation security, leadership, and honors.

All this awaits Philadelphia Christians in a Laodicean era.

Chapter 112

BLESS HIM BY NIGHT

*P*SALM 134 IS a very short psalm with a very tall order: "Bless ye the Lord…by night" (v. 1). Some Christians won't comply.

Others will. After being saved, they willingly become God's "servants" (v. 1). Rather than let sin, selfishness, or people control them, they consistently choose to serve the Father's pleasure—as His greatest Servant did "always" (John 8:29). They "stand" (Ps. 134:1), firmly fixed in God's ways—devotion, faith, love, holiness, faithfulness, intercession—while others fall or compromise. Their spiritual stance is in God's "house" (v. 1), where His presence and people are. They seek God's presence daily and gather, learn, and pray with His people regularly. In these private and public "sanctuaries," they "lift up" their hands (v. 2), worshipping their caring Father freely in full surrender and readiness to receive instruction, comfort, guidance, and provisions from Him. There they grow spiritually mature, as they learn to consistently "bless the LORD" (v. 2).

To "bless" God is to *give Him joy*. We do this by thanking, praising, or honoring Him with expressions, statements, or songs of adoration. We also do so by living right—in obedience, humility, diligence, charity, service, and patient suffering—because godliness pleases Him. Psalm 134, however, specifically requests visible and audible expressions of worship: "Lift up your hands…bless the LORD." When?

"By night" (v. 1). At nighttime the sun and its work and blessings are temporarily hidden, while darkness prevails. In spiritual night Jesus, the "Sun of righteousness" (Mal. 4:2), temporarily hides His works and blessings. The result is a strange, difficult, discouraging time, in which the "rulers of the darkness of this world" (Eph. 6:12) have their way, causing injustice, falsehood, and deception to thrive. The "triumphing of the wicked" (Job 20:5) progresses, and the cause of the righteous regresses. Why? It's the "hour, and the power of darkness" (Luke 22:53) and "no man can work" (John 9:4)—for now. God intentionally permits this dark season to test and grow our faith, patience, and loyalty to Him and train us to live by His Word, not appearances, at all times.

Nighttime falls in our lives when God permits the "Sun's" blessings to fade away and ominous adversities to cover us. We're misunderstood, slandered, and misjudged. Our rights, property, or respect is stripped away. Family members turn on us or walk away. Christian friends betray us. Our church splits. Our resources run dry. Illness overshadows us or loved ones. All our hard work produces little results. Everything we've believed in and prayed for appears defeated, finished—and God does nothing! While we remain undelivered, unhelped, and grieving, the night goes on. Yet, graciously, God doesn't withdraw our best blessing: His presence and voice. He faithfully draws near to manifest His nearness and speak to our hearts every time we draw near Him and His Word in the "night seasons" (Ps. 16:7). And He hopes we won't deny Him His best blessing.

That sweet joy is our lips continuing to bless Him, even in our night of sorrow: "By night...lift up your hands...and bless the LORD" (Ps. 134:2). This costly sacrifice of praise requires that we:

- Give God complete surrender
- Abandon our desires and rights, till God intervenes
- Accept God's right to test us
- Resolve to not let the night defeat us

Will God respond?

Absolutely! "The LORD...[shall] bless thee" (v. 3). As we bless God, He will lavish upon us the "treasures of darkness" (Isa. 45:3)—valuable insights from His Word, priceless proofs of His promises, wealthy revelations of His plan, enriching manifestations of His presence, gems of wisdom, and crystal-clear visions of "things to come" (John 16:13). Not everyone complies and receives these treasures. But Jesus and Jehoshaphat did.

John tells us Judas went out to betray Jesus, and then adds, "And it was night" (John 13:30). That nightfall was natural and spiritual. In its awful, thick darkness Jesus blessed His Father by singing a "hymn" with His disciples (Matt. 26:30–31). When the nighttime of a terrifying national invasion covered Judah, King Jehoshaphat ordered his people to bless the Lord: "Praise the LORD...with a loud voice" (2 Chron. 20:20–22). You can follow their example.

Are you God's servant? Standing faithfully in His house? Yet has spiritual night fallen in your life? When day returns, with its bright answers to prayer and signs of the "Sun's" work and favor, it will be too late to obey

Psalm 134. Your present nighttime is a great opportunity—a short season to comply with God's tall order. Finish maturing your faith and character.

Lift up your hands, and bless Him by night.

Chapter 113

SHAKE OFF THAT DUST!

*A*FTER BEING EXPELLED from Antioch of Pisidia by the disbelieving Jews, Paul and Barnabas "shook off the dust of their feet against them" and departed (Acts 13:51). What did this gesture mean?

One commentator notes, "Often Jews would shake the dust off their feet when leaving a Gentile town on the way back to their own land. This symbolized cleansing themselves from the contamination of those who did not worship God. For Paul and Barnabas to do this to Jews demonstrated that Jews who rejected the Good News were not truly part of Israel and were no better than pagans."[1]

Truly, many Jews in Antioch of Pisidia had fully heard, fully pondered, and now, fully rejected the gospel of God's grace (Acts 13:14–43). So as the apostles left, they shook off Antioch's dust from their sandals for two reasons. First, they were obeying Christ's command (Luke 10:11). Second, their actions were:

- A SIGN OF GOD'S REJECTION. God the Holy Spirit, who sent and inspired the apostles (Acts 13:2, 4), now rejects those who have "insulted and disdained" His offer of grace (Heb. 10:29, NLT).

- A TESTIMONY. The hallowed dust of Christ's kingdom now rested on Antioch's Christ-rejecters. At their judgment it will be an exhibit against them testifying that, truly, the King's messengers came near offering life, but they refused. (See Mark 6:11; Luke 10:11.)

- A DISCLAIMER. This dust will also be an exhibit at Paul's and Barnabas' judgments, proving that, indeed, they discharged their duty to evangelize the Pisidians and are no longer responsible for their souls.

This dusty process continues.

Every generation God faithfully sends messengers to present His gracious gospel to nations, cities, and dead churches. If after sufficient time

His messengers' offer is stubbornly rejected, He prompts them to move on: "When they persecute you in this city, flee into another" (Matt. 10:23). By doing so, they, like Paul, "shake off the dust of their feet against them." Nothing further can be done for now to convert these Christ-rejecting societies and groups, though individuals may still come to Christ, as a blind man did in Bethsaida when it too had rejected Jesus (Mark 8:22–26).

At the judgment this dust will rest on and testify against all who've rejected Jesus. But not them alone. It will also rest on kingdom messengers—Christians—if we refuse to share God's truth, when so led, or receive it. Are you dusty?

Got the dust of neglected evangelism? Have you feared or refused to share the gospel when an unbeliever has shown interest in Christ, His way, or His Word? Shake it off by sharing God's redeeming love and inviting them to repent and receive Jesus.

Got the dust of neglected exhortation? Have you avoided speaking out to try to restore a Christian who you've noticed is slipping back into apathy or sin? Shake it off by faithfully "exhort[ing]" them "daily" with heartfelt warnings and encouragements so sin won't "harden" them (Heb. 3:13).

Got the dust of rejected counsel? Has God sent someone to speak His loving correction, warning, or encouragement to you, yet you've stubbornly rejected it? Shake it off by humbly obeying the counsel.

Got the dust of undue condemnation? Have you faithfully evangelized or exhorted someone with God's Word, only to see them faithlessly reject it and walk away? Has their life taken a turn for the worse? Do you find yourself feeling responsible for their condition, though you know you've told them "all the counsel of God" (Acts 20:27)? Shake off this undeserved guilt by remembering and confessing that they, not you, are responsible. You didn't refuse to help; they refused help!

Satan tried to put this depressing dust on the prophet Elijah through the words of King Ahab. When Ahab, whose promotion of Baal worship throughout Israel caused a devastating drought, asked Elijah, "Art thou he who troubleth Israel?" Elijah immediately shook off the false accusation (1 Kings 18:17). He answered, "I have not troubled Israel; but thou, and thy father's house, in that ye have…followed Baalim" (v. 18). Thus the truth, recalled and repeated aloud, set Elijah free from the unjust condemnation the accuser of the brethren cast upon him. It's time for spiritual spring cleaning.

Spiritual dust-busting begins with prayer and honest self-examination. If you know individuals, churches, cities, or nations that are covered with the dust of rejecting Jesus or His truth, pray that God in His mercy may yet give them repentance. If upon reflection you realize you are dusty with neglected evangelism or exhortation, rejected counsel, undue condemnation, or any other negligence, don't wait. Act now.

Shake off that dust!

Chapter 114

MISTAKEN, MESMERIZING,
MADDENING MATERIALISM

*P*ROPHETICALLY, JESUS' MESSAGE to the Laodicean Christians addresses Christians in this final period of the Church Age (Rev. 3:14–22).

Historic Laodicea was a crossroads city in Asia Minor that, due to its thriving textile, medical, and banking industries,[1] became very wealthy—so much that when an earthquake leveled the city in AD 60, the Laodiceans refused Nero's aid and financed their city's reconstruction themselves. Good for them! But all the wealth the Laodicean Christians possessed eventually possessed them. Not good for them! Their words betray a deadly disease.

Jesus said they boasted, "I am rich, and increased with goods, and have need of nothing" (Rev. 3:17). These words confirm these twice-born people suffered from once-born thinking and values. Instead of serving God's will, they served theirs. They were "lukewarm," or uncommitted to and easily swayed from the absolute spiritual and moral truths of God's Word (v. 16). In their pursuit of gain, they lost interest in trusting God for their needs; they wanted fortunes, not faith. Consumers first and Christians second, they consistently put their financial business before the Father's business. Rather than living "by every word" of God, they lived by every increase in wealth. Instead of seeking God's presence daily, they sought more property. Soon they valued their estates more than God's kingdom. Their decisions were money-made not Messiah-led. If God's guidance risked diminishing their income or wealth, they spurned it to spare their mammon. Deceived by their denarii, they mistook their net worth for their spiritual worth.

Jesus' inspired diagnosis exposed their self-deception: "[Thou] knowest not that thou are wretched, and miserable, and poor, and blind, and naked" (Rev. 3:17). His opinion was precisely the opposite of theirs. They thought they were just fine; rich, increasing, and needing "nothing," thank you (v. 17)! Their smugly blind contentment with monies and material things proved their hearts were spiritually desolate and seriously ill. But the Healer persisted.

Like a modern CAT scan, His penetrating discernment revealed materialism's harmful effects. The Laodiceans were mistaken, or incorrect in

306

their view of what they were like and needed; mesmerized, or entranced by greedy consumerism; and spiritually maddened, or out of touch with biblically sound thinking. Their malady—materialism—is ageless.

It's alive and well today and ruling far too many Christians. Embedded in our old nature, materialism afflicts Christians in all socioeconomic groups. Why is it mistaken?

Materialism ignores seven vital Christ-facts:

1. JESUS' TEACHING. Jesus expressly taught us not to "treasure" or "lay up" worldly wealth to trust in, but rather, once saved by grace, to stockpile good works that will bring heavenly rewards (Matt. 6:19–21). If we disobey our Messiah, "mammon" is our god (v. 24).[2]

2. JESUS' WARNING AND PROVERB. Jesus solemnly warned us to watch for greed arising in our hearts: "Take heed, and beware of covetousness" (Luke 12:15). He also spoke a proverb declaring abundant wealth is not abundant life: "A man's life consisteth not in the abundance of the things which he possesseth" (v. 15).[3]

3. JESUS' PARABLE. His following parable shows how foolish it is to seek rich gains and goods instead of a rich relationship to God (vv. 16–21).

4. JESUS' LIFESTYLE. Jesus was void of materialistic ambition, owning neither lands, houses, nor even "where to lay his head" (Luke 9:58). If materialism is success, He was a miserable failure.

5. JESUS' MESSENGERS. Jesus prompted His apostle to tell us that desiring riches is a destructive trap (1 Tim. 6:9); also, that not possessing but loving money is a great taproot nourishing "all kinds of evil" in us (v. 10, NIV).

6. JESUS' SUCCESSORS. After Jesus' ascension, the apostles took up leading and feeding His sheep with merciful, not materialistic, motives: "Silver and gold have I none, but, such as I have, give I thee" (Acts 3:6).[4]

7. JESUS' CORRECTIVE CHALLENGE. Jesus challenged the Laodiceans to switch from "buying" natural to spiritual

"gold"—faith in and knowledge of God that's proven, purified, and priceless—so they would be eternally "rich" (Rev. 3:18).

After the Laodiceans yielded to materialism, it mesmerized, maddened, and mastered them. Eventually their consumerism consumed their Christianity. Christ's corrective challenge, however, proves there was still hope for them. And there's hope for us.

This side of the industrial revolution, materialism is more alluring than ever. But it's still a deadly malady and deceitful idol. Are you merely using money and material things or trusting in them? Living on or for them? Spiritually or financially motivated? If you ponder, learn, and practice the Christ-facts above, you'll master materialism—and be liberated to serve your true Master!

Today's the day to be free from mistaken, mesmerizing, maddening materialism.

Chapter 115

MARVELOUS MUNICIPAL MIRACLES MANIFESTING

C AN YOU IMAGINE an entire city panting for God's Word? It's happened before and will happen again! Luke described one of these marvelous municipal miracles.

When Paul first preached in the synagogue of Antioch of Pisidia, Jews and proselytes urgently asked him to teach more of God's Word: "The Gentiles begged that these words might be preached to them the next Sabbath" (Acts 13:42, NKJV). After a week of growing public interest, stunningly, nearly all Antioch attended Paul's Bible teaching: "Almost the whole city [came] together to hear the word" (v. 44). Instead of mockingly dismissing God's Word, as the Athenians later did (Acts 17:32), the Antiochians joyfully received it: "When the Gentiles heard this, they were glad" (Acts 13:48). They also honored God's Word, thinking and speaking of it with highest admiration: "When the Gentiles heard...they glorified [honored] the word of the Lord" (v. 48). Then the gospel took off, spreading through the region like a rushing river: "The word of the Lord was published throughout all the region [Galatia]" (v. 49). Thus this city hungered for, heard, honored, and heralded God's Word.

Again, note the Antiochians' focus. They came not to discover how to get rich, become popular, or generate miracles. They didn't rush in to meet gladiators, magicians, actors, singers, or oracles. They weren't interested in philosophy or politics. No, only one thing drew them. They wanted "to hear the Word of God" proclaimed, explained, and applied.

This was a marvelous municipal miracle manifesting—unmistakable evidence that God was working wondrously in a city. Why? Only God's Spirit creates interest in God's Word. All other religious or worldly spirits promote other interests. Anything but Scripture! The other attractions noted above appeal to our natural worldly interests, but Word-hunger is unique. It's spiritual, or created in us by the Holy Spirit!

When drawing sinners, the Spirit makes them curious about Jesus and the Bible. Once converted, they have a new, insatiable love for God's Word. They can't get enough of it. Suddenly God's Book becomes their spiritual food and drink (Luke 4:4), comfort in affliction (Ps. 119:50), joy (Jer. 15:16), peace-giving meditation (Ps. 1:2), guiding light (Ps. 119:105), inner strength (v. 28), reviving inspiration (v. 154), soul honey (Ps. 19:10), sustaining hope (Ps. 119:81), portrait of Jesus (the Gospels), "right" standard (Ps. 119:172), corrective counsel (vv. 9, 67), true riches (Prov. 8:19), and voice of the Lord. Antioch was not the first city engrossed with the Word.

Twice Jerusalem was similarly gripped. The apostles' Bible teaching "filled" the Jewish capital (Acts 5:28). Earlier, during the post-exile period, thousands gathered in Jerusalem's streets for an all-day Bible teaching led by Ezra the scribe. From "the morning until midday" their purpose was one: to be "attentive unto the book of the law...to understand the law...to understand the reading" (Neh. 8:3, 7–8). Afterward they went home rejoicing, "because they had understood the words" Ezra exposited (v. 12). Other municipalities also craved God's Word.

Ephesus was filled with interest in "the word of the Lord Jesus" during Paul's extended teaching ministry there (Acts 19:9–10). The Word also captivated Corinth, where Paul "continued...a year and six months, teaching the word of God" (Acts 18:9–11).

Today we're so distracted with worldly controversies and interests, it's remarkable when even one *church* becomes caught up with God's Word, much less a whole city! But God will again engross whole cities with Bible exposition. While you're thinking this can't happen in modern times, let me remind you, it has!

During Charles G. Finney's renowned revivals in Rochester, New York (1830–1831), the Spirit riveted the city's population on Finney's preaching of God's Word. One author notes:

> Such was the power of God on Finney's work that the entire business district often shut down to attend his meetings. Great crowds followed Finney as he preached from church to church.[1]

Similarly inspired citywide Word-fests occurred during many of Billy Graham's remarkable evangelistic crusades, chiefly, in Los Angeles, California (1949), and Seoul, South Korea (1973). What God has done in these cities, He can do in any city. Not by our marketing might or political power, but "by my Spirit" (Zech. 4:6).

When the Spirit visits again, we'll see marvelous municipal miracles manifesting like those seen in Antioch, Jerusalem, Rochester, Los Angeles, and Seoul. Masses will gather in arenas, stadiums, amphitheaters, or open fields, gripped by one powerful hunger—to hear God's Word taught and preached! Which cities? How many? In what regions, countries, continents? We can't say. Perhaps your city or church will be the next to hunger for, hear, honor, and herald God's Word!

Patiently pray, prepare yourself, and expect to see marvelous municipal miracles manifesting.

Chapter 116

ARE YOU AWAKE TO GOD'S PLAN?

*P*AUL PRAYED FOR the Ephesians, and us, "Be ye not unwise but understanding what the will of the Lord is" (Eph. 5:17). One key part of the will of the Lord is God's plan for the church.

Do we realize God has a plan for His people in this age—a plan of salvation and after salvation? If so, we'll stop trying to conceive plans for His church. God doesn't need our planning, just our recognition and execution of His plan. If we understand and pursue His plan, we're spiritually awake. If not, we're asleep, like the ten virgins, who "all slumbered and slept" (Matt. 25:5). As a slumbering man is temporarily unaware of his responsibilities and not discharging them, so we're unaware of and inattentive to ours. We're ignorant or forgetful of, or distracted from, the heavenly plan we're responsible to study, pray for, and execute on earth.

The New Testament reveals God's plan for His church. Here are some of its essential, nonnegotiable points. The will of the Lord is to:

- SANCTIFY AND UNIFY US. John 17:17–23 is God's blueprint, the heart of His plan. Jesus prayed we'd be "sanctified," or set apart for His fellowship and use, by learning and obeying His Word. He also requested we'd become perfectly "one," or as lovingly unified with each other as He was with His Father.

- MATURE US. Ephesians 4:11–16 says Christ "gave" the fivefold ministry to "perfect," or spiritually mature, us. Why? So we'll fulfill our personal ministries and build up Christ's entire body in the faith and knowledge of God (v. 13). Mature ministers' steady teaching and counsel produce spiritually mature disciples who discern heretics and deceivers (v. 14) and assert God's truth graciously but uncompromisingly (v. 15).

- DEEPLY PURIFY US. Ephesians 5:25–27 reveals Jesus "gave" Himself to make the church His "glorious[ly]" pure eternal wife, or soul mate. As we receive teaching and correction, and patiently endure tests and crosses, the Holy Spirit removes our "spots" of carnality, "wrinkles" of reliance on human wisdom and ways, and "blemishes" of wrong attitudes or actions.

- CONFORM US. Romans 8:28–29 says God causes "all things" to work together for the "good" of "conform[ing]" us to Christ's character "image." This miraculous inner molding occurs as we react to every situation by trusting, obeying, and praising God—as Jesus did.

- ESTABLISH US. Peter prayed that after sufficient teaching, testing, and suffering, we'd be "established" (1 Pet. 5:10), or fixed in a stable, close walk with Jesus while still in this unstable, Christ-rejecting world.

- ENRICH US. In Revelation 3:18 Jesus urges us to "buy of me gold," or pay the price to gain life's most precious commodity—proven faith in and knowledge of Christ. Since we buy this spiritual wealth "in the fire," fiery trials are part of God's plan. Since we buy it to "be rich," Jesus wants us to become wealthy with spiritual "gold."

- EVACUATE US. After we complete the steps above, Jesus will suddenly appear and take us to live and reign with Him forever (John 14:1–3; 1 Thess. 4:16–18). This evacuation will keep us "from" the world's (and Israel's) final "hour" of testing (Rev. 3:10; Luke 21:36). Why? We'll already be tested.

But this plan won't be completed without a fight. Why?

God's adversary, Satan, has a counterplan: "Resist every part of God's plan!"

Instead of our becoming sanctified and unified, Satan wants us unsanctified, alienated from believers, and joined with sinners. Instead of us being mature and discerning, he wants us childish and gullible. Instead of us being pure in heart and life, he wants us polluted with carnal lusts and un-Christlike attitudes. Instead of us being conformed to Christ's image, he wants us molded to his image—proud, stubborn, envious, covetous, power hungry, vengeful, prejudiced, selfish, etc. Instead of us being established in a close walk with Jesus, he wants us living unstably and far from Christ. Instead of us pursuing spiritual wealth first, he wants us preoccupied with materialism. Instead of us being ready for Jesus' appearing, he wants us unprepared—and left behind. This counterplan will succeed if we: (1) don't know God's plan, (2) forget it, or (3) get distracted or entangled with other causes.

Many admirable good causes—politics, government reform, social work, humanitarianism—may "entangle" and divert us from pursuing God's plan first (2 Tim. 2:4). By focusing on them more than God's plan, we forward Satan's counterplan—and fall asleep spiritually.

Now that you understand what the will of the Lord is, are you passive or pursuing it? Asleep or awake to God's plan?

Chapter 117

HE HASN'T GIVEN UP ON US

*F*ULLY COMMITTED, BIBLICALLY taught, historically informed, spiritually discerning Christians who examine current Christianity may fear we're too lukewarm to ever return to New Testament Christianity. But we needn't despair.

Jesus hasn't given up on us. Why am I sure? The same Bible that asserts He's unchanging—"the same yesterday, and today, and forever" (Heb. 13:8)—also reveals He didn't give up on the lukewarm Laodiceans. Let's examine their condition and His response.

Spiritually and morally lukewarm, the ancient Laodiceans were uncommitted to God's truth, righteousness, and holiness. Their moral teachings were relative, not absolute, and they compromised them whenever necessary to avoid their society's ire. This lack of conviction sickened Jesus, who rejected their fellowship and service: "Because thou are lukewarm...I will spew [vomit] thee out of my mouth" (Rev. 3:16). They were materialists, pursuing riches and goods more than Christ and His will and relying on their earthly fortunes more than their heavenly Father (v. 17). Lacking humility, they boasted that they were independently wealthy: "I am rich, and increased with goods, and have need of nothing" (v. 17). Failing to seriously apply Christ's teachings to their personal living, they became self-deceived "hearers only" (James 1:22). While they claimed their spiritual condition was excellent, Jesus said they were:

- HYPOCRITICAL, living for outward appearances (of prosperity) instead of Jesus' approval (implied, Rev. 3:17)
- SPIRITUALLY BANKRUPT, or inwardly "wretched, and miserable, and poor" in heart (v. 17)
- SPIRITUALLY BLIND (v. 17), unable to distinguish God's servants, works, and messages from Satan's
- SPIRITUALLY NAKED, with their old carnal nature's (the "flesh's") control shamefully exposed (v. 17)

315

Yet here's an amazing fact: though Jesus abhorred their condition, He didn't abandon them. If He had, He would have stopped speaking to them.

When King Saul persisted in stubborn disobedience, the Lord eventually stopped communicating with him. Before his death Saul acknowledged, "God...answereth me no more, neither by prophets, nor by dreams" (1 Sam. 28:15). After Herod Antipas executed John the Baptist—who was God's "voice" to Herod—God said nothing further to the corrupt king. When Herod later interrogated Jesus, "He answered...nothing" (Luke 23:9). So the fact that Jesus continued counseling the Laodiceans proves He hadn't forsaken them. They still had a chance to change.

"I counsel thee..." (Rev. 3:18). Every word of Jesus' counsel implies hope by illuminating a way out for these Christians who had lost their way. Let's consider His optimistic instructions (vv. 18–21).

Jesus urged them to face and endure the tests they had previously evaded by compromising. By doing so, they could now become truly "rich," possessing the spiritual "gold" of faith and knowledge of God proven in fiery tests (v. 18). So they didn't have to remain spiritually poor. They could become spiritually wealthy!

He charged them to buy "white raiment" (v. 18) by working out His grace-given righteousness in their daily actions. This would "clothe" them with the garment of Christlike works they needed to attend the marriage supper of the Lamb (Rev. 19:7–8). So they didn't have to remain "naked," or shamefully carnal. They could be clothed with godly living!

Jesus implied successful testing would "anoint" their eyes to "see" spiritual truths and understand their circumstances as never before: "Anoint thine eyes...that thou mayest see" (Rev. 3:18). (Compare Hebrews 5:14.) So they didn't have to remain blind. They could have spiritual insight!

He reassured them His chastening demonstrated His love: "As many as I love, I rebuke and chasten" (Rev. 3:19). So though He deplored their condition, He still desired them!

He ordered them to "be zealous" and "repent" (v. 19), and His commands are His enablings! So they didn't have to remain apathetic. They could become "hot"—fervently devoted to Him and uncompromisingly loyal to His Word (v. 15)!

He pledged to personally visit with responders: "If any man hear my voice, and open the door, I will come in to him, and will sup with him" (v. 20). So they didn't have to remain distant. They could have sweet, close fellowship with Him!

He challenged them to overcome, offering responders leadership authority: "To him that overcometh will I grant to sit with me in my throne" (v. 21). So they didn't have to remain spiritually defeated. They could conquer sin and self and qualify to lead and help God's people (v. 12)!

Prophetically, these lukewarm Laodiceans, the last church Jesus addressed before suddenly transporting John to heaven (Rev. 4:1–2), symbolize last-day Christians living just before the Rapture. Us! Like the Laodiceans, many churches today have modified their beliefs and practices to accommodate our culture's increasing sinfulness. But Jesus is offering us a chance to change.

So let's obey His counsel and praise Him that He hasn't given up on us.

Chapter 118

LORD, FULLY ENLIGHTEN ME!

O PASS THROUGH this sin-darkened world safely and productively, we need the wonder of light. The disadvantages of darkness are discouraging and dangerous.

In darkness we can't see the ground we stand on. Forced to crawl or feel our way along, we walk slowly and insecurely at best. We can't see paths, roads, or goals. Not knowing which is the right way or objective, we wander aimlessly and helplessly. We can't recognize people. So we can't fellowship, work, or minister with them sweetly and fruitfully. We don't detect objects, pits, or traps. Thus our forward progress is often interrupted by stumbling, falling, or entrapment. We can't see our hands or things we're working on. So our works are slow and mistake-ridden, unhelpful to man and unpleasing to God. Besides discouraging and endangering us, these disadvantages of darkness ultimately defeat us: We can't finish God's will in darkness! So at life's finish line we'll be discouraged, unproductive, disapproved failures.

Recognizing this, David looked to God for spiritual light and expressed confidence God would give it: "Thou wilt light my lamp; the LORD...will lighten my darkness" (Ps. 18:28). David's faith was twofold.

First, he was confident God would light the "lamp" of his soul—his human spirit—with a personal touch from the fervently bright divine flame of God's own "consuming fire" (Heb. 12:29). This would bring illumination to the very core of his inner man, his soul, and give him a deeply satisfying spiritual life.

Second, David was sure the Father of light would "lighten my [outward] darkness," or illuminate his external earthly life. One translation reads, "My God brightens the darkness around me" (NCV). David believed God would release a broad irresistible light beam from above to penetrate the dark uncertainties in his circumstances, present, past, and future, and give him insights, explanations, orientation, purpose, guidance, confidence, and rest from all fear. Thus he thanked the Light of this world, "Lord, You will fill my whole life with Your light—illuminating the lamp of my inner soul life and the obscurities of my outer life."

God did this for the Israelites in the wilderness. The Law lit their hearts with the knowledge of God and His will, ways, and worship. The "pillar of the cloud" gave them "light by night" (Exod. 14:19–20), or full illumination and orientation in the otherwise black desert nights and wayless days. Thus God enlightened their inner and outer lives as they trekked through their dark "valley of the shadow," the Sinai desert.

He did so again when He sent Jesus—"the light of the world" (John 8:12)—to visit Israel. When Jesus launched His ministry in Capernaum, Jews and Gentiles saw that "great light." Matthew records, "The people who sat in darkness saw great light, and to them who sat in the region and shadow of death, light is sprung up" (Matt. 4:16). Jesus' presence, preaching, and power blessed Israel like a joyful, clarifying sunrise after their long, dark, confusing night of Pharisaim. The "Sun of righteousness" (Mal. 4:2) arose with spiritual and physical healing in "his wings," or light beams. He then lit inner soul-lamps with His words and calls and brightened outward lives with His deliverances and healings. The same Son-rise can be ours.

Our Son-shine begins when Christ lights our inner soul-lamp with the floodlight of His Word: "The entrance of thy words giveth light" (Ps. 119:130). This truth, or Word-light, dispels the darkness of our false conceptions of God. He also shines other light-beams. For instance, the light of His:

- RIGHTEOUSNESS. "His righteousness" (Matt. 6:33) reveals the darkness of our sin, immorality, and injustice.

- LOVE. His love exposes the darkness of our hatred, envy, strife, apathy, and unforgiveness.

- WISDOM. His wisdom pierces the dark shadows of our indecision and foolish, self-opposing actions.

- INSIGHT. His insight helps us discern the darkness of false teachings, movements, and causes.

- GUIDANCE. With His guidance we distinguish right life-paths from wrong.

- JOY. His joy dispels the darkness of our hopelessness and despair.

- HUMBLE SELF-EXAMINATION. His humility illuminates our consciences to see ourselves accurately—with no dark shadows of pride.

- FAVOR. His approval shines His blessing on our efforts and turns people, even enemies, toward us.

Illuminating us inwardly and outwardly, these light beams help us "walk in the light," free from the dangerous disadvantages of darkness (1 John 1:7). We safely and steadily pass through the shadowy valley of this world and finish God's will with joy! Want this full enlightenment?

Follow David's example. For a hope-giving, life-changing Son-rise with a full array of spiritual light beams, pray, "Lord, fully enlighten me!"

Chapter 119

ONLY FIFTY MILES TO DERBE!

*P*AUL'S FIRST MISSION to Galatia wasn't just challenging. It was cruel—one painful persecution after another! But he persevered through his pain.

After Paul sowed God's Word in Antioch of Pisidia, the local Jews "raised persecution" and "expelled" him (Acts 13:50). Moving on, Paul preached in Iconium, converting a "great multitude" as "signs and wonders" confirmed his message (Acts 14:1–3). But, again, local Jews resisted. When Paul learned city leaders were plotting to stone him, he moved on, this time to Lystra—with the Jews still pursuing (vv. 5–6). After establishing a church, working a miracle, and denouncing idolatry there, Paul received more mistreatment. Urged by Jews from Antioch and Iconium, the Lystrans stoned Paul and dragged his apparently dead body out of town (v. 19).

Thus far Paul's Galatian tour was "stony"—entering and being expelled from three cities, with two attempted and one successful stonings! Paul's stoning left him brutally injured and broken in body. But not in spirit.

Up "the next day," Paul "departed with Barnabas to Derbe" (Acts 14:20). Derbe was approximately fifty miles away. That Paul walked this distance so soon after stoning implies the Holy Spirit miraculously healed and strengthened him. Even more remarkable was Paul's persevering attitude!

After three successive cities abused him, he was still willing to minister to another "the next day"—without rebellion, wavering, timidity, or self-pity. Paul's faithfulness was like a rock. He was unmovable, as firm in ministry as his enemies were in mischief! He embodied his writings: "Steadfast, unmovable, always abounding in the work of the Lord" (1 Cor. 15:58). Such steadiness implies obedience.

Paul must have "cast down imaginations" while traveling to Derbe (2 Cor. 10:5). When fears of more persecution pressed in, he quickly rejected them, knowing God never sends "a spirit of fear" (2 Tim. 1:7). When rebellious thoughts arose, he dispatched them by yielding to God's sovereignty. If God let him suffer again in Derbe, so be it; God's grace would again be "sufficient" (2 Cor. 12:9). Carnal reasonings surely assaulted him: "After three Galatian cities rejected you, Paul, you're crazy to expect acceptance in the next; God can't be leading you!" But Paul trusted the Holy Spirit with "all his heart" (Prov. 3:5), knowing if he shouldn't visit Derbe, the Spirit would check (Acts 16:6–7). Offense tried him: "You're fervent and faithful, Paul. Why did God permit your cruel stoning?" Humble, Paul chose to wait patiently for God's explanation. Self-pity appealed: "Poor Paul, you should feel sorry for yourself; no apostle has suffered so much!" The Lystran Christians possibly tried to dissuade him: "Don't go to Derbe! You need a sabbatical, not more travel and trouble!" But, remembering God's unmistakable call to this mission (Acts 13:2, 4), Paul determined to finish it! So he walked on—fifty miles!

The three-to-six-day trek[1] afforded Paul plenty of time to turn back. But whenever he pondered this, he chose to go on! Once in Derbe, he was glad he persevered.

Assuming Paul's stoning was lethal, his Jewish enemies didn't pursue him to Derbe. Thus his work there flourished. He "preached the gospel to that city" without protest or persecution and for weeks, perhaps months, trained "many disciples" (14:21, NAS) in God's Word and ways.

How different, and delightful, this was! Instead of suffering stony persecution, he harvested sweet fruit. It was a "Manasseh" moment.[2] God's sweet blessings made Paul forget his bitter sufferings—all because Paul persevered, pressing through imaginations, fears, reasonings, pain, weariness, and discouraging counsels for fifty long miles!

Have you met stony rejection in God's service? Ostracism? Harassment? Slander? Injustice? Dishonor? Abandonment? Abuse? Are you considering quitting your mission? Don't! Remember when God called you and persevere immediately (your "next day"), without:

- Offense at God for letting you suffer
- Crippling self-pity
- Hesitating timidity
- Doubtful reasonings
- Half-hearted "weariness in well doing" (Gal. 6:9)

This will make you, like Paul, as faithful as a rock in your calling. Why wait?

Begin working toward your "Derbe," and God will begin working for you. His grace will be sufficient and presence comforting, as they were for Paul. Once in Derbe—your next task, position, ministry, or mission—Christ will renew your strength and bless your work. You'll experience a Manasseh moment. You'll forget your cruel spiritual "stonings" and the challenging "fifty miles" it took to get there—those lonely, monotonous days or years of faithful preparation and service in humble, painful circumstances. So go on.

Follow Paul's perseverance. Press through your pain. Take the first step onward, and then the next, giving thanks that there remain not five hundred but only fifty miles to Derbe!

Chapter 120

ARE YOU ROOTED?

$\mathcal{A}$FTER PAUL AND Barnabas' first persecution-filled pass through Galatia, they returned to three Galatian cities that had expelled them: Lystra, Iconium, and Antioch of Pisidia (Acts 14:21). Why?

Primarily, they went to "confirm" (v. 22), or support further,[1] those converted through their earlier evangelism (Acts 13:44–14:20). Wisely watchful, Paul knew these lambs of Christ, though saved, lacked spiritual knowledge, experience, organization, and discerning leaders. Thus they were vulnerable to satanic attacks of persecution, heresy, sin, or other wiles. Since he and Barnabas were the most spiritually mature leaders in Galatia, they were best suited to help these new churches. So, for love of their heavenly Shepherd and His earthly sheep, back into the Galatian inferno they went—with one chief objective.

Spiritual rooting! Those who had been spiritually born must now be raised to spiritual maturity. For this they needed a well-established spiritual root system. Jesus warned that insufficiently rooted Christians would "fall away" during testing (Luke 8:13). To prevent this, He called us to "continue" in His Word (John 8:31).

It was with this in mind that Paul exhorted the Galatians to "continue in the faith" (Acts 14:22) and then fed their faith with steady, Spirit-illuminated Bible teaching. He surely challenged them, as he did Timothy, to "study to show thyself approved unto God…rightly dividing the word of truth" (2 Tim. 2:15). As he informed and nourished them with biblical expositions, and they pursued personal Scripture studies, God's Word began rooting in their minds.

Paul and Barnabas further confirmed the believers by counsel, guiding their key decisions with Spirit-chosen Scripture references that perfectly fit and explained their trying situations. They trained them to pray about every problem—"In everything by prayer…let your requests be made known unto God" (Phil. 4:6–7)—and prayed with them, individually and in groups. They fellowshipped with them daily, breaking bread in daily meals and Communion. Finally they appointed the most mature among them as elders and charged them to continue feeding the Galatians God's Word after their departure (Acts 14:23). Thus God's Word took root in the Galatians' minds. But this intellectual rooting wasn't enough. Their spiritual roots had to go deeper.

For this, continuing obedience was necessary. So, omnipotent, God personally arranged the Galatians' daily circumstances to test their obedience to His Word and guidance. Every time they yielded and obeyed Him in life situations, the Word took deeper root—spreading from their minds down into their hearts, wills, and the deepest recesses of their souls. Thus God's grip on them, and theirs on Him, increased. The more they received teaching, studied, and worked out the Word by obedience, the deeper their soul roots grew. Eventually they became widely and deeply rooted in God.

This rooting facilitated continuous spiritual nourishment. Just as roots absorb the water and minerals that feed plants, by feeding on God's expounded Word and drinking in His Spirit during prayer, the Galatians absorbed the spiritual nutrients that made them strong and confident in Christ. Steadily nourished, they grew. The Holy Spirit transformed them into Christ's character image as they increasingly produced the gracious, Christlike "fruit of the Spirit" (Gal. 5:22–23). As roots anchor plants, enabling them to stand upright, this steady edification inspired the Galatians to live uprightly without falling into unbelief, offense, or ungodliness. As they continued trusting and obeying God, they grew new, even deeper roots. Like prop roots buttressing cypress trees against strong winds, these extra roots held the Galatians firm in powerful storms of persecution and heresy (Gal. 5:10). As roots also store water and minerals for a plant's future needs, the Galatians' roots reserved extra spiritual nourishment to help them endure droughts of blessing, success, or favor. Thus they remained faithful to the heavenly Sower in even the longest, hardest tests. (See Revelation 3:10.) Why? They were deeply rooted in God!

Are you firmly grounded in Bible study? Deeply rooted in God by obedience? Putting down new roots? If so, stay "planted" close by the river of the Spirit flowing in God's Word and prayer, and you'll become a tree of righteousness—upright, stable, and fruitful (Ps. 1:1–3)—enduring every storm and drought in restful trust, sustaining hope, and faithful service. This rooted life is the blessed life!

> Blessed is the man who trusteth in the LORD...whose hope the
> LORD is...he shall be like a tree planted by the waters...that
> spreadeth out her roots by the river, and shall not see [weakness

or harm] when heat cometh, but her leaf shall be green [healthy]; and shall not be anxious in the year of drought, neither...cease from yielding fruit.

—JEREMIAH 17:7–8

Are you so blessed? Are you rooted?

Chapter 121

IF GOD CONVERTED PAUL...

CTS DESCRIBES PAUL'S conversion more than anyone else's—
three times! (See Acts 9:1–19; 22:1–16; 26:9–18.) There are several reasons for this emphasis.

It shows that, like his subsequent life and ministry, Paul's (Saul of
Tarsus') conversion was extraordinary. It also suggests his spiritual rebirth
is a model for study, teaching us about:

- THE POWER OF INTERCESSION, as Paul's conversion resulted
  partly from Stephen's prayer for his executioners (Acts 7:58–
  60; 9:1–9)

- THE BAPTISM WITH THE SPIRIT, which Paul received not at
  conversion but three days afterward (vv. 9, 17)

- FORGIVENESS, as Ananias ministered kindly to his now-peni-
  tent "brother" (v. 17) despite Paul's past cruelties

- HEALING, as Paul's eyes were divinely healed when Ananias
  prayed for him (v. 18)

- ISRAEL'S FUTURE CONVERSION, as Saul's sudden conversion at
  Jesus' appearing foreshadows Israel's sudden conversion after
  the Rapture[1]

But there's another reason. Paul's impossible yet true about-face
gives us hope for the stubborn, Christ-rejecting sinners and backslidden
Christians for whom we pray. The logic is simple: if God changed *Paul*, He
can change anybody! Let's examine Paul's condition when converted.

Trained by Israel's leading rabbi, Gamaliel, young Paul (Saul) was a
rising leader in Christianity's most hostile rival religion, Christ-rejecting
Pharisaic Judaism. On the Damascus road he was at the height of his anti-
Jesus persecutions, seething with hatred for Christ's "way" (Acts 22:4). "Saul,
yet breathing out threatenings and slaughter against the disciples of the
Lord" (Acts 9:1). "Exceedingly mad" (Acts 26:11) with self-righteous rage,
he was completely deceived about Jesus and convinced he should "do many
things contrary" to His name (v. 9). He was so hardened that he imprisoned,

brutally whipped, or executed "many" Christians, including women, without remorse (Acts 22:4). Insatiable, his obsession couldn't be satisfied with hurting Christians in Israel. It drove him to hunt them down in foreign cities (Acts 26:11).

Yet in one flash of divine intervention Jesus turned this malicious monster into His meek servant, praying, "Lord, what wilt thou have me to do?" (Acts 9:6). How? By God's presence, God's Word, and prayer.

Prayer encircled Paul. Churches everywhere were praying fervently for relief from his unrelenting persecutions. So to end Paul's campaign of terror, Jesus stopped him at Damascus' gates—by His presence. The Light of the world suddenly appeared "above the brightness of the sun" (Acts 26:13)—and instantly Paul fell, overwhelmed, dumb, and docile at His feet. He then seeded and saved Paul's heart with His life-giving Word: "Saul, Saul, why persecutest thou me?...I am Jesus" (vv. 14–15). Suddenly Paul the disbeliever believed and obeyed the Light, repeatedly calling Him "Lord" (Acts 22:8, 10). This shouldn't surprise us.

Prayer releases the same irresistible power upon those for whom we pray. The Holy Spirit's presence softens hard hearts like a "consuming fire" melts wax (Heb. 12:29). And God's Word, once spoken, pounds even the proudest, most stubborn consciences like a relentless spiritual hammer until they break: "Is not my word...like a hammer that breaketh the rock?" (Jer. 23:29). Paul's wasn't the first hard case Jesus broke.

He also smashed King Nebuchadnezzar's adamant pride, Mary Magdalene's demonic hardness, Zacchaeus' unresponsive conscience, Simon Magus' vain occultism, the Ninevites' hardened unbelief, the Ephesians' established idolatry, and Sosthenes' stiff resistance to Paul's gospel. Speaking for all, Nebuchadnezzar concluded, "Those that walk in pride he is able to abase" (Dan. 4:37). God has broken countless other belligerent spirits, yet none was ever harder than Paul's, the self-declared "chief" of sinners (1 Tim. 1:15) who prophesied everyone, saved and lost, will ultimately bow to the Light and acknowledge His lordship at the judgment (Phil. 2:10–11).[2] Do you share Paul's confidence in Christ's omnipotence? "Believe ye that I am able to do this?" (Matt. 9:28). Or are you doubting? Discouraged? Despairing?

Is your confidence in the heavenly Converter's supernatural power flagging because you see only stubbornness in those for whom you're praying? You see nothing but your son or daughter's growing secular beliefs? Your friend's relapse into drug or alcohol abuse? A backslider's many remorseful confessions—yet still without meaningful change? A fellow Christian's rebellion against his pastor's godly counsel? A hostile family member who has begun reproaching and slandering you without cause? A lukewarm friend who, despite your intercessions, seems blissfully unconcerned about her spiritual or moral compromise? Or your hard case may be different—but not harder than Paul!

If you focus on your hard case, you'll remain doubtful and your prayers powerless. If you meditate on Jesus' amazing converting power, your faith will soar, heart rest, and prayers produce lasting conversions in God's time and way. Don't let doubt defeat you.

When discouraged, keep praying, remembering, "If God converted Paul..."

Chapter 122

IF JOHN WERE HERE...

HE PROPHETS DECLARED that before Messiah came, God would send a forerunning prophet like Elijah to prepare Israel to receive Him: "Behold, I will send you Elijah the prophet, before the...day of the Lord" (Mal. 4:5).[1] The Gospels agree this "man sent from God" was John the Baptist (John 1:6).

But there's more. As God sent John before Christ's first coming, He'll send ministers like John before Christ's second coming. They'll turn, revive, and reform Christ's body until we're "a people prepared for the [Lord's]" appearing (Luke 1:17). These "little Johns" will bear similarities to their larger-than-life predecessor.

To understand them, therefore, let's consider John. If John lived among us, what would he be like? Preach? Do? Let's review the Bible's description of John and project onto the screens of our imaginations an image of a modern John—the man, his message, and his mission.

If John were here, he wouldn't rise from among the world's political or religious elite, today's "Tiberiuses" or "Caiaphases" (Luke 3:1–2), but he'd be "great" in God's sight, extraordinarily Spirit-filled and anointed with the rare church- and nation-turning "power of Elijah" (Luke 1:15–17). An atypical minister, he'd be trained apart from the religious mainstream and hidden in the ecclesiastical "wilderness" (Luke 3:2) until the "day of his showing" (Luke 1:80). Probably unaffiliated and uncredentialed, he'd live very close to, hear very clearly from, and be profoundly taught of God (Luke 3:2). Thus he'd be free from sectarian indoctrination. A simple man of monastic devotion, casual dress, plain diet, and humble means, he'd call Christians to a baptism of penitence, not prosperity (v. 3). Purged of pride, he'd ignore flattery and meekly redirect all praise to Jesus (vv. 15–17). Wise, he'd call us to repentant action, not mere words, and warn us never to presume our religious heritage, however godly, will spare us divine chastening (v. 8). His message?

Apolitical, his themes would be biblical, spiritual, and practical, not political, nationalistic, or ideological. Focused, his "message from God" (Luke 3:2, NLT) would primarily address God's people—born-again Christians—not secular rulers or legislatures. He'd trumpet Messiah Jesus' imminent appearing and urge us to refocus on His coming kingdom, not our passing nations and their endless problems (Matt. 3:1–2). While ministering water baptism, he'd emphasize Spirit-baptism, identifying Jesus as the heavenly Baptizer and heart purification as His primary goal (Luke 3:16–17). Holy, and thus unable to ignore sin, he'd reprove us for disregarding biblical regulations concerning marriage, divorce, and remarriage: "It is not lawful for thee to have thy brother's wife" (Mark 6:18). Without fear or prejudice he'd correct the poor and powerful alike—and suffer for it (vv. 17–26). Like King Herod, ungodly politicians, compromised clerics, and apostate Christians would likely conspire to silence his message—or him (v. 27)! And John's mission?

As stated above, his primary mission would be to "prepare…the way of the Lord" (Luke 3:4), or work to get Christians into such sanctified unity that Christ can freely visit, move among, and use us any way and time He pleases. Thus we'll be ready for Him to reveal Himself among us now and "rapture" us later, just before the Tribulation. To build this Revival Road or Visitation Way in our lives, our John would deal with our sins at not the fruit but the "root" level (v. 9). With the Spirit's guidance and aid he'd correct not just our bad behavior but also the bad attitudes that cause it. He'd challenge and instruct us how to:

- RAISE our "valley" (low) attitudes of fear, despair, and worthlessness (v. 5)
- LOWER our "mountain" (high) attitudes of pride, vanity, and worldly ambition (v. 5)
- STRAIGHTEN our "crooked" behaviors of injustice, immorality, and dishonesty (v. 5)
- SMOOTH our "rough" words and actions until we consistently interact with others patiently and kindly (v. 5)

Knowing godly correction constructs this corridor for revival, his corrections would be specific, practical, and personal, never vague, euphemistic, or misdirected (vv. 10–14). Though labeled invasive and negative, these deep reproofs would bring the loftiest reward, a visitation of God's glory—*Jesus* living, teaching, preaching, healing, and counseling among us (Isa. 40:5)! This is the kind of man, message, and mission God has promised to send us in these last days. And here's some good news.

He's done it! John's ministry anointing—the very "spirit and power of

Elijah"—is already working through thousands of brave, uncompromising ministers worldwide (Luke 1:17). But here's the key question: will we receive their corrective messages and counsels? Will we let God build a Visitation Way, a Revival Road, in our hearts, families, churches, and ministries?

Prepare now to respond, if John were here…

NOTES

3: Christian Abandonment

1. Oswald Chambers, *My Utmost for His Highest* (New York: Dodd, Mead, and Co., 1935), 73.

8: Let's Go!

1. Beginning in 1727, Moravians in Herrnhut, Saxony, began praying in shifts twenty-four hours a day seven days a week for God to birth missions and for other means to spread the gospel and grow Christianity. This prayer meeting extraordinaire lasted more than one hundred years. [Leslie K. Tarr, "A Prayer Meeting That Lasted 100 Years," *Christian History*, January 1, 1982, http://www.ctlibrary.com/ch/1982/issue1/118.html (accessed January 16, 2013).]

11: The First Duty of the Faithful

1. The Avalon Project, "First Inaugural Address of Franklin D. Roosevelt, Saturday, March 4, 1933," http://avalon.law.yale.edu/20th_century/froos1.asp (accessed January 18, 2013).

12: Sing While You Suffer

1. The Hebrew word *hallēl* means "praise thou." [A. C. Myers, *The Eerdmans Bible Dictionary* (Grand Rapids, MI: Eerdmans, 1987).]
2. C. S. Keener, *The IVP Bible Background Commentary: New Testament* (Downers Grove, IL: InterVarsity Press, 1993).
3. "John Hus," *Christian History*, issue 68, vol. 19, no. 4, 2000, 18.
4. "Bound for Canaan," *Christian History*, issue 62, vol. 18, no. 2, 1999, 18.

13: Seeking Spiritual Unity

1. I've borrowed this thought from the insightful writings of the late Dr. Fuchsia Pickett, *The Next Move of God* (Lake Mary, FL: Creation House, 1994), 149.

14: Are You on Fire?

1. Matthew Henry, *Commentary on the Whole Bible (in One Volume)* (Grand Rapids, MI: Zondervan Publishing House, 1961), 1640.
2. Howard Vos, *Exploring Church History* (Nashville: Thomas Nelson, 1994), 5.

19: A Fresh Revelation of Jesus Is Near!

1. See Deuteronomy 28:12.
2. Christ's high priestly prayer is recorded in John 17. The prophetic portraits of the church's final glory are found in Ephesians, where the Spirit inspired Paul's vision of the church ultimately becoming a Spirit-filled temple church, fully indwelt by the Spirit (Eph. 2:19–22); a mature-man church, of the same spiritual stature as Christ (Eph. 4:11–16); and a purified bride church, cleansed of every sin and fault, ready to be presented and wedded to Jesus (Eph. 5:25–27; Rev. 19:7–9).

22: The Benefits of Cross Bearing

1. In the text (Luke 14:27) and virtually throughout the New Testament the word *disciple* is taken from the Greek *mathētēs*, meaning "student, pupil, follower." [J. Swanson, *Dictionary of Biblical Languages With Semantic Domains: Greek (New Testament)*, electronic ed. (Oak Harbor: Logos Research Systems, Inc., 1997).]

25: Courageous Faith!

1. Oswald Chambers, *Run Today's Race* (Fort Washington, PA: Crusade Literature Crusade, 1976), 55.

26: Unmoved by Satan's Subtlety

1. *Webster's Encyclopedic Unabridged Dictionary of the English Language* (New York: Gramercy Books, 1996,) s.v. "subtle."
2. Abishag had been King David's concubine. In ancient times, marrying a king's daughter or concubine strengthened one's claim to the throne. Had Adonijah married Abishag, he could have made a claim to Solomon's throne. Solomon perceived this to be his intent and executed him for breaking his former agreement to not seek the throne (1 Kings 1:52).

30: Strengthen Your Hull

1. Keener, *The IVP Bible Background Commentary: New Testament.*
2. For more information on the hull failures of Liberty ships in the Second World War, see "Problems" in "Liberty Ship," http://en.wikipedia.org/wiki/Liberty_ship (accessed June 15, 2012).

31: Secret Believers

1. Swanson, *Dictionary of Biblical Languages With Semantic Domains: Greek (New Testament).*
2. Henry, *Commentary on the Whole Bible (in One Volume)*, 1357.

35: They Watched Him—and Watch Us

1. This sign was the Roman *titulus*, or charge, a placard worn around the condemned person's neck specifying his criminal charges and sometimes, as in Jesus' case, nailed to the top of his cross.

40: Walking Alone to Assos

1. Keener, *The IVP Bible Background Commentary: New Testament.*
2. W. W. Wiersbe, *The Bible Exposition Commentary* (Wheaton, IL: Victor Books, 1996).

41: The Wayless Wilderness

1. As God so preciously promises us in 1 Corinthians 10:13.

42: Don't Keep Jesus in a Tomb!

1. Warren Wiersbe notes: "All of this was of God, for now it was impossible for anyone—friend or foe—to steal the body. Without realizing it, the Jewish leaders and the Roman government joined forces to help prove the resurrection of Jesus Christ." [Wiersbe, *The Bible Exposition Commentary*.]
2. Some "classical cessationists" are more moderate, allowing that some miracles occasionally occur under specified conditions. The opposing view to cessationism is continuationism, which holds that the miraculous gifts and operations of the Holy Spirit have continued to operate since Pentecost.
3. As asserted by the apostle Paul in 1 Thessalonians 4:13–18 and 1 Corinthians 15:50–53.

44: Revival, the Simple Way

1. This is not to say God can't or won't sovereignly pour out His Spirit on us even when our obedience is lagging. He sometimes does. But we can't pray confidently for such showers of blessing unless we obey Him.

46: Complete Your Spiritual Résumé

1. A well-instructed rabbi, Paul was well versed in not only the Jewish law (Torah) and prophets but also the writings, which included the Book of Proverbs.

47: Ready to Rise?

1. Sharon is Israel's fertile coastal plain bordering the Mediterranean and extending some fifty miles south to north and ten miles wide.

50: Transformative Teaching

1. The Greek word here is *mathēteuō*. [Swanson, *Dictionary of Biblical Languages with Semantic Domains: Greek (New Testament).*]

51: Calling Christian Armor-Bearers!

1. "John Knox, the Thundering Scot," *Christian History*, issue 45, vol. 14, no. 2.
2. Armor-bearers have the spiritual gift of "helps" (1 Cor. 12:28).

53: Holding Jesus—Tightly!

1. H. Liddell, *A Lexicon: Abridged From Liddell and Scott's Greek-English Lexicon* (Oak Harbor, WA: Logos Research Systems, Inc., 1996).
2. The Diaspora were the Jews driven from Palestine and scattered or dispersed throughout the Gentile nations by the Babylonians and later by the Romans.

60: Pentecostal Peril

1. Edgar J. Goodspeed, *The New Testament: An American Translation* (Chicago, IL: University of Chicago Press, 1923).

61: A Few Thoughts on Self-Pity

1. John Gill, *Exposition of the Entire Bible*, public domain, s.v. "Matthew 16:22," http://gill.biblecommenter.com/matthew/16.htm (accessed January 20, 2013).
2. BibleCommentator.com, "King James Translators' Notes: Matthew 16," http://kjt.biblecommenter.com/matthew/16.htm (accessed January 20, 2013).

62: Shadowed by the Savior

1. Keener, *The IVP Bible Background Commentary: New Testament.*

79: The New Wine Is Better

1. According to ancient Jewish custom, young men, during the betrothal process, would first agree to the terms of marriage with their bride and her father. The groom would then pay the father the bride price and, to seal the marriage contract, drink a glass of wine with his bride. Thus Jesus sealed His marriage to the church by sharing literal wine with her representatives at the Last Supper and spiritual wine with her original congregation at Pentecost.
2. First-century Jews typically drank wine diluted, one part wine to two or three parts water, and only with meals, thus diminishing its intoxicating effects.

83: He Knows Where to Find You

1. GPS is the acronym for Global Positioning System, the United States government's space-based satellite navigation system commonly used by the public to help travelers realize exact coordinates and determine precisely how to find their desired destination.
2. Henry, *Commentary on the Whole Bible (in One Volume)*, 1670.

84: Refocusing on the Family of God

1. Fuchsia Pickett, *The Next Move of God* (Lake Mary, FL: Creation House, 1994), 103–104.

86: Our Original Denominations

1. Merrill C. Tenny and Moises Silva, *The Zondervan Encyclopedia of the Bible*, rev. ed., vol. 1 (Grand Rapids, MI: Zondervan Corp., 2009), 831.
2. J. Strong, *A Concise Dictionary of the Words in the Greek Testament and the Hebrew Bible* (Bellingham, WA: Logos Bible Software, 2009).
3. R. L. Thomas, *New American Standard Hebrew-Aramaic and Greek Dictionaries*, updated edition (Anaheim, CA: Foundation Publications, Inc., 1998).

87: Just a Mustard Seed

1. Keener, *The IVP Bible Background Commentary: New Testament*.
2. Oswald Chambers, *My Utmost for His Highest: Selections for the Year* (Grand Rapids, MI: Oswald Chambers Publications, 1986), 251.

88: Ananias' Extraordinary Character

1. Wiersbe, *The Bible Exposition Commentary*.

89: Go With a Straight Course!

1. Tacking refers to the zigzagging courses sailing vessels set when sailing into the wind. Though required to sail windward, tacking makes a journey longer and more time consuming.

91: The Walls Will Come Down!

1. Wiersbe, *The Bible Exposition Commentary*.

92: Memorial Day Is Coming!

1. So estimates one source. [J. F. Walvoord, R. B. Zuck, and Dallas Theological Seminary, *The Bible Knowledge Commentary: An Exposition of the Scriptures* (Wheaton, IL: Victor Books, 1985).]
2. "Herrnhut" means *the Lord's Watch*. Saxony is now part of Germany.
3. S. Smith and J. Cornwall, *The Exhaustive Dictionary of Bible Names* (North Brunswick, NJ: Bridge-Logos, 1998).

93: Reestablishing the Head

1. In order these references are: 1 Corinthians 11:3; Ephesians 1:22–23; 4:15; 5:23; Colossians 1:18; 2:19.
2. A. W. Tozer, (1978). *The Best of A. W. Tozer* (Harrisburg, PA: Christian Publications, Inc., 1978), 88.

94: All That Call on Thy Name

1. For another usage, see Acts 9:21.

97: Ecclesiastical Excellence

1. The Greek word *ekklēsia* (ek-lay-SEE-ah), used in antiquity to describe assemblies of citizens summoned to render decisions on civic issues, is used in the New Testament to describe the church or its assemblies.

98: Re-Crown Him Lord of All

1. Kathleen M. Chambers, *Oswald Chambers: The Best From All His Books* (Nashville: Oliver-Nelson Books, 1987), 315–316.

101: Praying Until…

1. "Seasons of the Spirit," *Christian History*, vol. 8, no. 3, issue 23, 1989, 7.

102: Be Christian or Die!

1. "Be Christian or Die," *Christian History*, vol. 18, no 3, issue 63, 1999, 16.
2. Tenny and Silva, *The Zonderan Encyclopedia of the Bible*, 831.

103: He Gives Light in Prisons

1. Luther's confinement began May 25, 1521, with the Edict of Worms, and ended March 6, 1522, when he returned to Wittenburg.

104: Obey Your Angel!

1. Thomas, *New American Standard Hebrew-Aramaic and Greek Dictionaries*.
2. For similar usages in the same passage, see Revelation 2:8, 12, 18; 3:1, 7, 14.
3. For more on Elijah's departure from Elisha, read 2 Kings 2:3, 11–12.

105: Sleeping the Sleep of Folly?

1. Sleep also symbolizes a very desirable spiritual condition—the complete rest of faith. We see this in Jesus sleeping during a terrifying Galilean storm (Mark 4:38) and Peter resting in serene confidence in Christ though scheduled for execution the next morning (Acts 12:6). In this chapter, however, we address only the undesirable sleep of folly.

106: On the Sidelines?

1. The evangelist Philip resided in Caesarea, as did the new church leader Cornelius.

107: Seek Confirmation

1. To compare Paul's Jerusalem experience with Stephen's, read Acts 6:8–12.

108: Rapid Righteous Reversals

1. So indicates the original language (Greek *kakoō*). Swanson, *Dictionary of Biblical Languages With Semantic Domains: Greek (New Testament)*.
2. The Jewish historian Josephus reveals Herod suffered five days before succumbing. [F. Josephus and W. Whiston, *The Works of Josephus: Complete and Unabridged* (Peabody, MA: Hendrickson, 1987).]
3. The "gallows" (Esther 5:14) Haman erected was more likely an impaling pole, as this gruesome manner of execution was commonly used in ancient Persia. [Walvoord, Zuck, and Dallas Theological Seminary, *The Bible Knowledge Commentary: An Exposition of the Scriptures*.]

109: Lord, Open My Eyes!

1. Elymas was an occultist/wise man (Greek *magos*) who probably practiced a mix of sorcery, magic, and astrology.

110: Whose Heart Are You After?

1. The original statement, quoted here by Paul in Antioch of Pisidia, is found in 1 Samuel 13:14.
2. This Simon described in Acts 8 is Simon Magus, who is purportedly the father of the heretical group called Gnostics. "Simony," the attempt to purchase or sell church offices, privileges, or spiritual blessings, is named for him, since he offered Peter money in a futile attempt to obtain the Holy Spirit (Acts 8:18–24).

111: Philadelphia Christians in a Laodicean Era

1. Smith and Cornwall, *The Exhaustive Dictionary of Bible Names.*
2. Attalus II was nicknamed "Philadelphus." [Myers, *The Eerdmans Bible Dictionary.*]
3. The *New Bible Dictionary* notes, "As Philadelphus was renowned for his loyalty to his brother, so the church, the true Philadelphia, inherits and fulfils his character by its steadfast loyalty to Christ (vv. 8, 10)." [D. R. W. Wood and I. H. Marshall, *New Bible Dictionary*, 3rd ed. (Downers Grove, IL: InterVarsity Press, 1996).]

113: Shake Off That Dust!

1. Excerpted from Acts 13:51 note, *The Life Application Study Bible* (Wheaton, IL: Tyndale House Publishers, 2004), 1851.

114: Mistaken, Mesmerizing, Maddening Materialism

1. Laodicean glossy black wool garments were renowned and sold worldwide. The city's medical school, famous for ophthalmology, produced a highly regarded eye salve. Located on the major East-West highway in Asia Minor, its trade thrived, making it a natural center for banking and eventually a very wealthy city. For more information, see Wood and Marshall, *New Bible Dictionary.*
2. Mammon is *worldly wealth trusted in* and loved as a god instead of God. The Greek word *mamōnas* means "worldly wealth" and is derived from a word meaning "that in which one trusts." See G. Kittel, G. Friedrich, and G. W. Bromiley, *Theological Dictionary of the New Testament* (Grand Rapids, MI: W. B. Eerdmans, 1985).
3. Several modern versions render Luke 12:15 excellently: "Life is not measured by how much one owns" (NCV); or, "Your true life is not made up of the things you own" (GNT); or, "Life is not about having a lot of material possessions" (GW).
4. Other passages commending ministerial mercy and condemning ministerial greed are 1 Peter 5:1–2; 1 Timothy 3:3, 8; 6:5–11.

115: Marvelous Municipal Miracles Manifesting

1. William P. Farley, "Charles Finney: The Controversial Evangelist," *Enrichment Journal*, Winter 2006, http://enrichmentjournal.ag.org/200601/200601_118_Finney.cfm (accessed January 21, 2013).

119: Only Fifty Miles to Derbe!

1. An average male in good physical condition could walk about fifteen miles per day under normal circumstances. Considering Paul's condition, he may have taken five or

even six days to cover the approximately fifty to fifty-four miles to Derbe. See "Travel," in Tenny and Silva, *The Zondervan Encyclopedia of the Bible*, 915.

2. See Genesis 41:51.

120: Are You Rooted?

1. Strong, *A Concise Dictionary of the Words in the Greek Testament and the Hebrew Bible*.

121: If God Converted Paul...

1. Israel's coming national conversion will be sparked primarily by (1) the tremendous impact of the Rapture of the true church, and (2) Christ's personal appearance to convert and commission 144,000 specially called Jewish believers (Rev. 7:1–8; 14:1; Rom. 11:25–26). *The New Scofield Study Bible's* annotation (#3) on 1 Corinthians 15:8 states, "Paul thinks of himself here as an Israelite whose time to be born again had not come nationally, so that his conversion by the appearing of the Lord in glory (Acts 9:3–6) was an illustration, or instance, before the time of the future national conversion of Israel." Thus Paul's conversion foreshadows Israel's future conversion.

2. This is not to say all will ultimately be saved, but that all, even the lost, will give glory to Christ by confessing His lordship when they stand before Him.

122: If John Were Here...

1. See also Isaiah 40:3–5.

CONTACT THE AUTHOR

Greg Hinnant Ministries
P. O. Box 788
High Point, NC 27261
TELEPHONE: (336) 882-1645
E-MAIL: rghministries@aol.com
WEBSITE: www.greghinnantministries.org

OTHER BOOKS BY THIS AUTHOR

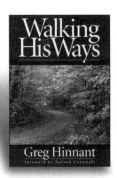

Walking in His Ways

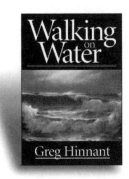

Walking on Water

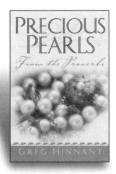

*Precious Pearls
From the Proverbs*

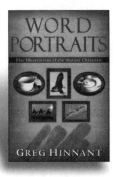

*Word Portraits: Five
Illustrations of the
Mature Christian*

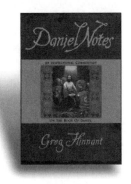

*DanielNotes: An
Inspirational Commentary
on the Book of Daniel*

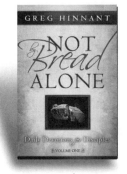

*Not by Bread Alone:
Daily Devotions for
Disciples, Volume 1*

*Gold Tried in the
Fire: Tested Truths
for Trying Times*

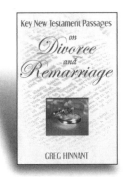

*Key New Testament
Passages on Divorce
and Remarriage*

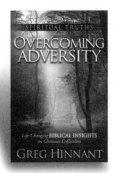

*Spiritual Truths
for Overcoming
Adversity*

Notes

Notes

Notes

Notes

Notes

Notes

Notes

Notes